Interpreting Modern Political Philo~

Interpreting Modern Political Philosophy

From Machiavelli to Marx

Edited by

Alistair Edwards

and

Jules Townshend

First published 2002 by
PALGRAVE MACMILLAN
Houndmills, Basingstoke, Hampshire RG21 6XS and
175 Fifth Avenue, New York, N.Y. 10010
Companies and representatives throughout the world

PALGRAVE MACMILLAN is the global academic imprint of the Palgrave
Macmillan division of St. Martin's Press, LLC and of Palgrave Macmillan Ltd.
Macmillan® is a registered trademark in the United States, United Kingdom
and other countries. Palgrave is a registered trademark in the European
Union and other countries.

ISBN 13: 978-0-3337-7242-3 paperback
ISBN 13: 978-0-3337-7241-6 hardback

This book is printed on paper suitable for recycling and made from fully managed
and sustained forest sources. Logging, pulping and manufacturing processes are
expected to conform to the environmental regulations of the country of origin.

A catalogue record for this book is available from the British Library.

Library of Congress Cataloging-in-Publication Data
Interpreting modern political philosophy: from Machiavelli to
Marx / edited by Alistair Edwards and Jules Townshend.
        p. cm.
    Includes bibliographical references and index.
    ISBN 0–333–77241–5—ISBN 0–333–77242–3 (pbk.)
    1. Political science—History. I. Edwards, Alistair, 1949—II. Townshend,
Jules, 1945–
JA83 .I58 2002
320'.01—dc21   2002019087

Printed and bound in Great Britain by
Cpod, Trowbridge, Wiltshire

Contents

Notes on the Contributors

Alan Apperley is Senior Lecturer in Media, Communications and Cultural Studies at the University of Wolverhampton. His latest articles have been on democracy, liberalism and autonomy.

Anthony Burns is Senior Lecturer in Philosophy and Politics at Nottingham Trent University. His publications include *Natural Law and Political Ideology in the Philosophy of Hegel* and *The Hegel–Marx Connection* (co-edited with I. Fraser).

Alistair Edwards is Lecturer in Political Thought in the Department of Government at the University of Manchester. He has written *A New Dictionary of Political Analysis* (with Geoffrey Roberts). His recent articles include work on democratisation, problems of explanation in political science, and the history of political thought.

Katrin Flikschuh teaches in the Philosophy Department at the University of Essex, and is author of *Kant and Modern Political Philosophy*.

Timothy Kenyon is Honorary Research Fellow, Department of Government, University of Manchester, and is author of *Utopian Communism and Political Thought in Early Modern England* and is the editor of *The Ricardian Socialists: Collected Works*.

Maureen Ramsay is a Senior Lecturer in Political Theory at the University of Leeds. Her recent publications include *Human Needs and The Market, What's Wrong with Liberalism? A Radical Critique of Liberal Political Philosophy* and *Democracy and the Politics of Lying* (with L. Cliffe and D. Bartlett).

John Salter is a Senior Lecturer in the School of Economic Studies at the University of Manchester. His publications include work on property and consent, justice and due share and theories of punishment in leading journals.

Jonathan Seglow is Lecturer in Politics at Royal Holloway, University of London, has written on pluralism and liberalism, and is author of a forthcoming volume on *Political Concepts*.

David P. Shugarman is a Professor and Director of the York University Centre for Practical Ethics, Master of McLaughlin College at York University and a member of the Department of Political Science at York (Canada). His recent publications include *Honest Politics: Seeking Integrity in Canadian Public Life* (co-authored with Ian Greene) and *Cruelty and Deception: The Controversy Over Dirty Hands in Politics* (co-edited with Paul Rynard).

Jules Townshend is Reader in Politics at Manchester Metropolitan University, and is author of *J. A. Hobson, The Politics of Marxism* and *C. B. Macpherson and the Problem of Liberal Democracy*.

Acknowledgements

Many individuals helped contribute to the production of this volume, especially colleagues from the editors' respective university departments at Manchester Victoria and Manchester Metropolitan Universities, as well as members of the various contributors' departments. To all these we are extremely grateful.

Sadly, Liam O'Sullivan, who was to be a contributor to this volume, died in 2001. In the world of political thought scholarship, he was one of its most convivial and subversive spirits.

ALISTAIR EDWARDS
JULES TOWNSHEND

Introduction

ALISTAIR EDWARDS AND JULES TOWNSHEND

This books aims to meet a pressing need for students of modern political philosophy: the need to access an ever increasing, sophisticated and diverse range of interpretations of the great modern political philosophers – from Machiavelli to Marx. The remarkable flowering of commentary over the past thirty years or so is in part attributable to the way academic life has become somewhat industrialised: production is encouraged, specialisation and the division of labour become intensified. But it is also evidence of something else. All these thinkers remain obstinately relevant. They have provided much of the language and concepts – the building blocks – of contemporary political discourse. And they all offer deep insights into the nature of political life as well as supplying arguments justifying or criticising political action, state institutions and public policy. Even where their vision is limited by their inherited assumptions and theoretical frameworks, as well as by the particular worlds they inhabited, often their ideas can be adapted to shed light on current concerns. These philosophers form a living presence in our own ideological universe, upholding the values of individual liberty, democracy, tradition, property, order, community, equality, and so on. They continue to provoke awe, inspiration, sometimes hostility, but hardly ever contempt.

Yet the perennial fascination with these great thinkers in producing an abundance of commentary also has a downside, particularly for undergraduate students coming fresh to the texts and debates. The problem is not just the exponential growth in the volume of material. It lies more in its increasingly specialised nature. Until fairly recently, the study of political thought required no copious introduction. Papers published in the journals were accessible even to undergraduate students just beginning their engagement with the great writers. Indeed, the titles of the essays written by undergraduates would be similar to the titles of the papers they were expected to use. If a student had asked then, 'Why does everyone ask these questions of the texts?' the answer would have been, 'Because those are the questions that leap from the page, and they are central questions of politics.' The same question asked today would receive a much more guarded response, largely because the questions have become increasingly refined and specialised, narrower in their focus, and more demanding of background knowledge. The response might now be, 'Because a host of different questions have been pursued over the last thirty years and we'll consider the particulars of those developments when you've read up enough on the various paths travelled.'

This book – the first of its kind – is intended to make that response less daunting by summarising and evaluating the key differences between interpretive responses.

Developments in Interpretation

Whatever the institutional and professional demands put on academics, there is little doubt that this blossoming in the study of the history of modern political thought owes much to the enthusiasm of the so-called 'Cambridge School' of Quentin Skinner, Peter Laslett, John Dunn, John Pocock and others, who set new standards in methodological sophistication in attempting a truly *historical* understanding of a thinker. More than thirty years ago, Quentin Skinner claimed to have identified common assumptions that had resulted in the implicit acceptance of false 'mythological' views about political philosophers (Skinner, 1969). Most notably, it was tacitly assumed that all the great writers were dealing with the same range of perennial problems and that each would have their own distinctive ideas about them. In addition, the study of these writers was insufficiently informed by historical understanding. Often the historical context would be ignored completely and the text would be assumed to speak timelessly for itself or, where the historical context was invoked, it would be in terms of broad socio-economic developments without much attention paid to whether these developments were the subject of actual political concern and debate.

Skinner's early pronouncements did not go unchallenged. They may have been stated too sweepingly, or misunderstood as more damning than they were intended to be. But they did carry weight and identified shortcomings. It appears with hindsight that the field lacked clearly stated interpretive frameworks, let alone an agreed methodological orientation to the history of political thought. The dominance, in the Anglophone world at least, of analytical philosophy had hindered this. Texts were picked over in painstaking detail. In most cases, far more time was given to the reformulation of the arguments than the authors had ever devoted to their original versions. Certainly, more time was given to the words written on the page than was given to the study of the historical context in which those words were written. The principle methodological position appeared to be that these were great authors and that their texts must therefore make, or be forced to make, full and consistent sense. As Oakeshott commented, this presumes consistency to have had the same value in the past as it has in current philosophical work (Oakeshott, 1960, p. li and p. lviii).

Of course, the field was not utterly bereft of methodological positions or historical concerns. Arthur Lovejoy proposed that the history of thought be constructed from 'unit ideas': recurrent images or assumptions that combine and recombine in various forms over the ages (Lovejoy, 1956, pp. 3–23). Leo Strauss suggested a hidden layer of meaning to be found in great philosophical writing, a layer deliberately hidden by authors fearful both of their own vulnerability to persecution and of the dangers of vulgar use of the truth: the great writers hid their true meaning by employing an esoteric code (Strauss, 1952 chapters 1 and 11; Strauss, 1953, pp. 206–11, pp. 246–7). C. B. Macpherson became a chief target for later criticism but had himself made a serious attempt to contextualise great writers within the submerged assumptions of their epochs (Macpherson, 1962, pp. 4–8). More broadly, Michael Oakeshott located writers within traditions that transcended the mundane ideological boundaries and made some progress towards a proper historical contextualisation (Oakeshott, 1960). But the major leap forward came in beguilingly simple form. Peter Laslett traced Locke's *Two Treatises of Government* back from their publication in 1690 to their composition at least ten years earlier (Laslett, 1960, 1998).

At a stroke, the reading of a central but always troublesome text was transformed; it had been mistaken by interpreters in a fundamental sense. A text of this kind, written post-1688, after the Glorious Revolution, was a cosy justification of the status quo. The same text, now identified as written much earlier, became a revolutionary call to arms. This most basic assertion of historical fact helped to turn the study of political thought towards a more contextualist focus. Although it took some time for this message to make itself fully felt, its importance for later contextualist developments cannot be overstated.

It was clear that our knowledge of the conditions under which a text was written must have impact on our understanding, not least in the sense that 'language' can be unstable and varies over time. The growing feeling that there was much to be gained from reading these texts more as time-bound, and as offering answers to specific historically pressing questions, entailed a rethinking of the mode of inquiry. Two major contributions to the study of thought wrought a rapid transformation of the field.

John Pocock suggested that political thought should be viewed as a 'continuum of discourse' containing a number of paradigmatic languages or idioms. Each paradigm provides the linguistic tools for the expression of political views but it does so selectively. Different paradigmatic languages will offer different perspectives on political life and will lend themselves more easily to the expression of some issues than others (Pocock, 1985, pp. 1–34). This sounds distressingly abstract. But, like most of the progenitors of such ideas, Pocock had more concrete ideas of the actual processes. Modern thought has been dominated by two major paradigms: natural law and classical republicanism (or 'civic humanism'). Each has its own distinctive language and concerns. Natural law has provided the main vehicle for modern political discourse with its concern for the protection of private rights and liberties and in its focus on the individual. Civic humanism displays different values: citizenship; the liberty of the free man to participate in the public sphere; and the cultivation of civic virtue through participation (Pocock, 1985, pp. 37–50).

Skinner, perhaps more closely influenced by the example of Laslett, put the matter slightly differently: the first task should be to identify 'authorial intentions'. This suggestion has been widely misunderstood. It sounds like an instruction to make positive engagement with the subjective mental state of the individual author. In fact, it is closer to Pocock's position than this. Skinner is asking us to identify the 'illocutionary' force intended by the author. This requires us to identify what the author was doing in writing the text, not what the author intended to achieve by writing that text (the perlocutionary force). I might, for instance, recount a fanciful tale about a particularly self-important and cruel monarch. I might have all sorts of intentions to achieve effects on my readers. I might want them to react with repugnance to authoritarian rule, or I might just want them to laugh. But what I want is not the first or main concern of the historian of ideas. The primary concern is to identify the act I am performing in writing this tale. Am I recounting fact? Or am I engaging in satire? (Back to Laslett for a moment: am I reassuring people about the acceptability of existing arrangements or am I challenging the present power structure?) I am attempting to communicate with readers, so my writing should bear the imprint of the different ways in which linguistic conventions govern the expression of these two quite different endeavours. Thus the primary focus goes beyond the individual author to the wider linguistic context, within which we find the conventions that allow us to distinguish between straightforward story telling and satire. We also find ourselves engaged in a much more negative process, eliminating what the author could not have been doing, where the text may fail to fit any identifiable conventional expression of that kind of act. The example of Laslett is too simple in that there a simple redating changes our view of the kind of expression embodied in the text. Most alternatives will be less easily resolved. In most cases we must study the language of the period to weed out those interpretations that could not have been intended by the author since no such meaning could have been attributed to the text by contemporary readers.

These contextualist moves proved of great value. Although their claims to confront 'the meaning' of texts had a sectarian ring, suggesting the exclusion of the other traditional concerns of political theory, their main exponents were usually careful to limit their own claims to the historical dimension of interpretation, leaving the way clear for other interests and concerns, for other flowers to bloom. Many gaps were filled: Skinner on the development of the idea of 'state' in Renaissance Italy; Pocock on the *Ancient Constitution* and the *Machiavellian Moment*; the locating of the more immediate political, intellectual and religious concerns of Hobbes and Locke by Skinner, Tully, Tuck and Dunn. This positive effect was most radically felt in the field of eighteenth-century thought where the deeper interrogation of writers like David Hume and Adam Smith, not at first sight enthusiasts for classical republican values, revealed them to be (in part) users of that language, sharing in some of its concerns but mainly offering a defence of modern commercial society against criticism.

Moves such as these are generally accepted to have solved problems. But they have created others. One problem is that a single writer has to be taken to be moving between linguistic paradigms. Getting the paradigm straight has proved an impossible task in many cases. This is a problem to be reflected on at a high level. But the more immediate problem is that these moves made access to the debates about the texts much more difficult. Not only were the arguments resting upon tricky notions of meaning and appropriate method, they were also demanding of extensive historical knowledge in their application to concrete interpretive questions. We should also note that whatever the 'Cambridge School's' importance has been (and is) for the study of the history of political thought, the reader will soon discover as they move through this book that other sophisticated interpretive frameworks are on offer, some focusing more readily on political, economic and social context, others on psychological motivation, or more exclusively on the text itself. These diverse approaches therefore raised daunting questions, and invite a book like this to ease newcomers to the subject into a lively, worthwhile and rewarding field of debate.

The Structure of the Book

We have used a uniform scheme in the presentation of the material. Each thinker will be dealt with under five headings: introduction; problems and issues; why conflicting interpretations? conflicting interpretations; evaluation. Each *introduction* will explain the importance of the writer in terms of his immediate preoccupations and interests, indicating the various contexts in which his ideas arose and giving a flavour of the main ideas without attempting to offer anything like a full or balanced summary of those ideas (the reader should consult other works for such summaries). The section on *problems and issues* will outline the main difficulties that arise from the texts, difficulties that create the space for differing interpretations. No piece of political theory can hope to achieve complete transparency or avoid all ambiguity in its treatment of problems. Indeed, as the foregoing has suggested, many of the difficulties encountered in understanding texts, particularly texts written in a context different from our own, arise from the gap that exists between different sets of expectations. We all approach the world with different questions in mind, so different aspects of the world appear salient in answering these questions.

Why Conflicting Interpretations?

Some of the answers to this question stem immediately from the preceding section. Ambiguity begets difference. But there are other sources of disagreement. All readers are interpreters: you, me and the authors of the books and articles with which we are concerned. Interpreters always bring some agenda of their own to the work they examine. We don't just read the texts; we are reading them for a purpose, with some particular points in mind. Think about this. You are, as a student, directed in your reading in so far as you are given essay questions, tutorial topics, key questions, and so on. You further bring to bear your own interests. It is in these terms that you explore the text. Like the writers of the original texts, their interpreters will bring the same kind of interests to bear. Foremost of these, we suspect, are their own political leanings. Interpreters sometimes seem to be fighting ideological battles by proxy. We can, for instance, see the effects of the reaction against totalitarianism in western scholarship. Some commentators, most famously Karl Popper, divided political philosophers into 'good guys' and 'bad guys'. The 'good guys' (especially Locke, Hume, Burke, Kant and J. S. Mill) contributed to the development of liberalism, either directly or through their opposition to radical change inspired by abstract plans. The 'bad guys' sowed the seeds of dictatorship and repression, beginning with Plato and continuing into the modern world through Rousseau, Hegel and Marx.

Commentators have also realised that their hero might be flawed in some way, and have therefore come to their aid with a theoretical 'makeover' rendering their argument more robust. This is particularly so for liberals in the case of Mill and, to a lesser extent, Locke. Those who wanted radical heroes engaged in a similar activity when analysing Rousseau and Marx. Less heroically, some of the ideas of these thinkers were borrowed in order to resolve or analyse contemporary political issues. This has obviously been the case with Marx, as a critic of liberal capitalist democracy. Mill's *On Liberty* has been invoked to deal with issues of public policy relating to various kinds of individual self-expression, whether in the media, culture or sexual relations. And Machiavelli's *The Prince* is never far away when it comes to questions concerning the connection between power (including violence) and ethics, whilst his *Discourses* embodies the civic humanism explored by Quentin Skinner. Just as significantly, contemporary American liberal political philosophy rests heavily on two thinkers in this volume. Locke's *Second Treatise of Government* provides the basis for Nozick's property owning libertarian utopia outlined in his provocative *Anarchy, State and Utopia*. Perhaps more importantly, Kant supplied the framework for Rawls's welfare liberalism in his magisterial *Theory of Justice*. Kant also informs contemporary thinking on cosmopolitan justice. And we should not forget Hegel. Communitarians such as Charles Taylor have used his ideas, and he has more than just a walk-on part in Fukuyama's widely read *The End of History and the Last Man*, which celebrated the victory of liberal democratic capitalism over its Communist (and Fascist) adversaries.

Other considerations might also motivate scholars, especially the use of novel interpretive frameworks referred to above. In this regard a far more historical approach has often been adopted. By stressing the intellectual/linguistic tradition within which a thinker wittingly or unwittingly works, we can see just how the natural law tradition impacted on a number of political thinkers, especially Locke, but less obviously, and perhaps more controversially, Hobbes, Hume, Rousseau, Burke, Kant and Hegel. The civic humanist or classical republican tradition has also been recognised as a significant current within the history of political thought, particularly in the case of Machiavelli, Rousseau and the Scottish Enlightenment, of which Hume was a part. Locating a thinker within a certain intellectual or linguistic context, much favoured by Quentin Skinner and the 'Cambridge school' referred to above, helps us to avoid the trap of anachronism, of assuming in timeless fashion that what they meant and intended can be gained from reading only the raw text. Political contextualisation may also enrich our understanding of the circumstances in which a text was written, adding to our knowledge of the author's intention and meaning. Machiavelli and Locke in particular have been the subjects of this line of interrogation.

Adopting such an approach may help to resolve disagreement; all may become clear once the context is properly understood. But it can also create disagreement of its own. There are many contexts and traditions that can be used in this way. It will seldom be clear which of these is appropriate, if any single one ever is. Conflict will therefore arise between contextualist interpretations. Equally, knowledge of the political context can reinforce interpretive difficulty if the author was possibly seeking to gain, or keep favour with, a patron, as with Machiavelli and possibly Burke. Or, more speculatively, the writer might have feared persecution or loss of a job, as with Hobbes, Locke and Hegel, leading them to write in a coded way so as not to give offence. Here Strauss's influence has been important.

Another form of contextualist approach might add less to our comprehension of an author's self-understanding but could help in appreciating the problems with which they were consciously or unconsciously attempting to grapple. Here the socio-economic context, favoured especially by Marxist-influenced commentators such as C. B. Macpherson, is seen as relevant in terms of viewing a particular thinker in relation to underlying socio-economic changes. An equally and potentially conjectural approach is psychoanalysis, the search for hidden motivations. Here Rousseau and Burke have been obvious candidates, although Marx too has been put on the psychiatrist's couch. Thus, conscious, authorial intention can become a less important focus of inquiry. Indeed, different kinds of historical approach may be adopted for another reason: to comprehend more fully the significance of a thinker for understanding present political philosophies and ideologies, which may have little or nothing to do with an author's intention or self-understanding. So for example we may want to understand Hobbes's or Locke's significance for the later liberal tradition, with the subsequent meaning of the term 'liberal' totally obscure from their point of view. In much broader terms we may wish to explore a particular thinker's contribution to modernity, characterised by secularism, science and different forms of individualism, all the product of a post-agrarian and post-theocentric society.

Finally, we may note that the problem of textual interpretation may have little to do with the interpretive agendas of the commentators themselves. These political philosophers may be just plain inconsistent. They can change their mind as their thought develops, so we get the 'young' and 'old' Marx. And of course they may have just forgotten what they said previously, mindful that consistency can be an overrated virtue and valued differently at different times. More specifically, interpretive differences may also arise because thinkers offer inconsistent or ambiguous meanings of key terms, as with Machiavelli's *'virtù'* and *'fortuna'*, Locke's definition of 'property', or

Marx's 'forces' and 'relations of production'. Equally prosaic: commentators may be unaware of the existence of key texts. Machiavelli's *The Discourses* did not become widely known until the eighteenth century, and Marx's early works were not readily available until the 1950s in the Anglophone world.

Conflicting Interpretations

This speaks for itself. Here you will find the main body of each chapter, summarising the main points of contention as they have arisen. This summary is necessarily selective. It picks out the main points of contention in a way that should be accessible to the reader who has some knowledge of the immediate appearance of the argument in the original text. Having read a text for the first time, you may find yourself thinking 'OK. But what do I have to say about this?' This section will introduce you to the kinds of things that commentators have said. More pointedly, you might react to your first reading by wondering why you're being told this. This section will give you a number of alternative answers to your question by showing how different interpreters had different ideas about the motives prompting the ideas expressed. We all have our own ideas about which answers are the better ones, so the final section allows each of our authors to express this as an *evaluation* of the interpretations on offer.

The Treatments Offered

To give a flavour of what you will encounter in the following chapters, we will briefly outline the key interpretive issues that have arisen in relation to each thinker. Although commentators could agree, as Maureen Ramsay indicates, that *Machiavelli* aimed to establish a strong and independent state in a corrupt Renaissance Italy, different textual interpretations can in part be put down to Machiavelli himself, if inadvertently. He seemed to advocate different forms of government in *The Prince* (rule by a single individual) and *The Discourses* (rule by the few and the many) and compounded this inconsistency by neither signing nor dating his manuscripts, making the exact context in which he wrote these pieces uncertain. Moreover, he was not intent on writing a formal treatise for contemporary academics to sink their teeth into; he wanted to move his reader, often through rhetoric. As a consequence, he never settled on precise and stable meanings of '*virtù*' and '*fortuna*', the two fundamental, organising concepts in his work. In truth, Machiavelli spoke with many voices, and many interpreters wanted to listen to only one of them.

This unwillingness to listen to all his voices may be attributable to the different interests and passions of the interpreters themselves. In the sixteenth and seventeenth centuries his writings upset the Catholic Church which was then embattled in the Reformation and Counter Reformation and having to face the rise of the secular state. The Church was outraged by his explicit notion that the Ten Commandments could not be used as a ready-reckoner for political calculation. Yet Italian nationalists warmly embraced him in the nineteenth century. And from the mid-twentieth century he became the focus of scholarly attention. In apparently adopting a value-free, empirical, inductive method in order to uncover the laws governing political behaviour he was heralded as a forerunner of modern political science. Yet scholars began to take textual and contextual matters more seri-ously, attempting to make sense of Machiavelli's seeming inconsistencies in his discussions of *virtù* and *fortuna*, and between the *Prince* and the *Discourses*. Interpreters were fascinated by Machiavelli, because he posed in starkest terms one of the most fundamental problems of political life: the problem of 'dirty hands', the way in which the principles informing politi-cal conduct were far removed from those governing individual, day-to-day dealings. Did Machiavelli divorce politics from ethics? Was he immoral or amoral, holding that the end justified the means, the champion of *realpolitik*? Or was he saying that politics demanded an ethics of a new type (utilitari-anism), that looked towards the beneficial consequences (the common good) of a political act, irrespective of the morality of the act itself? Perhaps the jury is still out on this question, if only because the problem of Machiavelli is the problem of politics. Not much better resolved is the issue that loomed behind many of the interpretive agendas: Machiavelli's moder-nity. Do we see him as a thinker looking backwards to ancient republican *virtù* and mystical notions of *fortuna*, or forwards as one of the first truly secular thinkers attempting to ground politics on the observable facts of human behaviour?

With *Hobbes*, interpreters could agree about his purposes and the broad outline of his argument – he seemed to articulate a disarmingly simple theory – yet differences emerge partly because he offered different presen-tations of the same argument, and also because of tensions within texts, especially with respect to the power of the sovereign and extent of individ-ual rights. As Alistair Edwards suggests, his argument 'creaks'. (2:44) And then there are the research agendas of the different commentators, with some at least wanting to cast him in a favourable (liberal) light. Others, explicitly or implicitly concerned with Hobbes's historical significance, pose an intriguing question because he stood on the 'cusp of modernity', in the early modern period of political, intellectual and economic transition, which saw him looking forwards and backwards, a modernist and a traditionalist. His modernism stemmed from his individualism, his attempt to ground his theory of obligation primarily on observable human traits and his self-conscious effort to employ scientific methods, with theological justification taking a back seat. Nevertheless, Hobbes sought to defend the traditional social and political order and its values, and he often spoke in the language of natural law. Yet, some commentators – both left and right wing – have detected in his theory of human nature evidence of bourgeois individualism, although others have been keen to stress that his individualism should be given no preconceived class content. And whilst Hobbes was clear that the individual had the right to resist the sovereign, based upon the right of self-preservation, there still remained the question of whether Hobbes wanted the power of the sovereign to be self-limiting, as a ruler through law, which seemed to propel him in a liberal direction. The question of a self-limiting sovereign in turn rests on the larger issue of the status of his laws of nature. Were they merely prudential and therefore modern, or were they Christian? Depending on that answer is whether Hobbes consistently held to a psychological egoist view of human nature. Also at stake in grappling with Hobbes' conception of the sovereign's power is the tension between Hobbes' own personal preferences in wanting an enlightened sovereign and the logic of his own theory. Yet whatever these textual tensions we have to look closely at his understanding of an evolving English political tradition and of seventeenth-century conflicts if we are to get an informed view of his intentions.

Given his foundational role in transatlantic liberal political culture, controversies over *Locke* inevitably have a currently relevant ideological inflection. Whilst most commentators could agree that Locke was a liberal, consensus evaporated as soon as the question sharpened to, 'a liberal of what stripe?' And this question in part hinged on what precisely Locke meant by the 'preservation of property', who and/or what is Locke seeking to preserve, for what reason and by which means? Conclusive answers to these questions were difficult because the texts were 'messy' (3:62), not merely in relation to the meaning of property. What Locke's priorities were in the *Two Treatises of Government* are not clear, oscillating between a political manifesto and a philosophical inquiry into the nature of government in general, as well as between natural law arguments and more detailed constitutional proposals. Equally, whether the *Two Treatises of Government* should be understood as part of a broader philosophical project is not clear. Then we also have to appreciate that, as Timothy Kenyon indicates, Locke was influenced by a range of interwoven contexts. (3:78–9) Commentators focusing on one context in order to explain his intentions,

ɔk the part for the whole, and unsurprisingly came up with
.erpretations that were vulnerable to the charge of attributing a
on to him. Most challenged the standard view of him as simply
a consu̇ṫ̇ṫional Whig and celebrator of the 'Glorious Revolution' of 1688.
From the 1960s onwards interpreters looked more closely at Locke within
various contexts. Those who took the political context as important emphasised Locke's radicalism, and even went so far as to lodge him within the
Leveller tradition, politically a liberal democrat. Those who stressed the
socio-economic backdrop painted him as a bourgeois liberal ideologue,
combining Christianity and capitalism, economically a neo-liberal.
Scholars underlining the intellectual environment portrayed him as a
Christian natural law thinker, for whom property ownership carried social
obligations, rendering him in effect a welfare liberal.

Others, in attempting to uncover the meaning of the *Two Treatises* and
other works, preferred to move into decontextualised waters, being quite
happy with textual analysis and examining the extent to which Locke was a
coherent thinker. For example, could his empiricist epistemology which
pointed towards scepticism be reconciled with his natural law affiliation
which presupposed a high degree of certainty? Some commentators were
concerned to show how Locke's inconsistencies revealed liberalism's inherent tensions, while others acknowledged his inconsistencies and proceeded
to reconstruct his argument in order to develop a coherent and politically relevant theory of property, whether of a neo-liberal or welfare liberal variety.

Until recently *Hume*, whose scepticism owed much to Locke's empiricist
epistemology, was known principally as an opponent of social contract
theory. Since the 1970s, however, interest in other aspects of his political philosophy have developed as a result of neo-liberal theorists' enthusiasm for
unintended consequence theory and its origins in the Scottish Enlightenment,
with which Hume was closely associated. As John Salter shows, interpreters
have in effect demonstrated that Hume's political philosophy was far from
simple. There were clear textual differences between his *Treatise on Human
Nature* and his *Enquiry Concerning the Principles of Morals* over his understanding of the origins of justice. The traditional view of Hume's epistemological scepticism was that it reflected his attempt to undermine the natural
law tradition, based upon reason. Rather, he argued, social rules stemmed
from convention. This position seemed to flow from his desire to limit the
right of resistance to rulers by denying natural rights arguments that could
easily take a revolutionary turn. More recent accounts, however, argue that
his prime intention was the modernisation of natural law and that his explanation of the origins of justice rested upon a secularised version of natural
law. He was influenced by a secular reading of Grotius, who, along with

Pufendorf and others, propounded a theory of limited resistance to government in contrast with more popular versions of natural law theory. And the rights of possession, for example, originated 'naturally', from within the family. More generally, Hume was concerned to establish the 'natural' psychological bases of moral sentiment. An implication of this interpretation was that Hume's real target of criticism was not natural law as such, but its theological underpinnings. Yet commentators who stressed his natural law affinity also wanted to underline his commitment to 'convention' as well. In combining both 'nature' and 'convention' he was a true moderate within the political context of the Hanoverian regime in the early eighteenth century. Hence he upheld both 'political' liberty unique to the British constitution, as well as a more universalistic liberty provided by absolutist regimes, which consisted of freedom under law.

Another interpretive framework viewed Hume's ambiguities from a different angle. This standpoint associated him with the civic humanist tradition, which saw active citizenship – 'political virtue' – as essential in establishing a militarily strong state. He seemed uncertain as to whether the advent of a commercial society would corrupt the political process or enhance it. The growth of public credit could generate social instability in the form of fostering a powerful financial/stockholder class with no particular loyalty to the state. On the other hand, commercial society brought to the fore a public-spirited middle class, as well as more moderate conduct in political life. And the development of the industrial 'arts' would increase the nation's military strength.

In stark contrast to Hume, *Rousseau* has little reputation as a political moderate. In helping to inspire the French Revolution of 1789 and the Reign of Terror that followed, he was perceived as a dangerous thinker, and to this day his thought has the capacity to inflame the passions. As Alan Apperly shows, Rousseau provided plenty of ammunition for radicals to criticise capitalist liberal democracy, as if he were a kind of proto-Marxist. Rousseau also supplied a well-stocked arsenal for liberals and conservatives to damn radicals as incipient totalitarians, as enemies of the 'open society'. Yet somewhere above the fray could be found sympathetic liberals who saw Rousseau as a forerunner of Kant, the most intellectually sophisticated liberal of all. That Rousseau was open to such diverse interpretations was partly down to Rousseau himself who, in seeking to reconcile individual liberty and order, had a fondness for paradox. This was best exemplified in his idea that good laws were needed to socialise citizens into virtue, but virtue itself was required to make good laws. The 'effect' would have to become the 'cause'. Perhaps (in)famously connected to this promotion of virtue is the paradoxical notion of 'forcing' a citizen to be 'free'. And although he championed direct democracy he maintained that the general will could differ from the majority of actual wills as expressed in the 'will of all'. At his most pessimistic he held democracy as an unattainable ideal, whilst in his more optimistic moments he maintained that some form of lawgiver could manipulate the people into democratic virtue. Those hostile to Rousseau held that these paradoxes concealed inconsistencies, whilst those sympathetic to him tried to make sense of, or explain them. Nevertheless, in historical terms his effect has been paradoxical, his individualism inspiring the French revolutionaries' defence of the Rights of Man in 1789, and his republican collectivism used to justify the subsequent Jacobin reign of Terror.

His *Social Contract* provided much of the data for a totalitarian interpretation of his position. His notion of moral liberty implied the 'politicisation of private life' (5:106) and therefore the abandonment of 'negative liberty'. On the one hand, Berlin, whose views exemplified the Cold War liberal response to Rousseau, saw him as an upholder of 'positive liberty', which assumed a 'real' or 'rational will' to which an elite had privileged access. Radicals, on the other hand, were inspired not merely by his argument for direct democracy, but by his *Second Discourse*. In this, Rousseau criticised modern society, with its competitiveness leading to a loss of personal authenticity, and its socio-economic inequality that diminished personal freedom through the loss of autonomy. Certain kinds of liberal were sympathetic to Rousseau, seeing in him a deep preference for individual liberty and the rule of law, as well as upholding the liberal distinction between freedom and licence. His liberalism was of a perfectionist kind, with the general will, although moralising, always open to question. The general will therefore required traditional liberal freedoms of speech, thought, the press and so on. Not surprisingly, given the politically motivated nature of the discussion, much of Rousseau got left on the 'cutting room floor' (5:119), telling us more about commentators' preoccupations than about Rousseau.

If Rousseau is famous for his radicalism, *Burke* is well known as one of conservative thought's main inspirations. Yet, as with Rousseau, David Shugarman indicates that a simple portrait of him is not possible. We do not have to spend much time to tease out his inconsistencies. His contemporaries were astonished by his instant transformation from a progressive Whig politician into a raging opponent of the French Revolution. Not only do we have the 'young' and 'old' Burke, but even his most famous text *Reflections on the Revolution in France* is hardly written from the viewpoint of considered reflection with carefully thought out lines of argument. Not surprisingly, some analysts of Burke see him as an inconsistent dualist, whose economic and political ideas seem grounded upon opposed liberal and conservative principles. He seemed both a critic and supporter of the existing social, economic and political order, a critic and supporter of both the aristocracy and the bourgeoisie. This left commentators undecided as to whether he was a liberal conservative or a conservative liberal. However, other Burke interpreters whose analysis took a more contextualist inflection maintained that the two Burkes were after all one, especially if the market economy was seen as part and parcel of the traditional order. A more unified Burke is offered by those who stress his liberal credentials in opposing the abuses of power. This constituted the mainspring of his politics, even if at times he had to conceal his true beliefs. Yet this perspective has been contested by those who see Burke as illiberal insofar as he was anti-democratic and intolerant of the 'swinish multitude', Jews and atheists.

Burke's commentators attempting to comprehend the nature of Burke's conservatism have been undecided about his attitude towards abstract theory. Some have viewed him as an archetypal sceptic when it came to the problem-solving powers of reason in human affairs, whilst others have regarded him as a natural law conservative whose position was grounded on metaphysical principles derived from Aristotle and Aquinas. This viewpoint has been rejected by those who, apart from indicating his anti-theoreticism, point to his emphasis, firstly on the way constitutions evolve spontaneously as unintended consequences and, secondly, on the role of pragmatic leadership. Moreover, he often adopted a utilitarian criterion in assessing the goodness of a constitution. Finally, there are interpreters, perhaps under the influence of literary theory, who prefer not to take any of Burke's political positions seriously. He was in their eyes merely a rhetorician or a dramatist, for whom the whole world was a stage. Yet whatever different images of Burke there are on offer, the contemporary political concerns of many of these commentators, especially those who wanted to recruit him to the anti-radical Cold War cause, were not far away.

Interest in *Kant's* political writings and its complexities is a relatively recent phenomenon. This has been prompted by John Rawls's indebtedness to him, as well as by the current need to think about the normative implications of globalisation, especially in terms of transnational justice and other forms of cosmopolitanism. Although Kant was a rigorous thinker, as Katrin Flikschuh demonstrates, he provided fertile grounds for interpretive difference, depending on which elements of his philosophy are emphasised – his epistemological or moral theory, or his theory of history. So far there have been at least five different schools of interpretation. The first suggests that Kant separated politics from ethics in such a way as to offer a quasi-Hobbesian account of political motivation, that is, one based upon rational self-interest. The state's sanctions gave everyone an interest in upholding the moral requirements of justice, with a social contract necessary to guarantee each other's freedom. And the centrality of self-interest in political life ultimately led to his call for a 'federation of free republics' at the international level, rather than a world government. A second interpretation stresses the moral dimension of motivation. Although Kant's political theory is portrayed as contractualist and the ethics/politics distinction is endorsed, this distinction was internal to morality. Thus obligation was based upon the state's moral authority in upholding the universal principle of justice as the 'principle of self-legislation'. Property rights rested upon the mutual recognition of all citizens that they were needed for external freedom. His cosmopolitan idea of lasting peace also rested on the moral motivation necessary to maintain the institutions of peace.

The third, 'teleological' interpretation was also grounded upon the ethics/politics distinction, with politics as the 'helpmate' of Kant's ethical, end-in-themselves doctrine. The state enabled individuals to realise freedom, and as such was founded not on a self-interested social contract, but as a consequence of objective capacity for individual self-realisation. The teleological imprint was also apparent at the international level, with cosmopolitanism an historical product of the human race searching for peace, the evolving, collective reflection upon the consequences of war and competition. Another interpretation saw Kant running with two theories of obligation, his 'real' one articulated in terms of natural law rather than social contract. Political obligation stemmed from the idea of property as the product of a mutual recognition of everyone's survival needs, forming a 'natural will' upon which the general will is grounded. Survival needs also formed the basis of a state's territorial rights in relation to other states, as well as the property rights of foreigners who passed through a state's territories. Nevertheless, peaceful interstate dealings had to be based upon a voluntaristic acceptance of the principles of justice, according to the requirements of natural law, and only republics were equipped to do this. The final, 'constructivist' perspective on Kant developed a cosmopolitan approach, applying his categorical imperative to interstate relations. This is, in a sense, the grounds for what may be called an 'ethical foreign policy', in which lying and coercion entail logical contradiction.

Traditionally *Hegel* is perceived, in contrast to Kant, as a deeply illiberal thinker, as an apologist for early nineteenth-century Prussian absolutism, as a critic of the French Revolution of 1789 and by the Cold War period as an enemy of the 'open society'. As Tony Burns illustrates, this view of Hegel could be supported in different ways. At the level of his metaphysics his philosophical idealism suggested that he was uncritical of reality and therefore a conservative; this was expressed most graphically in his famous assertion that 'what is rational is actual and what is actual is rational'. The corollary for Hegel was that the political and ethical principles that underlay the Prussian state marked the 'end of history'. In the *Philosophy of Right* he opposed democracy and its ignorant self-interested 'rabble' that had led to the French revolutionary terror, in favour of the bureaucracy's legislative wisdom. Although he vigorously defended private property as the basis of individual freedom and 'personality', he could be seen as illiberal in the sense that he opposed liberal social contract theory and the idea of freedom as doing what one wants, in favour of liberty as doing one's duty, effectively subordinating the individual to the state.

Over the last thirty years, however, some interpreters have portrayed Hegel as a liberal thinker. According to this reading Hegel is viewed as proponent of constitutional government and the rule of law, of a 'rational' state grounded in natural law and natural rights, and as close to Locke. Here he at least supports the French Revolution insofar as it upheld the Rights of Man. In the last twenty years some commentators have gone even further and portrayed him as a radical democrat, a secret supporter of the French revolution even in his maturity. They also took their cue from Marx's and Engels's interpretation of Hegel, distinguishing between his dialectical method and his metaphysical system, which, as an idealist, suggested that from the point of view of his method, history had not come to a full stop. The description in the *Philosophy of Right* was of a provisional sketch of the best state that had evolved so far in the process of world history. At least one commentator, in detaching Hegel's metaphysical idealism from his seemingly materialist account of politics and history, has suggested that, unknown to Marx, Hegel was a crypto-communist, who criticised capitalist private property relations.

These diverse interpretive positions were not solely attributable to the concerns and dispositions of the commentators themselves, but arise from Hegel's 'often ambiguous and obscure' use of language, (8:163) as when he says 'what is rational is actual, and what is actual is rational'. Second, this dialectical method of synthesising opposed positions means that he never seems to endorse or condemn one position outright, allowing interpreters to adopt different positions depending upon choice of emphasis. Finally, Hegel's meaning does not automatically spring from the page, in that the historical and political context of Prussian absolutism may have prompted him to communicate to his readers in a coded form.

With *Mill* the ambiguities do not have to be teased out of the text. Most accounts have noted the critical tension in *On Liberty* between his utilitarian affiliation to the greatest happiness principle, the product of loyalty to his father's teachings, and his heartfelt plea for individual liberty and toleration in a world of stifling conformity engendered by the growth of democracy. As Jonathan Seglow maintains, much of the debate turned upon the meaning of the 'harm principle' entailed in Mill's distinction between self-regarding and other-regarding acts as viewed through the prism of libertarianism or utilitarianism. Although a number of commentators took either his utilitarianism or his libertarianism to be the 'real' Mill, most acknowledged the existence of either a genuine or an apparent tension between these two principles. The traditional view is that he is palpably inconsistent. For example, there exists in his argument an implicit notion of 'morality-dependent harm', which according to his libertarian logic should not constitute grounds for state or society interference with individual taste or action. Yet on the utilitarian premise, to which Mill is also committed, all harms or disutilities must enter into the calculus. A number of revisionist schools have emerged seeking to portray Mill as coherent. Thus, for example, when Mill invokes the harm principle he is merely referring to the harming of another's 'interests'. Another interpretation suggests that the logic of Mill's utilitarianism means treating everyone with equal concern and respect. 'External preferences' resting upon a moralised belief as to how others should be treated and not merely oneself, which could lead to discrimination, therefore, should not be included within the calculus. An individual's freedom and opportunity would thereby be protected from the prejudices of others. A further utilitarian solution was to view prudential and aesthetic conduct as promoting happiness in the private sphere, and moral conduct, which involved the happiness of others, as properly belonging to the other-regarding, public sphere. A final attempt to square the circle was a proposal that for Mill individual freedom and happiness were inextricably linked. The harm principle is relevant in the sense that individual interests include autonomy as well as security; both are necessary for happiness.

Many of *Marx*'s sympathetic interpreters were similarly engaged in some kind of rescue mission, but within the context of hostile anti-Marxist criticism. As Jules Townshend suggests, the interpretive environment of Marx was highly politicised, given Marxism's ideological influence over a major part of the twentieth century. As a result, two criss-crossing interpretive agendas, often politically driven, emerged: Marx-as-truth, and the truth-about-Marx. Philosophers were keen to scrutinise the truth claims of Marxism, especially of Marx's own theories. Here the self-proclaimed scientific status of Marx's theory of history, known as 'historical materialism', came under the spotlight. Whilst critics suggested that historical materialism was unscientific because it was 'unfalsifiable', or incoherent because the meaning of the key concepts and the relation between them was unclear or implausible, defenders proposed that either Marx was a pragmatic thinker, or that he was a methodological pluralist. Others defended Marx's scientificity by suggesting that he was a structuralist or a functionalist. However, another group of Marx defenders, perhaps aiming to play down the a priori, scientific status of historical materialism because of its association with the totalitarian ideology of the Soviet Union, emphasised his empirical approach to understanding society and history as well as his debt to Hegel, especially to his dialectical methodology. Indeed, Marx's sympathisers, perhaps seeking to construct a non-Soviet Marxism, often went so far as ignoring his claims to science altogether, and portrayed the 'real' Marx as a political philosopher, a theorist of human 'self-alienation', of human freedom. This interpretive line also gave rise to less politically charged perspectives concerning the extent to which Marx was a normative theorist. Thus, we get different schools of interpreters emphasising the 'scientific' or 'ethical' Marx, resulting in a debate about his intellectual development and whether the 'young' or 'old' Marx was the 'real' Marx.

All this interpretive dissonance was of course aided, if unwittingly, by Marx himself. There were obvious tensions in his work between his Hegelian, teleological roots – the idea that 'history' has a purpose – and his commitment to empirically based, open-ended research, as well as between his desire to understand the world in a scientific and objective manner and his subjective, ethical commitment to proletarian self-emancipation. Then we can add to this the fact that definitions of key terms of historical materialism and their precise conceptual relationship with each other were either unclear or unstable. Finally, we have to note that as in the case of the treatment of some other thinkers in this volume, our picture of Marx radically changed as some of his less well known (early) texts became generally available.

We have now outlined the different interpretive glosses put on the thinkers included in this volume. We have not indicated how each contributor evaluates the relative strengths and weaknesses of these interpretations – some are clearly stronger than others. But there is usually a grain of truth in all of them, helping to kindle and rekindle endless argument. This volume is a snapshot of an irresistible conversation which can go in any, and many, directions, with some issues resolvable and others not, with new interpretive paradigms (deconstruction being quite possibly a future one) giving rise to new questions, and new political imperatives in the 'real' world demanding new philosophical bearings. We are party to an historical conversation between the past and the present. Yet we must acknowledge that the present is also 'history', with its own distinct priorities and questions. Consequently, the thinkers considered here may, at some future date, prove not to be quite so canonical – others may seem more relevant or insightful or analytically rigorous as the participants in political discourse become less male, middle and upper class, less white and less European. Just as societies change and move on, so does political thought, and in reflecting society it reflects back into society, helping shape the images of the world in which we live, relentlessly asking the question of where we, as political animals, ought to go and what we ought to do. Alternatively, time may tell us that the writings of these thinkers are in fact canonical, articulating truths and arguments that each generation can use, reshape and claim as its own.

1

Machiavelli (1469–1527)

MAUREEN RAMSAY

Introduction

Machiavelli is a pivotal figure in the history of political thought. His views of human nature, society and government mark a break with medieval philosophy and sixteenth-century political theory based on teleological assumptions about God's purposes for man. Machiavelli divorced politics from higher purposes, from Christian morality, from theology and from religion. He conceived the state as functioning solely for human purposes and constructed rules of conduct that were not moral rules, but which were informed by a realistic and practical view of the world gleaned from observation of events and examples drawn from history. Machiavelli radically secularised political thought and initiated new ways of looking at man and society. It is with Machiavelli, that modern social and political theory begins.

Machiavelli is best known for his two major political writings, *The Prince*, and *The Discourses on The First Ten Books of Titus Livy*. Although the *Art of War*, *The Discourses* and the *Florentine Histories* are relevant to his political thinking, it is the two former works and the relationship between them, which form the core of Machiavelli studies. Throughout all his political writings, Machiavelli claimed to have one fundamental purpose – to discover how to establish and maintain an independent state in corrupt Renaissance Italy. To do this, he intended to break with ancient and medieval thought with its theological and metaphysical underpinnings and to campaign against illusions about politics rooted in the Christian or the idealistic thought of his predecessors. He aimed to blaze a new trail of political analysis in order to reach the truth of practical politics.

Machiavelli saw himself as an innovator. In *The Prince* (hereafter *P*; see A. Gilbert, 1965), he announces that he is departing from 'the methods of others' in order to 'write something useful for him who comprehends it'. The novelty of Machiavelli's new method lay in his claim to be concerned with the 'truth of the matter as facts show rather than with any fanciful notion' (*P.* XV). *The Prince* was intended as a practical advice document in the genre of treatises dealing with the problem of princely rule. In the princely literature from the Middle Ages to the Renaissance, political moralists had compiled a list of cardinal and princely virtues it was the duty of a good prince to acquire. Machiavelli complained that such advice only applied to perfect princes in perfect states. He intended to discuss facts drawn from history and from his own political experience as a civil servant and diplomat in the government of Florence, in order to bring about what was typical and general in political conduct and so to establish rules and define maxims for successful political action.

Machiavelli took it as given that the ends of politics were the acquiring and keeping of power, the stability of the state, the preservation of order and general prosperity. Therefore, in order to provide useful advice, Machiavelli was concerned to establish from historical example and factual evidence the kinds of qualities rulers must have and the actions they must take in order to achieve political success. These qualities were psychological and social, rather than moral; these actions were governed by prudential rules rather than moral rules. Consequently, he overturns the idealised conception of the virtues found in the works of his predecessors. He exhorts the prince to act according to conventional virtues when he can. But the prince must be adaptable and 'have a mind to turn in any direction as Fortune's winds and the variety of affairs require ... he holds to what is right when he can and knows how to do wrong when he must' (*P.* XV11).

The prince must cultivate, not traditional virtue, but Machiavellian *virtù*. He must be bold, resolute, flexible, prepared to break promises and act against charity, truth, religion and humanity. The prince must combine the cunning of the fox with the strength of the lion and be devious, ruthless, violent or cruel as the situation demands. Political necessity frequently demands that the prince learns how not to be good. When the occasion requires it, the prince must adopt any means necessary. If princes succeed in conquest and in preserving states, they will be honoured and praised regardless of the means used since 'as to the actions of all men and especially those of princes ... everyone looks to their result' (*P.* XV111). Machiavelli's focus in *The Prince* was on monarchies and princely behaviour. In *The Discourses* (hereafter *D*; see A. Gilbert, 1965) he is mainly concerned with republican government. Here, he aimed to explain how the Roman republic managed to achieve greatness. As in *The Prince*, he applies his method using historical studies and his own experience to draw practical conclusions. He again emphasises that in times of political necessity, means must be adapted to circumstances. Actions, which display *virtù* rather than traditional moral virtues, are required to withstand the blows of Fortune. If a republic is to survive, rulers and citizens alike must possess *virtù*. Just as a ruler should not shrink from evil deeds, neither should citizens when the survival of the republic is at stake:

> because when it is absolutely a question of the safety of one's country, there must be no consideration of just or unjust, of merciful or cruel, of praiseworthy or disgraceful; instead setting aside every scruple, one must follow to the utmost any plan that will save her life and keep her liberty. (*D*. 111, 41)

Similarly, success excuses the deed because a prudent intellect will never 'censure anyone for any unlawful action used in organising a kingdom or setting up a republic – though the deed accuses him, the result should excuse him' (*D*. 111, 2).

In *The Discourses*, however, Machiavelli advances the view that though a single ruler is necessary to found and reform states, a republican government is better at maintaining them once they have been established (*D*. 111, 9). Their subsequent fortunes depend not on the virtue of one man, but on the civic virtue of citizens prepared to advance collective interests over their own private or sectional interests. Here, he claims that 'governments by the people are better than those by princes' (*D*. 1, 58) and that it is 'not individual good but common good that makes cities great. Yet without doubt this common good is thought important only in republics' (*D*. 11, 2).

Problems and Issues

Interpretations of Machiavelli are legion. No other political author has provoked either the same volume of critical responses or caused such sharp disagreement about his purposes. There are a bewildering array of conflicting interpretations about his political views which have continued to grow unabated from his own time to the present evidenced in Fiore's (1990) 600 page bibliography of modern Machiavelli scholarship.

In the interpretive literature Machiavelli is variously described as the Galileo of politics, the first political scientist, an anti-metaphysical empiricist, a positivist, a realist, a pragmatist, a cynic. Conversely, he is seen as lacking a scientific mind and a historical sense, more artistic and intuitive than scientific. Or, he is the founder of metapolitics, of *raison d'état*, an advocate of *realpolitik*, a cold technician of political life. He is condemned as an evil ideologue, a despot, an absolutist, a teacher of evil, an atheist, a pagan and an anti-Christian. He is hailed as heir to, a rebel against, and a representative of, Renaissance humanism. He is an anguished humanist, a radical critical humanist. He is admired as a moralist, a passionate patriot, the father of Italian Nationalism, a giant of the Enlightenment, a committed republican, and a proto-revolutionary.

In order to forge a way through the impenetrable mass of diverse opinions, the significant areas of dispute can be categorised, firstly into debates about Machiavelli's method and the scientific status of his work. Secondly, into conflicting interpretations about the relationship between politics and morality and, within this, debates about the meaning and significance of Machiavelli's political vocabulary. Thirdly, mirroring and related to the ethics–politics debate, into the rival view of the relationship between the advice given to the absolute ruler in *The Prince* and the apparent republican sentiments in *The Discourses*.

Why Conflicting Interpretations?

Few political writers have suffered from such polarised judgements as Machiavelli. A partial explanation for this lies in the textual status of his works. There are no original autographed manuscripts of the chief works. Translations and edited versions inevitably involve critical interpretation and they differ in tone, vocabulary and syntax, opening up possibilities for different readings. The lack of definitive texts also poses chronological puzzles, difficulties in accurately dating the major works and explaining their genesis and place in Machiavelli's thought. In the received texts difficulties in discerning Machiavelli's meaning are exacerbated by his own lack of rigour, by aspects of his prose style and by his limited political vocabulary. Machiavelli was not a systematic, analytic political theorist. He does not give any formal exposition of the features of his method nor explain their importance for understanding his doctrines. He does not define the principles underpinning his maxims nor sustain a case for why one type of government is better than another. As a vehicle for conveying his ideas, his prose style and his political concepts are problematic. Features of Machiavelli's prose ensure maximum impact, they startle and shock and they excite controversy. Machiavelli's key concepts such as *virtù* and *fortuna*, but also *ambizione, bontà, politica, stato, ordini, libertà, gloria* are used in a wide variety of contexts. They convey a plurality of meanings, undermining precise definition, making it difficult to establish his intentions. Moreover tensions, contradictions and ambiguities within and between the texts make them vulnerable to different readings, stubbornly resisting a definitive interpretation.

Different attitudes towards Machiavelli, however, are also a consequence of biased political and historical opinion. His early reputation as a diabolic advisor to princes, the appropriation of his name as a byword for cunning and duplicitous behaviour, his reinterpretations as republican patriot in the eighteenth and nineteenth centuries, reflect either the limited information available to commentators or their own political and moral preoccupations. The range of modern critical viewpoints still encompasses ancient accusations and positive appraisals of Machiavelli's ideas. Though these debates were re-focused by the new interpretations of Croce, Meinecke and Chabod in the 1920s, they have done little to stem disparate views about Machiavelli's relationship to politics and morality, his republicanism or his methods of analysis. More is now known about the details of Machiavelli's life and work and this has inspired a plethora of conjectures about the roots, development and meaning of Machiavelli's thought. Machiavelli has been dissected by theologians, moralists, philosophers, political scientist, linguists, literary critics and historians. These focus variously on his life and career, his maxims, his assumptions, his basic concepts, his method and conclusions, his style and use of language, his reading of classical authors, his understanding and use of history, his relationships with his predecessors and contemporaries, his experience as a statesman, his Chancery writings, his association with Renaissance humanists, the conditions in sixteenth-century Italy – the political, intellectual and cultural environment in which he lived. Different interpretations reflect the variety of disciplinary and methodological interests of the interpreters. They disagree because they impose different explanatory frameworks on Machiavelli's thought in an attempt to systematise his ideas and because they emphasise one aspect of his thought or a particular context over another.

Conflicting Interpretations

Political Method

A common modern interpretation of Machiavelli popular with scholars of a positivist persuasion and concurring with his own self-proclaimed novelty, champions Machiavelli as a pioneer of empiricism and the inductive method, and hails him as the founder of modern political science. Burnham (1943) for instance claims that Machiavelli shared the methods of Galileo and applied these to politics. His method consisted of describing and correlating

facts drawn from observation or political literature in order to discover constant patterns in history and on the basis of these, define rules or maxims for
successful political behaviour. For Cassirer (1946), Olschki (1945),
Renaudet (1942) and Hancock (1935), Machiavelli is an objective technician
of politics. Their thesis about the scientific character of Machiavelli's
thought also incorporates claims about his ethical neutrality. According to
Cassirer, Machiavelli 'studied political actions in the same way a chemist
studies chemical reactions ... he never blames or praises political actions:
he simply gives a descriptive analysis of them' (Cassirer, 1946, p. 154).
Renaudet describes his methods as 'purely positivist'. Olschki also sees in
Machiavelli a 'refined scientific instinct' who transformed history into an
empirical science and made of politics 'a system of universal rules' based on
the assumption 'that political as well as natural phenomena are ruled by
an inductive method of thinking' (Olschki, 1945, p. 22, p. 25, p. 29).

The notion of Machiavelli as a political scientist comes up against the
challenge that Machiavelli was a man of passion who lacked the emotional
detachment of a neutral impartial scientist, a challenge that resurfaces in the
politics–morality and realism–idealism debates (Chabod, 1958; Sasso,
1958). Others who question Machiavelli's status as a scientist, complain that
Machiavelli did not use or apply a scientific or inductive method. He did
not objectively examine historical data in order to draw practical lessons or
to formulate general laws. Rather he used historical sources as examples of
laws he had already formulated (Butterfield, 1940; Scaglione, 1956).
According to Hulliung 'Machiavelli unified theory and practice by ideology rather than science' using his own 'Machiavellian' reading of history
(Hulliung, 1983, p. 166). But it is Anglo (1969) who most savagely attacks
Machiavelli's methods to expose a number of fallacies. He demonstrates
that Machiavelli's technique as he applied it is at best a shoddy induction in
that his adherence to classical authors and use of recent history is selective,
his sources are uncollated and not used comparatively, and his general
theory is based on a few dubious examples. At worst, Machiavelli's technique
does not constitute a method at all and his induction is a spurious procedure. The essence of induction is that a conclusion should emerge from a
sifting through sources, but Machiavelli imposes conclusions on evidence,
fails to take account of completing theories and examples which would
invalidate his theory and misinterprets or even falsifies sources when they
do not fit his preconceptions. Anglo concludes that Machiavelli is not a scientist, but an artist whose perceptions and disturbing insights were intuitive
rather than the result of the application of any scientific method. His
method 'was not fundamental to his political observation; but was, rather,
an elaborate and irrelevant superstructure' (Anglo, 1969, p. 243).

Politics and Morality

Immoral or Amoral?

Machiavelli has been castigated as a man inspired by the devil, as an immoral writer, an anti-Christian, an evil ideologue and an advocate of tyranny. This was the view of most of the Elizabethan dramatists influenced by Gentillet and supported by the early denunciations of Cardinal Pole, Bodin and Frederick the Great. In recent times Maritain (1942) and Strauss (1958) restate this 'old fashioned and simple opinion that Machiavelli was indifferent to right and wrong and a knowing and a deliberate teacher of evil'. Strauss argues that Machiavelli sought 'a complete revolution in thinking about right and wrong' by leading the prince to accept the 'repulsive doctrine' that 'the end justifies the means' (Strauss, 1958: p. 14, p. 67). It is in this sense that popular culture understands 'Machiavellianism' as an immoral doctrine that licences the abandoning of all moral scruples in the quest for political power. Machiavelli's doctrines have also been seen as the recognition of the necessities and realities of political life and thus as amoral, objective or descriptive, rather than immoral. The most widely discussed thesis is that put forward by Croce in 1925. For Croce and his followers the association of Machiavelli with immorality is inappropriate. Machiavelli was an anguished humanist who did not deny the validity of Christian morality, but revealed the fundamental incompatibility between moral means and political ends. His greatest contribution to the philosophy of politics was his recognition of the 'autonomy of politics' a sphere of action with its own logic and laws 'beyond good and evil', exempt from moral considerations (Croce, 1925, pp. 60–5). Chabod agrees that Machiavelli 'divorces politics and ethics' and that he 'swept aside every criterion of action not suggested by *raison d'état*' (Chabod, 1958, p. 195). Meinecke (1957) also claims that Machiavelli was the first person to recognise the true nature of *raison d'état*, the element of necessity in political conduct. 'The striving for security and self-preservation at any price is behind all conduct according to *raison d'état*' (Meinecke, 1957, p. 265). *Raison d'état* refers to what a statesman must do, what it is logical and rational to do to preserve the interests of the state. Meinecke calls Machiavelli the forefather of modern politics and the pathbreaker of modern history, seen in the actual practice of the pursuit of power by any means.

Challenges to the Originality of Machiavelli's Realism

There are those who argue that Machiavelli is not as original as Meinecke claims. He was not the first to recognise the element of expediency in successful political action. This had been acknowledged at least since the time of Aristotle and was raised more explicitly in the princely literature of the fifteenth-century Italian humanists who were forerunners to Machiavelli (A. Gilbert, 1938; F. Gilbert, 1939). Moreover as Post (1964) has shown, the concept of *raison d'état* was familiar in the late Middle Ages and inherent in the practice of fifteenth-century politics. Political realism was reflected in the internal and external affairs of the medieval state and this had not escaped the attention of theologians and legal theorists who frequently used the notion 'necessity has no laws' to justify extraordinary means through force of circumstance (see also Anglo, 1969, chapter 7).

Descriptive or Ethically Neutral

Other commentators see Machiavelli's political realism as objective or descriptive without committing themselves to the view of the autonomy of politics. Herder, Ranke, Macaulay, Burd and, in recent times, Sasso (1958) argue that Machiavelli simply tells the truth about politics accurately describing the political relationships and strategies that are used to maintain and legitimise power. Others hail him as the first example of a value-free scientist rather than simply descriptive (Cassirer, 1946; Renaudet, 1942; Olschki, 1945; Hancock, 1935). According to this view, Machiavelli's doctrines are not immoral or amoral and he did not judge from a standpoint beyond good and evil. Rather, he provided a technical imperative of skill of the form 'if you want to achieve x, do y'. The ends themselves are neither rational nor good, the means to achieve them are neither praised nor blamed. They are advocated only to achieve the end in question. Machiavelli is ethically neutral and politically uncommitted.

A Different Morality

Others maintain that there is nothing immoral, amoral or ethically neutral about Machiavelli. He provides a justification for moral principles appropriate to political actions which is different from traditional or private moral values, but which is nonetheless moral. For instance, Berlin argues that it is a false antithesis to say that Machiavelli divorced politics and morality. Rather, he distinguishes two incompatible ways of life and therefore two moralities. Machiavelli contrasts the morality of the Graeco–Roman world where ultimate values are political, communal and social, with Judeo–Christian morality in which values are private and individual. According to Berlin, Machiavelli is a moral pluralist, announcing the need to choose between incompatible, but equally moral sets of ends 'either a good, virtuous private life, or a good, successful social existence, but not both' (Berlin, 1972, pp. 197–8). Germino (1966) proposes that Machiavelli can be seen as a proponent of what Weber called (in *Politik als Beruf*) 'the ethics of responsibility' as opposed to 'the ethics of intention'. Machiavelli endorses an 'ethic of responsibility' or 'consequences' in which it is irresponsible in politics to act out of pure motives of individual conscience without weighing the consequences that actually result.

Virtù *and* Fortuna

Virtù and *fortuna* are terms pivotal to Machiavelli's thought since together they comprise the polarities of, and the framework for, all human experience. His belief that *fortuna* controls half our lives and the need to display *virtù* as a countervailing force has important political and moral implications. It raises questions about political virtue – the kind of behaviour necessary for political success and about what kind of government best sustains *virtù* and vice versa. However, of all the basic concepts and contrasts in Machiavelli's political thought, *fortuna* and *virtù* are notoriously problematic and scholars have struggled to assess their precise meaning and significance. According to some interpreters, *fortuna* is a survival of a prelogical description of the world and represents a breakdown of reasoning in Machiavelli's thinking. When he could not explain events, he attributed them to the quasi-superstitious workings of fortune. Cassirer claims that Machiavelli resorted to *fortuna* as a half mythical power when he could not explain events in terms of reason (Cassirer, 1946, p. 157). Chabod largely shares the opinion that *fortuna* is at least half mythical and is regarded by Machiavelli as a mysterious, transcendent grouping of events whose incoherence is unintelligible to the human mind (Chabod, 1958, pp. 67–70).

Against these views of *fortuna* as mysterious or transcendental, Sasso (1952, p. 205) claims that fortune is simply the limitation of human nature which denies men control of certain historical situations. Olschki goes further. *Fortuna* is not a mythical or illogical concept, but an abstract, secular concept representing 'the passive conditions for political success' and '*virtù* is its active counterpart'. (Olschki, 1945, p. 378) Consistent with his interpretation of Machiavelli as a political scientist, Olschki argues that *virtù* and *fortuna* are 'technical terms of a rational system of political thought'. They are building blocks of a scientific analysis of human behaviour comparable to gravity and inertia in Newtonian physics. For Villari, Machiavelli 'always used the word *virtù* in the sense of courage or energy for both good and evil' (Villari, n.d., p. 92). Later scholars agreed but went further in distinguishing the senses in which Machiavelli used the term or in emphasising some senses over others. Wood (1967) prioritises the militaristic aspects of *virtù* and claims that Machiavelli transfers to politics the behaviour of soldiers in battle. Hannaford (1972) argues for a more political and less militaristic understanding of *virtù*, denying the equation between politics and war, which Wood found in Machiavelli. Instead, he highlights the connection between *virtù* and public, political purposes. Plamenatz (1972) distinguishes heroic and civic *virtù*, the former a quality of rulers, founders and restorers of states, the latter a corporate quality of citizens. Pitkin (1984) draws attention to Machiavelli's misogyny and to *virtù* as a masculine concept, denoting energy, effectiveness, virtuosity, force combined with ability. The antithesis of *virtù* is *fortuna*, explicitly a woman favouring young bold men, who to keep her in order must 'cuff and maul her' (*P*. XXV). Price (1973), however, shows *virtù* to be a much more extensive concept conveying a wider range of meanings than the above analyses allow. He argues that *virtù* is a complex cluster concept, one which included traditional, Christian moral virtue, purely militaristic virtue, purely political virtue, a combination of politico–military virtue, an instrumental virtue and a cultural virtue as well as ancient and modern virtue. It is perhaps this combination of meanings which led Whitfield to state that 'there is no doctrine of *virtù* in Machiavelli' (Whitfield, 1947, p. 95).

The Relationship of The Prince to The Discourses

Explaining away the Differences

Much scholarly attention has been devoted to reconciling Machiavelli's advice in *The Prince* with the republican ideas expressed in *The Discourses*. Eighteenth-century interpretations of Machiavelli as patriot, democrat and teacher of freedom explained away *The Prince* as a satire on princes, a warning against tyrants (Spinoza and Rousseau). A more historical relativist attitude in the early nineteenth century explained *The Prince* as a piece of special pleading written at a moment when only a saviour prince could free Italy from foreign domination, preserve her independence and begin her regeneration (Herder, Hegel, Fichte, Ranke). In the nineteenth and early twentieth century, it was Machiavelli's political realism that explained the differences. Meinecke argued that Machiavelli was a republican by ideal and inclination, but his political realism meant that his republican ideals had to give way to princely *realpolitik*. Therefore the contrast between his monarchical and republican attitudes was specious (Meinecke, 1957, p. 32f). Concentrating on the objectivity of Machiavelli's scientific method, other interpretations followed, claiming that Machiavelli's teaching fits a single harmonious pattern. Renaudet (1942) and Cassirer (1946) argued that Machiavelli was indifferent to the choice between absolute monarchy and republican liberty. He was merely interested in the techniques of politics.

The Genetic Approach

Chabod and Italian scholars agreed that there is a unity between the works, but not one attributable to unity of method. They objected to the conception of Machiavelli as a detached scientist applying his ideas in succession to two different subjects, principalities and republics. For Chabod, Machiavelli was a man of passion, whose ideas came from his experience as a politician. Chabod (1958) and Sasso (1958) adopted a 'genetic approach' tracing Machiavelli's development by studying the genesis of his ideas and their connection with his public experience and the events and ideas at the time of writing. Chabod's claim that *The Prince* and *The Discourses* were interrelated and inter-dependent aspects of an organically unified outlook was linked to his thesis about the dating of the two works. According to Chabod, the first half of the first book of *The Discourses* was written in 1513. It displays a strong republican confidence, which in chapters 16–18 gives way to an interest in the personal success of the prince, and the mood in which *The Prince* was composed. Given that at the time of writing restoring a republic was unrealistic and only a prince could restore a state, Chabod suggests that Machiavelli abandoned *The Discourses* after the eighteenth chapter to write *The Prince* between August and December 1513. Machiavelli then returned to work on *The Discourses* and finished in 1517 according to the original spirit of the work (Chabod, 1958, p. 21, pp. 36–41). These speculations about dating were supported by epistolary evidence, comparison with other writings, analysis of prefaces and dedications, references to historical events and the final chapter in *The Prince* and in particular cross-referencing between the works. Together these indicated that the second and third book of *The Discourses* must have been written after *The Prince* and the first book must be older than *The Prince*.

Machiavelli's Evolution as a Republican

Chabod's arguments were widely accepted by a number of scholars, notably Prezzolini (1967) and Ridolfi (1963). Among the minority who did not share this view was Baron (1961). He argued that the two works were not indissolubly joined, but had different messages. Machiavelli did not move from republican idealism to princely realism, but *The Prince* was an earlier phase in his evolution as a republican. He demonstrates the improbability of the first book of *The Discourses* being written before *The Prince*. He argues that the political realism of *The Prince* was not a moment or second step in Machiavelli's thought, but the result of fifteen years of practical politics in service of the republic, a synthesis of which he intended to offer the Medici prince. Baron stresses Machiavelli's subsequent enforced leisure after the restoration of the Medici and his dismissal from public office; his close contact with republicans and literati who he met for conversations in the Oricellari Gardens as well as the undisguised values of a republican citizen found in *The Discourses*. He concludes that although in *The Discourses* the central problem for Machiavelli is still the winning and defence of political power 'the sources are no longer sought in diplomatic craftsmanship exclusively, but in a social and constitutional fabric that allowed civic energies and a spirit of political devotion and sacrifice to develop in all classes of people' (Baron, 1961, p. 249). A revived and strengthened republicanism helped Machiavelli arrive at more profound answers to earlier questions. Skinner (1981) builds on Baron as well as F. Gilbert (1965) and Pocock (1975) seeking to understand Machiavelli by reconstructing both the intellectual context of civic humanism and the political context of Italian city–states. He claims that *The Prince* and *The Discourses* have different intentions. Machiavelli, in *The Prince* intended readers to focus on Florence at the time, but like Pocock he argues that Machiavelli's thought was consistently republican at both a practical and ideological level. The arguments of *The Discourses* resemble the early tradition of Italian republicanism, linking liberty, civic glory and greatness and the traditional belief in the common good. Viroli (1990) agrees that Machiavelli had as his goal the republican ideal of politics as the art of instituting and preserving community based on judgements about the common good. This possibility, however, depended on a truly political man capable of using the force of necessity and it was Machiavelli's purpose in *The Prince* to advise such a man.

Evaluation

Looking first at disputes over his method, Machiavelli was not a philosopher, nor a systematiser who carefully defined, distinguished and justified his ideas, and this militates against any definitive understanding of his intentions and any agreement about his status. Doubts about Machiavelli as a political scientist are partly attributable to his failure to engage in serious political analysis and strict logical argument. Consequently, those who draw attention to the fallacies and flaws in his method can challenge the 'scientific' interpretation by demonstrating that he did not actually use or apply what is now known as the inductive method, a process of inferring generalisations from observation of particular instances. Features of his prose style further undermine Machiavelli's scientific credentials. These are his sequential mode of presenting an argument; constructions which begin 'therefore', 'thus', 'because', 'hence'; his fondness for aphorisms; his pithy sentences, juxtapositions, dramatic statements, violent contrasts, disjunctive techniques presenting either/or formulations, and the use of antithesis. These features make Machiavelli's argument vivid, bold and arresting. They also function to plaster over the gaps, inaccuracies and inconsistencies in his argument and make it easy for interpreters to conclude that Machiavelli is an artist striving for effects rather than a serious political analyst. The opposing views of scientist or intuitive artist could only be resolved if it could be agreed that Machiavelli was not a methodical or analytic thinker. It is an exaggeration to describe Machiavelli as a political scientist because he was interested in facts rather than ideals or because he claims to support his conclusions with observation and experience. His methodology was not systematic or coherent enough to be called scientific in the manner of Galileo. But it would not be seriously misleading to see in Machiavelli the suggestion of more modern forms of political investigation. By maintaining that facts about political life and people's behaviour patterns were the only valid data on which to base political conclusions he created the basis for a transition to a more pragmatic approach to politics that rested on observable reality rather than Christian derived precepts, abstraction, speculation or utopian thinking.

On the perennial question of Machiavelli's attitude towards morality, his controversial reputation was first established through readers responding to the limited information that was historically available to them. Interpreters reading into the texts their own preoccupations or using them for their own ideological purposes compounded this. Early interpretations of Machiavelli as an advocate of tyranny and a teacher of evil tended to base their interpretation on readings of *The Prince* alone. Soon after publication in 1532 it became the subject of fierce political invective and moral condemnation. *The Prince*, like all Machiavelli's works, was placed on the Papal Index of Proscribed books in 1559 where it remained until 1890. In approximately 1539, Cardinal Pole denounced *The Prince* as 'a diabolic handbook for sinners'. The sixteenth-century political polemicist, Gentillet, whose book attacking Machiavelli spread his ideas throughout Europe, reinforced this view. Drawing on Gentillet, the murderous Machiavelli of the Elizabethan dramatists popularised Machiavelli's name as a byword for astute, cunning, unscrupulous political behaviour. The words 'Machiavellian' and 'Machiavellianism' entered and remain in the language as terms of reproach and dishonour. Interpretations of Machiavelli, both

negative and positive, reflect the issues of the age and the agendas of commentators. The anti-Machiavellianism of the sixteenth and seventeenth centuries was motivated by a desire to defend religious values against the rise
of the secular state in the Reformation and Counter Reformation. During
the Enlightenment the availability of *The Discourses* led to the reinvention
of Machiavelli as patriot, democrat and crypto-republican satirist. In the
nineteenth century the nationalist projections of the Risorgimento resulted
in the celebration of Machiavelli as patriotic hero, prophet and founder of
Italian unity. In the nineteenth and early twentieth century appropriation of
Machiavellianism as an amoral doctrine became a weapon that political
realists and the modern state could use to defend power politics, the power
state and the rationality of the politics of interests. Many of these responses
are recognised now as misconceptions, misrepresentations, deformed and
biased readings, but modern commentators on the morality–politics debate
still respond in disparate ways. These different interpretations might be
explained in terms of commentators' own efforts to wrestle with the moral
dilemmas that politics brings, and this may account for their attempts to
variously condemn Machiavelli's advice or to legitimise it as rational and
realistic, to neutralise it as explanatory or descriptive or to defend it by
dismissing the relevance of morality to politics.

A further complication is that even though different readings of the relationship between politics and morality can be attributed to interpreters' own
pre-occupations, there still remain tensions and ambiguities in the texts,
which make different judgements possible. In *The Prince* XVIII and *The
Discourses* 1, 9 Machiavelli says that in politics actions are judged by their
success. If this is taken to mean that any political end *justifies* any means and
the emphasis is placed on *success* however it is to be achieved, then it is not
difficult to see why Machiavelli's advice has been considered immoral. If the
message in these passages is taken to mean that political success *requires*
immoral means and the emphasis is on *necessity*, then Machiavellianism can
be interpreted as a recognition of the realities of political life. Consequently,
it is not surprising that interpreters have claimed that Machiavelli's advice is
amoral, descriptive or ethically neutral. Within the texts, there is also evidence that suggests a latent moral perspective. When Machiavelli discusses
the qualities that bring praise or blame he does not just say that conventional
vice may bring political success and conventional virtue may result in political ruin. In chapters XV–XVII of *The Prince* he illustrates the point that
morally good actions can lead to evil results and vice versa. For example, in
relation to cruelty and mercy, he writes:

> A wise prince then, who is not troubled about a reproach for cruelty is
> more merciful than those who, through too much mercy, let evils continue

and which result in murder or plunder because the latter commonly harm the whole group, but those executions that come from princes harm individuals only. (*P.* XV111)

Implicit in these arguments is the notion that failure to commit a moral wrong is often the greater of two evils. Meanness, cruelty and violence are not just more politically efficacious than the practice of conventional virtues, but can be more preserving of them in the long run. Those who argue that Machiavelli is the author of the doctrine 'the end justifies the means' overlook the fact that his prescriptions were not formulated in that terminology. He never employs the concept of justification in the sense that the ends make the means right or that political success vindicates the crime. Rather, he illustrates the consequences of not acting immorally if the occasion demands it. But to conclude from this that he was a scientist or a technician of political life, describing means to ends, unconcerned whether the end was rational or good, is to go too far. Machiavelli advocated ruthless strategies not to secure and preserve power in a vacuum or to achieve political success *per se*. The point was to create and maintain a strong state, the moral purpose of which was to secure the good of the whole community. If Machiavelli described the world as it is, he did not accept it. The point was to change it for the better. He called for a regeneration of his own society and advocated a republican order where civic virtue, liberty, personal security and co-operation for the common good could be realised.

Those who say Machiavelli divorced politics and ethics similarly overstate the case. Machiavelli's contrast between political and moral means is not simply a contrast between expediency and moral principle but a contrast between one type of morality and another. But Berlin's claim that Machiavelli was showing the incompatibility between pagan and Christian morality is simplistic and his attempt to turn Machiavelli into a liberal who recognises the plurality of competing values is implausible. Machiavelli implied that morality in politics must be consequentialist and he could be seen as an embryonic Utilitarian who demonstrated the incompatibility of consequentialist ethics with all other forms. Consequentialist ethics clash with Christian and traditional ethics, any kind of moral absolutism or idealism, any ethic that has as its source and criterion of value the word of God, eternal reason or the dictates of conscience, with ethics that stress intention, personal integrity or that embody abstract conceptions of justice, fairness or individual rights. Machiavelli's main concern was to call for the replacement of the one over all others.

Turning to the question of the meaning of *virtù* and *fortuna*, just as Machiavelli's lack of rigour and prose style leads to difficulties in interpretation, the limitations of his political vocabulary create further problems in discerning the precise meaning of his key terms. Disagreement about the meaning and place of *virtù* and *fortuna* in Machiavelli's thought are due to their overuse, to ambiguities in their use and in the relationship between them. *Fortuna* has been understood in different ways because *fortuna* is portrayed in different ways in the text. *Fortuna* is sometimes a mythical image and sometimes an abstract and elemental force, a flood that might be partly controlled (*P*. XXV). She is both a fickle goddess with a personality and purpose of her own who 'blinds the minds of men when she does not wish them to resist her power' (*D*. 11, 28); and a woman to be pummelled into obedience by audacious young men (*P*. XXV). *Fortuna* is also simply the unexpected and unforeseen, used to describe whatever is inexplicable in human affairs. *Virtù* can also be made to bear the multiple meanings interpreters have found in the word or conversely can collapse beneath their weight. This is because Machiavelli used one word for several different qualities and because there are ambiguities and confusions in its use. For instance, in one of the most widely discussed passages in chapter V111 of *The Prince*, Machiavelli argues that really wicked men – like Agathocles, the tyrant of Syracuse – who achieve their ambitions cannot be called virtuous. This is inconsistent with his general practice of attributing *virtù* to those who achieve their ends by evil means as well as good. Both Hannibal and Scipio had *virtù* even though they achieved success by different means. Scipio was loved for his 'mercy, loyalty and piety' and Hannibal feared for his 'cruelty, treachery and lack of religion' (*P*. XV11; *D*. 111, 21). Cesare Borgia is admired for his *virtù*, though his actions were no less ruthless, cruel or treacherous than the deeds of Agathocles. There are also confusions in the relation of *fortuna* to *virtù*. On the one hand, Machiavelli often urges *virtù* to stand up to *fortuna* and suggests that men of *virtù* can overwhelm her or win her favour. On the other hand, he pessimistically counsels that *fortuna* can have the last word. His admired men of *virtù* – Borgia, Hannibal and Scipio – are all in the end defeated by unpredictable circumstances suggesting that even men of extreme *virtù* cannot defeat her. *Virtù* and *fortuna* then, are radically unstable concepts and it is not surprising that scholars differ in their assessment of Machiavelli's attempt to organise his subject matter around these two polarities. However, it is not impossible to discern some coherent thread running through Machiavelli's usage of these terms. *Fortuna* usually represents contingency, chance, accident, the unpredictable. Observation and experience reveal, however, that there is sufficient correlation between behaviour and events to discover recurrent patterns and to see that the exercise of *virtù* can lead to favourable outcomes. Moreover it is clear that *virtù* is a consistent concept in so far as it embodies different qualities at different times, given what is necessary to attain goals in particular circumstances. Princely *virtù* embraces those qualities, capacities and dispositions necessary for a prince to establish, restore or maintain the security of the state. The *virtù* which survived in ancient Rome was the civic virtue of the masses and consisted of those qualities which helped to make the state strong, in particular, devotion to community, public spirit and respect for law. The core of *virtù* is pure efficacy, any quality that is politically effective, and this has devastating consequences for traditional morality as well as implications for who should rule. Republics are preferable to principalities because though it takes one man of *virtù* to found, preserve or restore a state, kingdoms depending on the *virtù* of one man are not lasting. Republics offer a wider range of people to adapt to changing circumstances and enjoy good fortune for a longer time (*D.* 11, 2).

In considering the relationship between *The Prince* and *The Discourses*, based upon a dating of the texts, any interpretation of the major works or the relationship between them comes up against the immediate problem of accessing the 'original' Machiavelli. There are no complete autographed manuscripts of *The Prince*, *The Discourses*, or *The Florentine Histories* so readers only have access to problematic contemporary manuscripts or else to translations or editions of them. Moreover, there is some evidence from surviving copies and earliest printed versions of *The Discourses* that the chapters are not in their original order of composition nor in the sequence finally agreed by Machiavelli (Anglo, 1969, p. 75). Cross-referencing between *The Prince* and *The Discourses* poses chronological puzzles and differences of opinion about the dating, conception and purpose of each. Nothing short of acquiring the original texts would suffice to resolve problems from variations in manuscripts, from editorial modernisations and discrepancies and from some of the difficulties arising from the order of composition. However, even if the question of dating could be settled, this would not establish the validity of the conclusions regarding the place and purpose of either work in Machiavelli's thought. If it could be proved that *The Discourses* were begun first, this alone is not evidence for Machiavelli moving from some kind of republican idealism to princely realism. By the same token, if we knew that *The Discourses* followed *The Prince* this alone would not demonstrate his progression from political expediency to republicanism because Machiavelli's intentions would still remain obscure.

Looking at the context or Machiavelli's method might help us understand *The Prince/Discourses* relationship. Yet contextual arguments alone are unable to resolve this matter because different interpretations result from conjectures which give emphasis to particular contexts and draw unwarranted conclusions from them. The view that Machiavelli moved from republican idealism to princely *realpolitik* depends on thinking that the immediate conditions in Italy at the time of *The Prince*'s composition are the most relevant factor in the explanation. The view that Machiavelli moved from a narrow view of political expediency and evolved as a republican depends on foregrounding the context of civic republicanism. Depending on the context highlighted a case is made for the unity, disunity or progression in Machiavelli's thought.

Similarly, if Machiavelli's method and objectivity rather than the context of his ideas are stressed, then a case can be made for the unity between the two works. Machiavelli can then be viewed as being concerned with the techniques of politics and the question of principalities or republics is subordinate to the unifying theme of the winning and defence of political power.

However, there is a kernel of agreement between the interpretations. They all accept that *The Prince* was the result of the frustration of Machiavelli's republican sympathies, of his desire for employment in the Medici regime, of his belief that founding a republic at that moment was unrealistic, of his hope in the founder of a new state and of his willingness to support any government that would preserve Florentine independence. This agreement underpins historical relativist, political realist and genetic explanations as well as Baron's evolutionary thesis. And even Baron, who insists on the differences between the works and Machiavelli's republicanism, agrees with those who see unity (both those who see Machiavelli as neutral and objective and the 'geneticists') to the extent that he concedes Machiavelli's overriding concern was the problem of acquiring and maintaining power in a hostile world. Harmony between these disparate interpretations could be produced in the sense that all have similar analyses of *The Prince* as a work of political realism and all recognise the application to republics the methods and conceptions of 'Machiavellianism' and the preoccupation with power in all his works. Recognising this, however, is not incompatible with maintaining that Machiavelli was fundamentally a republican in political outlook. Those who see *The Discourses* as a dispassionate analysis of republican rule, as simply another answer to the problem of government, overstate the case. They equate Machiavelli's wavering between different forms of government which different circumstances allow or prohibit, with their own hypothesis that he was neutral and impartial. In concentrating on his technical application of rules to politics, they give no weight to aspects of Machiavelli's thought, which others have shown to be consistently republican.

To conclude: almost every conflicting interpretation of Machiavelli's life and work still has its adherents and Machiavelli's ideas have proven to be resistant to confident categorisation, neat formulation or to a single definitive interpretation. The fundamental reason why Machiavelli can be interpreted in so many ways is because contradictions and oppositions within and between the texts support different readings of them. Machiavelli speaks in many voices. Threading their way through the texts are the voices of Machiavelli the career diplomat, the flattering courtier, the experienced and pragmatic politician, the methodological innovator, the messianic warrior, the radical critic of Christian and traditional morality, the admirer of ancient republics, the humanist and classical scholar, the political analyst and historian, the orator and rhetorical mystifier.

Responding to these voices are critics from a variety of disciplines each situating Machiavelli in a particular intellectual, theoretical, historical, political, cultural or literary context. Their interpretations pull in different directions depending on the context they emphasise, the generalisations they impose, the voices they privilege or the strands of argument they identify as significant. Exaggerating aspects of Machiavelli's life and thought in order to systematise or synthesise it, they further fragment it, concentrating on one facet of his thought or another as constituting the 'real' Machiavelli. When the part is mistaken for the whole, it becomes even more apparent that Machiavelli does not fit into any single category. Bridges could be built between interpretations if different aspects of Machiavelli's thought could be brought together without contradiction. We could see in Machiavelli a relatively new mode of political praxis and enquiry while at the same time recognising that the persuasive force of his argument is strengthened by rhetoric rather than logic; that his originality lies not in discovering the element of necessity in political action but in normalising it and in putting the case for political expediency in its starkest, most electrifying form. We could acknowledge that Machiavelli gives immoral, realistic and technical advice since these descriptions are not mutually exclusive and at the same time reconcile this with the glimmering of an ethic where actions are justified in terms of their consequences for the common good. We could accept that Machiavelli's realism is not the ideological antithesis of his idealism and that the texts' refusal to provide a universal rational for one form of government another is not inconsistent with his republican preferences. Even if these matters could be resolved, however, or some other synthesis found, different interpretations of Machiavelli will not be quelled. Part of his appeal is due to the dynamic way he expressed his ideas, overstating his case to achieve an effect. It is this which excites comment beyond the text. But it is the case itself, his demonstration of the collision between the demands of traditional morality and the requirement of power politics that will continue to stir passion and to provoke disparate judgements. Machiavelli will be damned, praised, revised, legitimised, excused and rescued as long as the relationship between means and ends in politics is thought to be a crucial and perennial problem in politics. Machiavelli's enduring contribution to political thought, policy and practice is the remarkably resilient idea that politics involves or even requires the transcendence or violation of ordinary moral principles, that politics presents dilemmas of dirty hands. As long as we retain the idea that there is something special and different about the political sphere that makes it difficult to apply conventional moral standards, the problem of Machiavelli will not be closed. In this sense Machiavellianism, if not Machiavelli himself, will remain a puzzle characterised by Croce (1949) as 'an enigma that perhaps will never be resolved'.

2

Hobbes (1588–1679)

ALISTAIR EDWARDS

Introduction

Hobbes's chief concern was with the nature of political authority and its role in maintaining social order. This concern is not surprising, coming from one born an Elizabethan in the year of the Armada and growing up during the fear and religious persecution of the Tudor period, followed by the uncertain transition from Tudor to Stuart rule. Most immediately, he was provoked by the sharpening political and religious sectarianism in his adult years, and the ensuing conflict between Charles I and Parliament, into a turn towards a new form of political writing in 1628 and a project that was to bear its most famous fruit in 1650 with the publication of *Leviathan*.

Hobbes's later political writings aimed to cut through the divisions they addressed, appealing to the religious convictions of those who had them, appealing more broadly to the capacity of reason he presumed on all sides. In this appeal he failed. Royalists saw his premises as pernicious. Republicans were unable to swallow his absolutist conclusions. Nearly all contemporaries were unwilling to accept an argument that appeared Godless and the most potent rejection of Hobbes centred on his (wrongly) alleged atheism.

This general concern for questions of order did not set Hobbes aside from his contemporaries. Indeed Hobbes's own early political writings may seem unremarkable and many of his later, more systematic, arguments closely resemble contemporary positions. But the later work established his position as one of the great political philosophers, if not in its parts then in its systematic whole. His aim, never fulfilled, was a complete and integrated account of politics, human nature, the physiological roots of human action, the physical components of human physiology, and so on, including an appraisal of human knowledge itself. It is thus easy to see why the project remained incomplete. Yet he made some headway in this, drawing on a curious mix of methods and models (psychological, physiological, geometrical, analytical, definitional, experimental, rational, and moral) to produce a theory of the body politic designed to drag his readers, kicking and screaming, to his conclusions. At its simplest, the design was to lay down unobjectionable analytical definitions and to rebuild these into a theory of the only system that would satisfy human desires. Find some fault in the logical construction of the system or some compelling objection to Hobbes's definitions: otherwise accept the conclusions.

Hobbes's basic argument can seem very simple. The most fundamental and overriding desire of each individual is for self-preservation. Considering mankind's 'natural condition' (or the 'state of nature'), removed from the constraints imposed by government and society, scarcity and competition must always be a feature of life. Even those whose desires are modest must strive endlessly in order to ensure their continued possession of the small amount that would satisfy them. There are no natural limits to what people may do to protect themselves. This lack of natural limit to the quest for power leads to continual conflict, 'a war of all against all', which is to the disadvantage of everyone (Hobbes, 1996, pp. 86–90).

The means to escape from this natural condition should be apparent to all rational beings. What nature has failed directly to provide, man must create. 'Laws of nature' enjoin men to create and abide by artificial obligations, such as promises: if men are to live in peace they must agree limits to their conduct and abide by these (*ibid.*, pp. 91–111). Of course, it is not quite so simple. For these obligations to protect individuals there must be general obedience to the agreed limits. The man who fails to grasp this will be easy prey for those who see that the maximum advantage can be gained where *they* continue to act completely free from constraint while *others* limit their actions. Here lies the problem: if there are no natural limits, then there are no natural reasons for abiding by artificial agreements. In the natural condition there can be no peace, because there can be no trust; and a lack of trust is no basis for relying on a promised peace. The only solution is to create an artificial power capable of enforcing these agreed limits. The only solution is the creation, by 'covenant', of a single, indivisible locus of power, the absolute sovereign (*ibid.*, pp. 111–29).

This is the untroubled way in which nearly all of us will first read Hobbes. But it is one thing to read this general message, quite another to appreciate the depth of analysis and the host of problems that lie behind it. Consideration of these may lead us to revise our first thoughts and to appreciate how differing views may emerge.

Problems and Issues

Where, to begin with, do we situate Hobbes? Timeless? Looking forwards? Looking back? Here we have a writer whose own declared interest was scientific; he claimed universal validity for his prescriptions, independent of time or place; he pursued his own interests with the help of the most up-to-date scientific methods he could find. But those interests were obviously sparked by contemporary problems; immediate threats to public order informed his thoughts, sectarian threats in particular. And his own experience of the broader features of a society at a particular point in its development cannot be ignored. He could be described in terms that suggest either that he was at the cutting edge of a new set of class interests or, even more boldly, that he anticipated the world-view of a class still being born at his time of writing. Certainly, a distinctively modern concern for the private interests of the individual can be discerned. Yet, in dealing with the problems of a more traditional world-view, he inevitably used some of *its* terms and values. Such problems are hardly surprising for one who wrote in these times. While some writers are easily located in a single set of problems, the more far-sighted will be difficult to fix.

A further problem arises from variations in Hobbes's own presentation of the same core argument. Although we will be concerned here with the best known version, offered in *Leviathan* (*ibid.*), other versions cannot be ignored. *Elements of Law* (Hobbes, 1928) and *De Cive* (Hobbes, 1983) are of clear and direct significance for the political reading of *Leviathan*. (Differences between the Latin and English versions of these works have also been drawn upon in disputes but will not be referred to here). Four main lines of difference have fed disputes. Firstly, although much of *Leviathan* displays the appearance and language of science, and although many students may be struck, or indeed baffled, by Hobbes's rigorous logical analysis, *Leviathan* is, in fact, a relatively flowery and ornate version of the argument, adorned with much metaphor and rhetorical flourish. *Elements of Law* and *De Cive* were deliberately presented in spare unadorned style. Secondly, and perhaps surprisingly in the light of this first difference, it is in *Leviathan* that we find an explicit commitment to a clearly scientific and mathematical analysis. This is absent from the earlier works. Thirdly, *Elements of Law* and *De Cive* are more clearly egoistic in their treatment of human nature than is *Leviathan*. Lastly, the '*authorisation*' of the sovereign is only worked out in detail in *Leviathan* (but perhaps still not fully worked out even there). Although it is mentioned in earlier works, it is certainly not integrated properly with the main argument about the obligation of subjects.

Beyond the problem of variation in textual sources there are tensions and ambiguities within the texts themselves. Some of these seem to arise from Hobbes's manner of presentation; he tends to move from the general to the particular without fussing too much about whether the particular case fully exemplifies the general principle. Other problems are of more clear and immediate importance to the main argument; he tells us that a key component in the argument can be understood in two different ways – it seems crucial to the argument as a whole *which* way it is understood but he fails to enlighten us about this.

Some of these ambiguities are central enough to raise doubts about the success of the argument. Does Hobbes succeed in deriving an unconditional obligation on subjects to obey the absolute sovereign? The jury is likely to remain out for some time on this one. For some, Hobbes succeeded on his own terms, but what those terms were may still be contested. Others have argued that the account is fundamentally flawed but good enough for Hobbes's purposes; for yet others it is riddled with incoherence. One thing is certain: there are fundamental tensions and it is not clear that Hobbes succeeded either in placing the sovereign fully above the law or in fully protecting him from the judgement of his subjects.

Given this fragility, it is hardly surprising that many of Hobbes's contemporaries who embraced his conclusions 'misliked' his reasoning. His conclusions required firm and unequivocal commitment. His reasoning was distressingly conditional, practical and lacking in absolutes.

All of this can be summed up as a set of compelling doubts about Hobbes's success in his endeavour. The argument simply doesn't quite work – at least, it doesn't work simply. It creaks. There are loose ends which, if pursued, lead to deep tensions. To adapt and generalise an acute judgement made by a commentator (Tuck, 1979, p. 131), there are many gaps in the argument that leave space into which competing interpretations can move.

Why Conflicting Interpretations?

How should we situate ourselves, as interpreters, in relation to Hobbes? Are we concerned to explore his historical identity in terms of the ideas of his time? Or are we concerned more with the significance of his work in developing traditions of thought and problems of continuing importance? In both cases, but particularly in the latter, our own preoccupations and interests may come into play. There are just so many traces of earlier patterns of thought and value in Hobbes's writings, and at the same time so many constructions that have been repeated and built upon as modern political thought has developed, that we should not be surprised to find a high degree of resonance with a great variety of both earlier and later writers and traditions. Choosing the most salient ideas, traditions or problems to provide a context for interpretation from amongst this variety has provoked debate.

Some interpreters have been concerned with writers and their texts as part of a route to the present. Some of these, it is probably fair to say, have been more concerned to tell a coherent story of such a journey than with the veracity of detail encountered along the way. In other words, the version of Hobbes sometimes encountered may have been adjusted to the needs of a particular account of centuries of historical development. Hobbes has been a prime target for this sort of perspective as a writer who was self-consciously innovative and modern at a relatively early stage. This general concern appears in a number of forms. Remarkably similar readings of Hobbes have been produced by both conservative and Marxist interpreters, united not only by their critical attitude to modern values and institutions but also by their interest in the social transformations that lead to and constitute modernity. Strauss's Hobbes is firmly rooted in differences between ancient and modern practices and in Strauss's own account of how these came about: aristocratic virtue and commercial prudence; moral certainty and relativism; political philosophy and social science (Strauss, 1952). Macpherson's Hobbes can be loosely described as the ideologist of proto-capitalism, theorising 'human nature' and its results on the basis of his own experience of emerging bourgeois attitudes and aspirations (Macpherson, 1962). From a more abstract point of view, Oakeshott read Hobbes as a part of a shift in the concern for order based on 'Reason and Nature' to one based on 'Will and Artifice' (Oakeshott, 1960, pp. x–xii). Alternatively, interpreters with a keen interest in the history of moral philosophy (Riley, 1982; Taylor, 1965; Warrender, 1957) seem to be most ready to identify Hobbes as a key figure in the move from traditional natural law theory to more modern Kantian constructions, and to emphasise as central those aspects in Hobbes's argument which bear upon this transition. Yet for those interested in the history and philosophy of science, different aspects of Hobbes's *method* have been used to explain how the argument should be understood, some claiming that Hobbes's political conclusions depend on, or are even determined by, his views on knowledge and scientific method (See, for instance, Goldsmith, 1966; Spragens, 1973; Watkins, 1965). This view is strongly contested by Sorell for whom Hobbes's civil philosophy has an autonomous status (Sorell, 1986).

Other concerns may be less historical and more purely philosophical. Where doubt exists about the success of Hobbes's enterprise in imposing artificial order on natural disorder, there is a strong temptation to complete his task for him or, at least, to develop the reading that appears most successful. The most obvious ways to achieve this might be to make individuals more sociable than other interpretations would have them be, or to show that the laws of nature can bind more strongly. There may be *other* very good reasons for both these moves, but the suspicion is that versions of Skinner's 'myths' of interpretation (see introduction, p. 2) are at work. Interpreters may be a bit in awe of their subjects, presuming that the major thinkers probably had their position pretty well straight, even if they couldn't properly express it to others. Or, perhaps, it is just that the more philosophical concern to get at the best answer intrudes upon the attempt to identify the answer actually offered by the text.

All of this assumes, of course, that there is general agreement about the nature of the *question* addressed by the text. This is by no means the case. Skinner's early work (for instance, Skinner, 1965) traces Hobbes's intentions to some very immediate and particular political concerns of the Civil War period whereas Macpherson tries to reconstruct Hobbes's tacit assumptions derived from a much broader social and economic milieu. Skinner's latest work moves beyond the immediate context in attempting to tease out in very abstract form the precise notion of the modern state that Hobbes was struggling to develop (Skinner, 1999).

The role played by normative commitment is sometimes clear. The stories in which Hobbes's argument plays its various roles are all of a piece with the political values of the storytellers. And all interpreters will tend to read a text *in relation to* their own interests and values, just because that is what they are interested *in* and their respective concerns may lead them to emphasise aspects of the text which appear to have some bearing on those concerns.

Having said that, there can be more obvious and direct ways in which political values inform interpretations. It sometimes seems that interpreters might be trying to pick the best players for their own side. But who would want Hobbes on their side? Who, these days, would think there was much to be gained by recruiting an irascible absolutist as even a central defender? There could be reasons, even for this. Some have tried to identify Hobbes as the provider of the essence of British legal sovereignty (Baumgold, 1988); others have tried to establish 'a more tolerant Hobbes' or Hobbes as an important component of the liberal tradition (Ryan, 1988a and 1988b). The sub-text here may be to establish liberal values as irremovable bricks in the wall of modern western thought. If even Hobbes the absolutist had to accept them, their place is secure.

We must also confront the problem of personal likes and dislikes. It is rare that an interpretation should display contempt and yet still command attention. An interpretation that engages an audience usually, like a good biography, embodies respect and fellow feeling for its subject. Most interpretations seem to conform to this generalisation. Some do not. For most of the twentieth century the standard edition of *Leviathan* (Pogson-Smith, 1909) bore an introduction that was fairly described as 'malicious' (Taylor, 1938, p. 406), betraying a real contempt for Hobbes and questioning his status as a serious thinker (We should be grateful that Hobbes survived this). More recently, Quentin Skinner has not shrunk from displaying his distaste for Hobbes's arrogance (Skinner, 1996, pp. 390–437). The two cases are not the same. Skinner clearly respects Hobbes, disliking only his manner of dealing with opponents and those of different religious persuasions. But they are comparable in that each draws attention to elements of Hobbes's argument that would be ignored by others or which would be treated more leniently in so far as they do not compromise the main points.

Without supposing that all interpretations can be understood in exactly the same way, perhaps this leads us, very speculatively, towards a rough outline of two main sources of disagreement. *Historically*, it is as if Hobbes rested on the edge of modernity, ostensibly offering a universal analysis that operates on equal terms on each side of the divide. His analysis reaches back to traditional forms of expression in order to reach forward into yet unexplored and not yet understood aspects of a society to come. His interpreters have not been content to leave him in this uncomfortable position. He makes insufficient sense in this position, which is to say that he only makes his own sense. Most have tried to push him forward into one or another aspect of modernity; some have pushed him back onto traditional concerns; others have simply left him in his own period and *its*, but not necessarily *his*, particular problems. *Politically*, Hobbes's recent interpreters are not themselves absolutists; yet all recognise the power of his insights. Interpreters may seek to retain sufficient of the argument to capture its insights but, unable to swallow the whole message, may look for those elements that seem most anathema and attempt to display their peripheral place. We will each have different grounds for this: some intellectual, some political, some personal. But the result will be the same: disputed interpretation.

How far are these disputes generated simply by different perspectives, interests and values and how many can be resolved by reasoned assessment of the textual and other historical evidence? To answer these questions we must turn to more detailed examples of the interpretations.

Conflicting Interpretations

The main disputes revolve around one or more of four areas of contention. Firstly, the basic problem: how does Hobbes root social conflict in *human nature*? How far does conflict arise from the nature of the human individual, or from the goods pursued by individuals, or from the situation in which individuals are placed? Secondly: the immediate means to a solution, the means Hobbes employs in characterising man's escape from the state of nature. How are we to interpret *the laws of nature* and enjoined covenant? What role, if any, does religious commitment play in the consequent obligation that subjects owe to their sovereign? Thirdly, *the extent of sovereignty*: just how far and how firmly does this unconditional obligation extend? Lastly, *the life of the citizen*: how should we regard Hobbes's commonwealth with respect to the solutions it produces for its subjects?

Each of these questions has evoked different and conflicting responses. By simplifying and selecting from positions, this framework can be used to present a roughly chronological account of how debate has evolved.

Human Nature

In describing the state of nature, Hobbes intended to convey the idea of an unpleasant condition. This much is agreed. But whence does this unpleasantness arise? Three main answers are possible: from the self-centred, competitive and irrational nature of human individuals; from the more particular goods that these individuals pursue; from the structured condition of life without sovereign political power. In most commentaries these alternatives do not constitute a stark choice; the interpretation offered is a matter of the emphasis given to one of these aspects.

Leo Strauss (Strauss, 1952), our first portrayer of call, endorsed much of this. His innovations were twofold. Firstly, he traced a development (better, a debasement) in Hobbes's own writing: from an Aristotelian concern for political virtue to a Platonic focus on the scientifically discovered realities of individual psychology and political power. Secondly, identifying Hobbes as a writer at the cusp of modernity, he argued that Hobbes recognised aspects of political virtue, notably the desire for glory, as a problem. The glory of public honour had become a self-seeking pride in material success. This problem could be solved only by a turn towards a system of justice that protected individuals from the excesses of pride-driven competition and, ultimately, from violent death at the hands of their competitors. Thus the public ideal of civic virtue was replaced by the private ideal of competitive prowess; the state was intended only to provide a robust protective framework for this competition; the nobility associated with the aristocrat was replaced by the material success of the merchant; and duty was replaced by individual right.

In Strauss's hands, this broad view was offered with an explicitly normative intent. Hobbes's role was degenerative. Hobbes was a part of the modern world's abandonment of spiritual values in favour of purely material pursuits. For later writers, this same story could be given a more progressive twist. Forget that the rejection of public virtue is of normative significance. Stick with the facts of modern history. Aristocratic values have, just as a matter of fact, been elbowed aside by the more material values of the commercial market place.

Macpherson (Macpherson, 1962) learned much from this but, much more explicitly than Strauss, built an account of Hobbes as an ideologist for the emerging bourgeoisie. Hobbes's insight went beyond the recognition of obsolescence in the traditional view of an ordered society in proceeding from a new and quite specific set of assumptions about the nature of man, the 'possessive individualist' of bourgeois society. This man does not just want to live; he wants to live well. The need for success in market competition was unrestrained by any natural moral feelings; a man's value was his 'price', determined by the market, in the face of which all other values fell away.

According to Macpherson, Hobbes's picture of 'natural man' is coloured by his own society and, perhaps, by his own acute perceptions of the emerging aspects of that society that were likely to become predominant. In short, Hobbes's natural condition of mankind was a picture of bourgeois man left unprotected by the removal of political and social institutions. This reading provoked, and continues to provoke, sharp criticism. On the one hand, writers like Skinner accepted that the text might bear this interpretation but rejected it on contextualist grounds as an anachronistic representation of Hobbes's possible intentions, a judgement also extended to the readings of Strauss, Warrender and Hood (Skinner, 1974, p. 229). On the other hand, Macpherson has also been attacked for paying selective attention to the text, ignoring, for instance, passages where Hobbes's discussion of the 'worth' of man goes beyond the idea of 'market price' (Thomas, 1965, pp. 230–1).

Both Strauss and Macpherson are notable for their concern with the social origins and character of Hobbes's ideas, and for the place of these ideas in a broad picture of historical change. In this they differ from many interpreters who are either uninterested in such issues or sceptical about their role in the study of political thought. But they also take up positions on matters of central interest to others, including those interested primarily in the basic logical structure of the argument. Their Hobbes was, above all, a natural *rights* theorist. Most of their immediate critics took a different view, emphasising the role of the *laws* of nature in Hobbes's argument. These laws have, for centuries, generated puzzlement and attracted criticism. Until fairly recently, nearly all interpreters had taken Hobbes to be a 'psychological egoist' in that he held all human action to be prompted by self-interest, by the desire to further our own well-being. The problem then arose of whether these laws are sufficiently compelling to bind men to obedience and, if they are, whether Hobbesian human nature was quite so self-seeking as it first appeared.

The Laws of Nature

Many commentators have followed the lines laid down by Nagel and Watkins (Nagel, 1959; Watkins, 1965, pp. 56–68) in regarding the laws of nature as prudential: statements of the conduct best suited to pursuing one's own interests. We should abide by our covenants and obey the sovereign because it is in our interests to do so. But this reading is widely questioned, not least because the obligation will not always hold. There must be situations where the self-interested individual will benefit from disobedience. The individual who is confident of escaping punishment for profitable disobedience will disobey. It appears Hobbes has failed to deliver the *unconditional* constraint that he intended. The obligations of subjects, derived from the laws of nature as prudential rules, must allow them to choose disobedience under certain conceivable conditions.

This difficulty has generated a number of interpretive responses. Taylor argued that Hobbes's egoism did not extend to his theory of obligation (Taylor, 1938, pp. 407–12). That theory bore comparison with Kant's in that it was deontological (concerned with moral duty rather than beneficial consequences). Although men were psychologically *motivated* to pursue their own interests, at an independently moral level they were *obliged* unconditionally to obey the laws of nature and always to obey: psychology is simply divorced from morality. Warrender took a slightly different line, though their accounts are often referred to jointly as the Taylor–Warrender thesis. For Warrender, the laws of nature produce a binding obligation, by virtue of their status as God's commands, a status common in traditional uses of the idea of natural law. Unlike Taylor, Warrender does not leave a radical disjunction between motive and duty; he brings the two areas more closely together by arguing that the overriding prudential motive is self-preservation and that this allows action according to duty only when certain 'validating conditions' are in place. Once the sovereign is established, disobedience threatens self-preservation more than it enhances it. Under these conditions we do have a valid moral duty, willed by God, to obey (Warrender, 1957, pp. 212–16).

Warrender's general strategy to resolve the problem of obligation constitutes a reappraisal of the status of the laws of nature. If these can be shown to oblige in the requisite sense, then perhaps the rest of the argument can be shown to follow from this. If we are already obliged to seek peace, not just conditionally and instrumentally in order to preserve ourselves, but as a basic moral duty to preserve life, then the disjunctive problem can be resolved, albeit at the cost of turning Hobbes back towards the more traditional use of natural law theory that he appears to reject. Warrender's adoption of this strategy takes off from an unorthodox reading of a single short passage in *Leviathan* (though it should be noted that parallel passages exist in other of Hobbes's works and that one, at least, may be more amenable to Warrender's reading).

> These dictates of reason, men used to call by the name of laws; but improperly: for they are but conclusions or theorems concerning what conduceth to the conservation and defence of themselves; whereas law, properly, is the word of him that by right hath command over others. But yet if we consider the same theorems as delivered in the word of God, that by right commandeth all things, then are they properly called laws (Hobbes, 1996, p. 111).

Most interpreters, and all Warrender's critics, take the first part of this passage as the encapsulation of Hobbes's own position. It is a mistake to treat the laws of nature as laws. They do not command. The second part is merely an aside, adding an extra layer of obligation applicable only to those with particular beliefs, perhaps inserted by Hobbes to stress the compatibility (but not identity) of his doctrine with orthodox Christianity. Warrender disagrees. Hobbes, he insists, was not the atheist he was often accused of being and he intended his audience to understand that these laws of nature were indeed God's commands, morally binding on all his creation (Warrender, 1957, pp. 97–8).

Of course, there is more at issue than just this short passage. Any thorough discussion of even the Warrender thesis must range over more material than this. On the one hand, unqualified references to the laws of nature are common in all of Hobbes's works, and references to God's authorship are not uncommon. On the other hand, it seems pretty clear that an egoistic psychology is Hobbes's starting-point, and that covenants operate as the fulcrum of the argument; to displace these is not especially appealing. So there is much more to be said about the textual evidence, one way or the other. But perhaps for all that, it still comes down to a reading of this passage. We are just looking more widely within the text for reasons in favour of one reading and against the other. The passage seems to distil what is at issue.

But examination of this dispute can take us beyond the text, to those who wish to correct our understanding of the problem addressed. Richard Tuck has put the matter in a particularly compelling way. As Filmer first noticed there is a central tension in Hobbes's use of certain key conceptions. Hobbes defines 'right' and 'law' as clearly distinct since the former consists in 'liberty to do, or to forbear' whereas the latter determines or binds to one of these. Unfortunately, Hobbes then goes on to define the right of nature in a way that suggests that we are not free to forbear from the preservation of our lives. Tuck claims that

> it is this discrepancy between the notion of a right as formally defined by Hobbes and the fact that men are apparently not at liberty to forbear to preserve themselves, which is at the heart of the case argued by Professor Warrender (Tuck, 1979, p. 130).

Here Warrender's basic claim about the status of natural law continues to occupy its central role, but Tuck is also concerned with Warrender's further claim that the right of nature proceeds from the dominant motives of self-interested individuals (self-preservation), whereas the law of nature states the duties of mankind in general (to preserve life). There remains a discrepancy in Hobbes's argument, but it is accounted for in terms of Hobbes's move from concerns of motivation to those of duty – a move that Hobbes misleadingly described in terms of the presence or absence of liberty of action.

Tuck then goes on to dismiss this aspect of Warrender's account by explaining how this misleading distinction really did occur. Warrender claims that it is the result of a hidden switch in an otherwise coherent transition from hypothetical and conditional to moral and unconditional imperatives. Tuck holds that it can be explained as a result of a series of pretty ramshackle and *ad hoc* amendments added to an argument developing over the years in response to criticism, and that these have little directly to do with the alleged problem of unconditional obligation (Tuck, 1979, pp. 131–2).

There is, of course, another way out of this problem and that is to deny that Hobbes was a psychological egoist at all. Included in his list of human passions we find, for instance, 'benevolence', 'charity' and 'pity' (Hobbes, 1996, pp. 37–46). These are not characteristics of pure egoists. It is true that each individual feels pleasure (or pain) according the satisfaction (or not) of these passions. But it would be self-defeating to describe an individual acting from pity as self-interested because he or she suffered pain at the sight of another's suffering. It is also true that Hobbes adds egoistic twists to his account: pity, for instance, arises from imagining that oneself might suffer a similar hurt. But this is not Hobbes's *definition* of pity. It is a physiological *cause* of it. Pity is simply defined as 'grief for the calamity of another', a definition perfectly in keeping with the view that people are capable of feeling the force of altruistic motives (*ibid.*, p. 43). This is not to say that the world according to Hobbes is populated entirely by altruists, far from it. Self-interested action may be common. It is likely to be more frequent where highly valued goods, especially lives, are threatened. And there may be some people who never act altruistically. But none of this excludes the general capacity to feel a concern for others. It only follows that altruism cannot simply and safely be presumed. All prudent individuals (and political theorists) must recognise this in their calculations.

This is broadly the line taken by McNeilly, Gert, Raphael and Sorell (Gert, 1996; McNeilly, 1968; Raphael, 1977; Sorell, 1986) and it is now quite widely accepted as a reading of *Leviathan*. Gert goes further than most in extending this to Hobbes's earlier works which other interpreters continue to identify as egoist (Gert, 1996, pp. 165–8). Each of these writers, and most other recent interpreters, have had no difficulty in allowing for some form of moral imperative without accepting the need for this to depend upon God. The now common general position is that Hobbes's argument supposes at least a natural obligation to deliberate and act reasonably. Somewhat surprisingly, Hood reaches similar conclusions despite holding that Christian themes and positions inform Hobbes's argument (Hood, 1964, p. 60). This is most robustly denied by McNeilly, for whom religious belief simply has no such role to play in *Leviathan* (McNeilly, 1968, pp. 211–12). Sorell's reading suggests that the laws of nature are closely related to an Aristotelian doctrine of virtue and that the commonwealth provides a world made safe for virtuous conduct (Sorell, 1986, pp. 107–8; 117–18).

All interpreters have recognised that these are central questions and problems. But for some they are not quite at the centre of Hobbes's argument, at least in the version set out in *Leviathan*. Gauthier and Tuck, for instance, treat *authorisation* as carrying more weight than the bare covenant to transfer rights. Hobbesian subjects have empowered their sovereign to make judgements on all matters, on their behalf. They are therefore the authors of the sovereign's acts. The sovereign's commands are their own commands and, says Hobbes, it would be 'absurd', contradictory, to try to act against one's own will (Hobbes, 1996, p. 93). Aside from adding a strange form of logical necessity to the obligation of subjects, this introduction of authorisation strengthens an argument that had earlier been presented in rather negative terms. In merely giving up rights, subjects undertook only not to impede or resist the sovereign. The introduction of authorisation is alleged to strengthen Hobbes's sovereign as a positive unity of his subjects (Gauthier, 1969, pp. 120–77; Tuck, 1979, p. 129).

This leads to the next area of debate: just how extensive are the sovereign's powers? That may seem an odd question. Hobbes's sovereign is absolute and all subjects have given up their natural rights in his, or its, favour. In line with the title of Hobbes's best known work and the description of the leviathan in the book of Job, we might think nothing could be more powerful. Again, things are not so simple.

The Extent of Sovereignty

There is no dispute about the *indivisibility* of sovereignty in Hobbes's theory. All political and juridical power is located at one single point in the system, with the sovereign. But division exists on the real extent of sovereign power, both as real ability and as rightful authority. A major worry is that the right of nature can never wholly be renounced. Hampton holds that Hobbes's argument fails to establish absolute sovereignty since subjects retain the right to judge when obedience may threaten their own preservation. The subject is perpetually in the position rightfully to decide whether or not to obey the sovereign and hence to determine 'whether or not he will continue to hold power' (Hampton, 1986, p. 206). Thus the right of resistance is much more extensive than that allowed by the absolutist intentions of the argument and this explains Hobbes's inconsistent flirtation with forms of moral obligation that might serve to paper over the cracks. Others have made similar points without needing to identify such obvious and central shortcomings. Sorell, for instance, points out that the sovereign's mismanagement can threaten his authority. If basic necessities of life are not legally obtainable, subjects 'commit no crime when they break the law and steal to feed themselves' (Sorell, 1986, p. 122). This general point, that the sovereign is only sovereign so long as his *de facto* power remains and is used to provide protection for his subjects, is one long accepted and its force is only sharpened by more recent interpretations.

On considering rightful authority as itself a problem, the first worry is natural law. Those taking the view that natural law itself imposes real duties recognise that these must also bear on the sovereign, at least in so far as the sovereign is a natural as well as an artificial person, a flesh and blood creature and not just the creation of the covenant. Martinich makes much more of this than most writers and provides a detailed account of the sovereign's duties under the law of nature, duties which are not expressions of 'mere piety' on the part of Hobbes nor 'a nod in the direction of conventional morality'. Rather, these are an important element in Hobbes's construction of a system that will provide public safety and the means to live the good life (Martinich, 1995, pp. 277–85). But a more common focus for dispute is the role of positive law. It appears that the sovereign can only rule through law. And, following from the definitions Hobbes provides, he must declare, in advance, what is required of his subjects, and must attach known punishments to disobedience (Hobbes, 1996, pp. 183–221). This is an undoubted benefit to his subjects. They can know what to do to avoid pain. They must obey the declared laws. But it seems to be a limit on sovereign power in that the sovereign cannot simply act as he pleases. He must act in the artificial form of law prescribed by Hobbes. Much rests on whether all of this can be sidelined as purely formal definition, or whether it imposes limits on sovereign action by precluding retrospective changes in the law.

Many, probably most, interpreters have passed this off as an insignificant element of the system. Even if the sovereign does not act through law he may rightfully (by virtue of his own right of nature) commit a simple act of hostility against his subjects (see, for instance, Goldsmith, 1966, p. 201). And furthermore, in appealing against an action of the sovereign, the sovereign's own judgement is all that counts. So if my land has been confiscated and the sovereign says this was done through and according to law, whether all reasonable people think that it wasn't can be of no account (McNeilly, 1968, p. 233). Others have disagreed.

Hampsher-Monk describes Hobbes's position as 'a weak and limited version of the rule of law' but nevertheless acknowledges that 'although Hobbes's point is definitional, it has teeth' and should modify the view of 'Hobbes as an enthusiastic defender of capricious absolutism or exploitative tyranny' (Hampsher-Monk, 1992, pp. 48–9). In a work subsequent to that cited above, Goldsmith seems to concur (Goldsmith, 1996, pp. 284–5). Hood had earlier taken up a position with similar implications in arguing that Hobbes's 'legal absolutism is not incompatible with what may be called a moral constitutionalism' (Hood, 1964, p. 180). This reading went so far as to treat Hobbes as a theorist of the English constitution, an arrangement where 'the only restrictions on a legally supreme sovereign authority must be self-imposed by moral restraint or by enlightened self interest', but where those restrictions had, for Hobbes, some real force (*ibid.*, p. 181). On this view, morality and/or prudence dictate that sovereign authorities should generate self-limiting rules.

This raises the final question of the general character of Hobbes's theory and of his commonwealth. To put it bluntly, is this a place where we would want to live?

The Life of the Citizen

Locke famously asked whether men were foolish enough to avoid the dangers of polecats or foxes by seeking safety in the custody of devouring lions. This is the popular image of Hobbes's sovereign, the licensed tyrant free to devour what he will. On this reading Hobbes offers a substantive constitutional theory that advocates the establishment of absolute political power. This is at odds with the view taken by nineteenth-century Utilitarians and some later writers (Goldsmith, 1980) for whom Hobbes provides little more than a logical analysis of the idea of sovereignty (Baumgold, 1988, pp. 56–79). If this is so, then the sovereign as licensed tyrant is pushed into the background taking Locke's worries with him.

This formal assurance aside, Locke's fears might be allayed either by establishing proper limits to the sovereign's powers of the kind noted above, or by some more general identification of an anti-tyrannical, tolerant, or even liberal–democratic element in the argument.

Macpherson provides a distinctly one-sided example of this. The commonwealth need not be politically oppressive since its aim is to make life safe for the pursuit of wealth. Possessive individualist assumptions, at their 'clearest and fullest in Hobbes', are a central part of modern liberal–democratic theory. Of course, this does not make the commonwealth an attractive place for all since its strongest appeal is essentially to the successful accumulators, to the bourgeoisie (Macpherson, 1962, pp. 264–71).

Broader assurances, even on the vexed and central question of religious belief, can be found. Ryan, accepting that the sovereign has the sole authority in these matters, points out that Hobbes supposes little intervention to be necessary. Religion is essentially a private matter and intervention will be required more to deter sectarian fanatics from imposing their views on others than to demand uniformity (Ryan, 1988a; see also Tuck, 1990). More generally, Ryan argues that Hobbes's scepticism on matters of knowledge leads to 'epistemological anti-authoritarianism and individualism', requiring a state in which each is free to pursue his own conception of the good (Ryan, 1988b). And yet, as Parry has stressed, Hobbes's concerns for the divisive potential of belief leads him to an authoritarian position on the control of education (Parry, 1998).

These readings give a liberal flavour to Hobbes's ideas. But there are also grounds for assimilating Hobbes into the *democratic* tradition of political thought, grounds that go beyond the mere compatibility of democratic government and Hobbesian sovereignty.

The early versions of Hobbes's argument treat quasi-democratic relations as a necessary step towards establishing the sovereign. A union of citizens must first be created and this union may then confer power on a single individual or group. And although the introduction of authorisation in *Leviathan* removes the need for this, reference is still made to it in the text (Goldsmith, 1966, pp. 156–61). More generally, sovereign power comes from the people and its use is the embodiment of their will (Hobbes, 1996, p. 120). Yet the mainstream position remains that this carries no real democratic substance (Watkins, 1965, pp. 116–18) and that any attempt to read Hobbes in this way introduces a sense of 'communal identity' which is quite alien to his thought (Baumgold, 1988, pp. 52–4).

The underlying issue is how far this 'real unity of will' must suppose a community of values, or whether it could rest on a mere aggregation of individuals in the mutual recognition of a common interest in security. This dilemma continues in all liberal debates.

Evaluation

Forty and fifty years on in some cases, most interpretations retain some bite. Strauss's reading is still stoutly maintained by Straussians but, more broadly, is recognised in the general acceptance of pre-modern elements in Hobbes's argument, and in its continuing ability to provoke fruitful debate. Its detailed claims have fared less well. Hobbes's direct use of aristocratic virtue is thin and marginal, and no major shift is apparent in his later work (Polin, 1953). Macpherson's Marxist reworking is treated as a touchstone for teaching purposes but is, beyond this, treated more seriously as a part of Macpherson's own considerable contribution to political theorising (see Townshend, 2000) than as a part of Hobbes scholarship. This is not to dismiss the broad perspective. Perversely, Strauss's reading may provide a better basis for a Marxist reading of Hobbes (Raphael, 1977, p. 90) and, had Macpherson chosen the language of commercialisation rather than stark class division, many of his critics might have been more sympathetic.

That Hobbes's work is marked by a progressive (really a degenerating) retreat from an attachment to aristocratic public virtue to a safer defence of the private bourgeois pursuit of wealth is no longer a tenable view, whether in its original backward-looking form, or in subsequent Marxist versions. At the same time, it is perfectly possible to pull out from Hobbes's general argument a continuity of concern for certain virtues, and these include both ancient and modern. We can therefore see the sense of examining Hobbes in these terms without thinking that we have to fix a firm bourgeois or possessive individualist label before proceeding with other questions.

Taking a slightly different though similarly structured view, it is possible to discern in Hobbes's writings a concern for the virtues of citizenship which goes beyond the demand for passive obedience and which treats citizens as more than the mere objects of authority. Nobody would claim this turns Hobbes into a classical republican, or even pushes him towards the position. Nobody needs to push him back towards that position. Nor does it push him forward to some more modern facsimile. For while this concern may be compatible with pluralist participation in public affairs, and with a degree of toleration for diversity, it by no means confers rights on any subjects in these areas. Even Alan Ryan's version of the Hobbesian sovereign seems to be issuing constant reminders to his subjects that their contributions to politics can only be at the level of advice (Ryan, 1988a, p. 105). Beyond that, when Ryan insists that '[M]ankind does not need to be told what ends to pursue, what the good life is, how private life is to be conducted', it is not an opinion backed by direct reference to Hobbes but rather to Michael Oakeshott's account of modern individualism and its consonance with Hobbes's views. At most this account must be counted as itself advice, to be picked up or ignored according to the judgement of the sovereign. In many accounts, Hobbes's own *preferences*, or what may be *allowed* by Hobbes's sovereign, become confused with what is *required* within Hobbes's theory. Hobbes may well have held all sorts of values consistent with either ancient virtue or modern liberalism, or both. He may even have envisaged an enlightened sovereign operating with these values in mind. But that does not mean he built a model of the political system that protected these values against encroachment and it is this *protection* that marks out the liberal theorist.

The godless Hobbes is simply wrong. We now know enough about the man to be fairly confident that he had religious belief. But this may have little bearing on his political writings. His scepticism cannot support any confident pronouncement about religious truth, sufficiently definite to command the agreement necessary to supply order. His position looks, in the end, close to the unashamed atheism of Hume: nothing can be known of God sufficient to have bearing on the contestable issues that divide his creation. The one judgement of his interpreters that must stand as unassailable is that in *Leviathan*, though not elsewhere, he took account of religious matters only to subordinate them to political power.

In retrospect it may seem that the attempts to reconstruct a satisfactory theory of obligation constitute an interpretive cul-de-sac, one entered only due to the crude egoist readings of Hobbes's psychology and the formalistic interpretations of sovereignty imposed by Utilitarians. In particular, Warrender's ascription of real divine authority to the laws of nature has received little support and may seem a very strained reading of the text. However, if we compare the relevant sections of *Leviathan* with those in the earlier *De Cive*, it does appear that Hobbes was concerned in the later work to emphasise God's authority and irresistible power (Martinich, 1995, pp. 176–81). And, more generally, there may be historical grounds for supposing that Hobbes intended to offer a universal theory of moral duty and that readings like Warrender's are not merely attempts to rescue the argument through reconstruction (Burgess, 1990, pp. 700–2).

In *Leviathan* and other writings, Hobbes systematised and theorised political relations at such a high level of abstraction that it is simply to miss the point to note his indebtedness to aspects of contemporary debate. Again we find contextualists who are able to trace the roots of parts of the argument elsewhere but whose attempts to reduce Hobbes to the level of his sources fail. His vision clearly transcended the immediate problems of the seventeenth century yet remained fixed on the case of England. Hobbes was trying to protect what he saw as already present in the English political tradition. He did not seek to innovate, except at the level of understanding what was already present. He sought to reassure us that near complete subjugation to the sovereign could never threaten our safety as much as the attempt directly to protect it by limiting sovereign power. In the context of seventeenth-century conflicts this produced a statist leaning, trusting the sovereign political power to protect the subject from the pressures of a deeply divided civil society. This made him appear anti-liberal to modern eyes. But his general drift matched the development of his own historical model. Morally and prudentially limited constitutionalism allowed civil society to resolve its own conflicts with only the occasional intervention of directly coercive sovereign power, much as Hobbes urged. If we are to seek a single characterisation of the political tone of this most radical of thinkers, he was a true conservative.

3

Locke (1632–1704)

Timothy Kenyon

Introduction

In *Two Treatises of Government* (1689) Locke promotes ideas on the rights of the individual and on limited government, since regarded as fundamental to liberal political theory. Locke argues that a government's legitimacy depends upon the origins of its power in individual consent. Individuals possess fundamental rights and sovereignty resides with the people. A free people will only willingly submit to government when it is in their interests to do so. In exercising sovereignty, government is entrusted by the people. A free people will not establish unlimited government. There is a right to resist tyranny. A government is rendered genuinely accountable only when the governed consent to its actions. It is necessary to constrain government through the separation of powers (most obviously into its legislative, executive and judicial functions). When these branches become too closely entwined good government is imperilled. Certain aspects of the human condition, religious conscience for example, should stand apart from governmental interference. The private sphere necessary for human individuality and flourishing should be protected through government's commitment to the doctrine of toleration.

Surprisingly, Locke did not always see things this way. His earlier political writings, such as the *Tract on Government* (1660), were as authoritarian as his view of human potential was pessimistic (see Goldie, 1997). Here he argued for strong government, particularly in defence of the Anglicanism of the Church of England restored as the 'official religion' alongside the Stuart monarchy. But defending authoritarian government generally entails regarding the regime's policies as acceptable. Under the later Stuarts a much-changed Locke found this not to be so.

As he awoke to its increasingly arbitrary and doctrinally intolerant lean-ings Locke became a radical opponent of the Stuart monarchy. He had good reason to become unnerved. As the monarchy freed itself from parliamen-tary constraint it revealed its Roman Catholic sympathies. Here lay the fear that motivated the opposition 'Whig faction' led by Locke's patron and mentor the Earl of Shaftesbury. By the early 1680s the Whigs believed that should Charles II's more Catholic brother James become king, England would slide towards absolutism of a kind being brought to its apogee in the France of Louis XIV. Political intimidation eventually drove many leading Whigs, Locke included, into exile in Holland.

The works for which Locke is most remembered were published in the immediate aftermath of the so-called 'Glorious Revolution' of 1688 by means of which James II was replaced by William and Mary. These monarchs co-operated with the constitutional views of the political group that set them on the throne. Locke was afforded the opportunity to return to England. His major philosophical work *An Essay Concerning Human Understanding*, the *Two Treatises of Government* and *A Letter Concern-ing Toleration* were published (the latter two anonymously) in 1689–90. *Some Thoughts Concerning Education* (1693) and *The Reasonable-ness of Christianity* (1695) followed. Each element of Locke's analysis of the human predicament is the product of years of intellectual reappraisal. Each is informed by a belief in humanity's overwhelming need to dis-cover salvation through its capacity to exercise rational intellect. In order to achieve this end a degree of personal integrity free from government interference is prerequisite. Locke is the last great political theorist to be preoccupied with the idea that salvation is humanity's fundamental objective.

In *Two Treatises* Locke attacks the absolutist theory of government advanced by the Civil War Royalist Sir Robert Filmer (Filmer, 1991). Filmer's writings (especially *Patriarcha* written circa 1632 but first pub-lished in 1680) were resurrected by royalists anxious to undermine consent-based theories of political obligation. Filmer's defence of evidently illiberal propositions assumes mankind's *natural inequality*. Such a notion appealed to many contemporaries as according with the social circumstances of the times. Filmer contends that: (i) political authority cannot be based upon the consent of the governed because successive generations cannot engage in contractual arrangements; (ii) property cannot be derived from some equal natural right of ownership in common because individual ownership would then require the consent of everybody and the problem referred to in (i) would again arise and (iii), following from (i) and (ii), exclusive property rights must therefore be sanctioned by laws representing the will of an absolute sovereign whose power is derived not from within the political community but extraneously through a grant from God.

Confronting this position, Locke argues that (i) people are *naturally equal* and successive generations can be embraced by a contractual relationship with political authority and (ii) there is no need for any one individual exercising a right of access to the earth in common and establishing a right of ownership to some part of the earth to seek the consent of all. By exercising a right to labour and by observing certain duties constraining what can be taken into private ownership it is possible to accumulate property without transgressing the equal rights of access of others. Crucially, argues Locke, *property*, derived in accordance with natural law, should be *preserved* by government. Government can be justifiably overthrown if it fails in this fundamental duty. In arguing the case for limited government Locke contends that various forms of individual rights, including political rights and rights of ownership, are inextricably connected.

Problems and Issues

Two Treatises is textually messy. It is far from obvious what Locke's *priorities* are. Locke's immediate political concerns are revealed but so too is a more systematic philosophical analysis of government. For example, Locke refers to 'The Fundamental Law of Nature' and states that this requires 'that all, as much as may be, should be preserved' (Locke, 1998, p. 183). However, it is not clear who or what Locke is seeking to have *preserved*, for what reasons and by what means. Troublesome statements of this kind riddle the text. Lack of clarity is particularly pronounced in Locke's consent-based theory of political obligation and his discussion of property.

Locke attempts to overcome Filmer's objections to the idea of government based on consent. Locke's response develops his belief in natural equality. Hence he argues that one generation cannot bind its successors (*ibid.*, p. 116). So Locke is committed to identifying what is to count as a declaration of consent. Too rigid a requirement, with too few opportunities to consent, would limit the extent of the political community. Hence Locke's distinction between 'express' and 'tacit' consent.

'Express' consent is the more explicit, being a voluntary act of submission to government which makes the individual 'a perfect Member of that Society, a Subject of that Government' (*ibid.*, p. 119). But Locke fails to provide explicit instances of express consent (for example, oaths of allegiance). He intimates that acquisition or inheritance of estate, 'upon the Conditions annex'd to the Possession of Land in that Country where it lies' (*ibid.*, p. 73

and see also p. 117) might count as a strong form of consent. However, here Locke is concerned to stress the importance of maintaining the territorial integrity of the state and the consequent conditions placed upon landowners not to secede. It is by no means clear that inheritance constitutes express consent to political obligations. Locke's lack of rigour has enabled interpreters to disagree over whether he took landownership as correlating with express consent (Parry, 1978, pp. 103–6 on Macpherson, 1962, pp. 247–51) or whether instead inheritance can be construed merely as a form of tacit consent (Dunn, 1969, pp. 134–8). In attempting to extend the consenting political community Locke admits that 'the difficulty is what ought to be look'd upon as tacit consent, and how far it binds,' the danger being that there will be 'no Expression of it at all' (Locke, 1998, p. 119). Nevertheless, Locke perseveres, contending that 'every Man, that hath any Possession, or Enjoyment, of any part of the Dominion of any Government, doth thereby give his tacit Consent, ... whether his Possession be of Land, ... or a Lodging only for a Week; or whether it be barely travelling freely on the Highway' (*ibid.*, p. 119).

The problems with these passages are manifold. For example, whereas it might be thought that landowners enjoying the protection of the state are placed under a considerable obligation it is less easy to regard walking down the street as an act of *consent*. This raises the question whether Locke envisaged a two-tiered political community – with different rights and obligations for the expressly-consenting propertied and the tacitly-consenting propertyless. Alternatively, Locke's conceptual imprecision can be taken as counting against such a hard and fast distinction.

Ambiguity is compounded by what Locke says about natural equality and the acquisition of property, particularly in land. On an initial reading it is not immediately clear what purpose Chapter V 'Of Property' serves or whether it is even necessary to Locke's case for limited government. One difficulty is in establishing how Locke's conceptualisation of ownership relates to his more specifically political preoccupations and if and how his concern with the 'preservation of property' is linked to his ideological critique of arbitrary government.

Locke's property theory is rights-based but is also influenced by the background noise of contemporary political economy: reflections upon the commercialization of society, the prosperity owing to the industrious and rational, and so on. Locke contends that government is established for 'the preservation of the property of all the Members of ... Society' (*ibid.*, p. 88). However, it is not always clear what Locke means by 'property'. And so there is uncertainty concerning what Locke wishes government to preserve. On occasions Locke defines property very broadly as 'Life, Liberty and Estate' (*ibid.*, p. 87) and thereby infers that all men are stakeholders and are somehow part of the political community. But he needs also to account for the acquisition of 'estate'.

Locke contends that God wills Man's wellbeing, requiring the pursuit of self-preservation. The earth represents a grant *in common* to all men each of whom has an *inclusive right* of access to its use. In the natural state there is no exclusive private dominion. But this leaves a problem: how is property to be individuated? Or is Man to starve? Locke's solution turns upon a theory of labour reinforced by God's will (*ibid.*, p. 32). The rights of labour, and the command to appropriate, accord with the Law of Reason. Here Locke confronts one of Filmer's most telling arguments (ridiculed by Locke, p. 29). Filmer asks, if the earth is a grant in common to *all* men, how can any one individual acquire a right to any thing without the consent of all others? Locke's answer is to contend that because men have a property in their own person, of which their labour is part, to labour on what is previously unowned is to create a right to whatever is produced. Through labour the common rights of others are excluded and a distinction is placed between appropriated property and what remains common. But in making this point Locke states confusingly that 'the Grass my Horse has bit; the Turfs my Servant has cut; and the Ore I have digged in any place where I have a right to them in common with others, become my Property, without the assignation or consent of any body' (*ibid.*, p. 28).

Locke's reference to the servant's labour is bemusing because it raises questions about his position on natural equality, the status of servants and their stake in the political community. Locke offers an insight into his understanding of the master–servant relationship: 'a Free-man makes himself a Servant to another, by selling him for a certain time, the Service he undertakes to do, in exchange for Wages' (*ibid.*, p. 85). Evidently, the master gains a temporary power, defined by contract. Service is not slavery and natural rights are not thereby alienated. But these are troublesome passages.

Locke seeks to balance the natural right of all to access the earth's resources against individual ownership by making appropriation conditional. One restriction is the 'use' or 'spoilage' limitation – not letting things waste (*ibid.*, p. 31). Another is the 'sufficiency' limitation – leaving 'enough and as good for others' (*ibid.*, p. 27). But Locke also seeks to account for extensive property-holdings, particularly in land (*ibid.*, p. 46). Several factors contribute to the emergence of large-scale ownership. These include tacit agreements to the introduction and use of money (thus affording the 'storage' of wealth to overcome the spoilage limitation), and the commensurate tacit agreement to countenance substantial holdings (*ibid.*, p. 36). Alongside the possibility of storing wealth through the medium of exchange, agreement to 'disproportionate and unequal Possession of the

Earth' (*ibid.*, p. 50) is a socially useful inducement to the industrious to accrue property. This is justified as promoting economic growth (*ibid.*, p. 37).

Locke travels a long way down the road from emphasising the inclusiveness of the natural right to labour and appropriate to extolling the merits of property-based economic activity. It is by no means clear which part of the story has the greater bearing upon Locke's political theory. He appears aware of this difficulty when he addresses the inter-generational connotation of his position. 'Late-comers', he contends, are not necessarily disadvantaged by there being no common land left for appropriation. Through industry and selling their labour they too are able to share in growing prosperity. And what of the needy? Locke commends moderation of possession and charitable giving.

Locke stands at the dawn of the Enlightenment but *Two Treatises* is influenced by the natural law theory of an earlier epoch. The critical problem thrown up by Locke's political thought is in determining the extent to which his advocacy of liberal ideas (looking forwards to commercial society and modern liberalism) is dependent upon the fundamental, but potentially outmoded, principles on which he drew (looking back to the language of natural law and natural rights). Elsewhere in his writings Locke struggled to demonstrate the credibility of foundational or *a priori* ideas such as eternal natural law and the prevalence of universal natural rights. The interpretation of Locke's political theory turns upon whether he delivered a coherent philosophical system upon which to base his politics and what consequences follow if he did not.

Why Conflicting Interpretations?

Methodology and Conflicting Values

Just as *Two Treatises* solicits conflict so too a range of interpretations appears plausible. The text is messy, it was drafted over a long period during which Locke became 'politicised', it is not even intact and it was cobbled together belatedly for publication. The difficulty of uncovering Locke's intentions is exacerbated by disagreements concerning the way to go about understanding *Two Treatises*. Furthermore, methodological disagreement has been compounded by conflicts of value amongst scholars either anxious to claim Locke as an adherent of their own political viewpoints or as an advocate of a position with which they take issue (the former is Ashcraft's defence of Locke's liberal credentials, the latter Macpherson's critique of Locke's economic liberalism).

Whereas there is substantial agreement that to understand *Two Treatises* the work must be contextualised, by identifying Locke's background assumptions, there is methodological disagreement over what most influenced Locke: prevailing socio-economic conditions, his political activism or his longer-term philosophical enquiries. But not all interpreters are proponents of the contextual approach. Some commentators believe that to *understand Two Treatises* it is necessary to evaluate the soundness of Locke's arguments.

Dispute often centres upon whether *Two Treatises* forms part of a broader philosophical project and whether Locke's other writings shed light on his politics. But looking beyond *Two Treatises* has often intensified conflict. Even when there is agreement on the significance of Locke's doctrine of natural law, disagreement persists over whether this provides a solid or a fragile basis for his political philosophy.

Locke's Foundations

Locke's thought reflects an age characterised by profound realignments in thinking about the human condition, informed particularly by the impact of scientific and cosmological discoveries upon theology. The retrospective/prophetic elements of *Two Treatises* fuel disagreement over whether Locke's eclecticism is an asset or a hindrance. Some critics (Tully 1980, 1993; Ashcraft, 1986, 1987) see Locke as successfully developing principles founded in natural law theory, such as natural equality, into modern liberalism. Locke thus provides a bridge to the modern world. Others (Dunn 1968, 1969, 1984; Lloyd-Thomas, 1995; Jolley, 1999) see Locke's liberalism as tainted by the failure of 'a priorism' (Porter, 2000): meaning that Locke's foundational principles are insubstantial – to the effect that *Two Treatises* is more a set of policy preferences than a political *philosophy*.

Locke's Liberalism

Two Treatises can be read as Locke's defence of basic liberal principle. But a question soon springs to mind. *Why* is Locke so animated to protect a sphere of individual action free from government interference? Possible responses involve attempting to identify what sort of liberal Locke is. These are: (i) Locke is just what he seems, a *political liberal* who emphasised toleration and freedom of individual conscience; (ii) certainly a political liberal but with a specific *ideological* purpose, namely the advancement of the Whig case in opposition; (iii) a *philosophical liberal* who attempted to develop a political theory from broader theoretical, often theological, foundations and (iv) wittingly or unwittingly an *economic liberal* – an apologist for the political ambitions of an emergent propertied class. Locke's interpreters take one view or another on what sort of liberal Locke is. But often, because they hold strong views on the merits or demerits of certain kinds of liberalism, having identified Locke as a particular type of liberal interpreters differ over whether or not Locke's project is a success.

Locke's theory of property, articulated in *Two Treatises*, supports contradictory appreciations of Locke's liberalism: favouring at the extremes either (i) individualism, highly differentiated exclusive rights of ownership and the minimalist state or (ii) collectivism, some degree of equalitarianism and the intervention of government in pursuit of 'social welfare'. Such disagreement is sustained by Locke's troublesome conceptualisation of ownership (various depictions are advanced by Macpherson (1966), Cohen (1995), Tully (1980, 1993), Nozick (1974) and Waldron (1979, 1982, 1983, 1988)). Locke's position in relation to the rise of capitalism, whether he argues for unlimited property rights (Strauss, 1953; Macpherson, 1966; Wood, 1984; Cohen, 1995; Waldron, 1979, 1982, 1983, 1998) or whether he advocates a version of ownership constrained by moral and social obligations (Dunn, 1968, 1969, 1984; Tully, 1980, 1993; Ashcraft, 1980, 1987) is pivotal to interpretive conflict.

Locke's ideas on property and the legitimacy of ownership often inform present-day debates on 'social justice'. Consideration of issues such as the rights of owners of property to consume, exchange or invest; the rights of labour to a share in the product; or the appropriate bases of 'social welfare' provision, regularly refer back to arguments advanced by Locke. Hence the depth of contention over how to interpret what Locke has to say, or appears to say, about social distribution. And hence, the emergence of conflicting interpretations to support the view that Locke condoned: (i) capitalist expropriation (Macpherson, 1962; Cohen, 1995; Waldron, 1979, 1982, 1983, 1988), (ii) social welfare sustained by a utilitarian 'trickle-down' effect (Tully, 1980, 1993; Ashcraft, 1987) and/or (iii) social redistribution derived from the duty of charity and the rights of access of the excluded propertyless (Dunn, 1968, 1969, 1984; Tully, 1980, 1993).

Conflicting Interpretations

Locke's Liberal Legacy

A commonplace and often popularised view of Locke, held for 250 years after the publication of *Two Treatises*, emphasises his defence of liberal tenets such as the 'rights of man' (Kendall, 1941; Seliger, 1968). This view regards Locke's political ideas as anticipating and vindicated by Enlightenment political philosophy and the advancement of liberty through the American and French revolutions. Until the mid-twentieth century there was a widespread (and mistaken) assumption that the *Second Treatise* is an apology for the 'Glorious Revolution' of 1688. As a result, Locke is depicted by some commentators (Gough, 1950; Franklin, 1978) as a political moderate whose message can be readily extrapolated to serve the liberal cause.

Locke as Economic Liberal (Strauss, Macpherson, Wood, Cohen)

By mid-century several critics were advancing the view that to fully understand Locke's politics it is necessary to regard him as fundamentally an economic liberal. The conservative–republican Strauss (1953) and the radical–democrat Macpherson (1962) share the view that Locke was a 'bourgeois liberal' – but differ in their reasons for regarding Locke's position as objectionable.

Strauss's interest in Locke stems from his contention that the 'crisis of modernity' has been occasioned by the departure from the principles (including 'natural duties') of traditional, classical, natural law. Strauss contends that this process involves a slide towards liberal relativism and, ultimately, nihilism. Utility is an insufficient foundation of a moral truth by which to live. Strauss sees Locke as following Hobbes's lead as an essentially 'modern' thinker who recognised mankind as selfish and acquisitive. Mankind may have innate natural rights (of self-preservation) but for Locke there are no natural duties (of charity). So Strauss insists that natural law could not have formed the philosophical basis of *Two Treatises* which should instead be read as an essentially civil work, a pragmatic defence of the Glorious Revolution. On this reading, Locke is seen as promoting the reasonableness of self-preservation and resistance to tyranny.

Strauss claims that Locke adhered only to a 'a partial law of nature' and cites his property theory as exemplifying this contention. Whereas prior to entering civil society ownership is constrained by the natural law, once civil society exists men must look to convention and positive law to preserve property. For Locke 'civil society has no other function but to serve its own creation' (Strauss, 1953, p. 235). Whereas pre-societally the natural law placed certain constraints upon appropriation, in civil society acquisitiveness is unleashed through market relations and money transactions. Men enter civil society to enlarge their possessions. So Locke defends appropriation devoid of concern for the needs of others. Labouring is not the only way of establishing property rights. For Strauss, Locke captured the spirit of capitalism and bequeathed a political ideology to the United States.

With much of this Macpherson's 'possessive individualist' interpretation, stressing minimal individual obligation to society, is in sympathy – except that Macpherson castigates Locke's liberalism from a radical socialist perspective. In representing Locke as having advanced the moral basis for capitalism, Macpherson instigated a heated debate that remains central to Lockean scholarship. Macpherson accepts that Locke is a liberal but contends that his thinking must be appropriately contextualised. To Macpherson, the assumption that Locke was simply a defender of liberty against tyranny is too superficial. Instead, Macpherson sees the meaning of *Two Treatises* as residing in Locke's 'unstated social assumptions' (Townshend, 2000). This methodological approach leads Macpherson to contend that Locke's position is influenced by contemporary socio-economic circumstances. According to Macpherson, Locke was witnessing the consolidation of 'bourgeois' property rights within a regime of capitalist exchange. It is hardly surprising, therefore, that far from defending universalisable liberal rights Locke was instead promoting a political doctrine designed to support more specific class-related ownership. Indeed, and very controversially, Macpherson contends that Locke could not have believed in the feasibility of universal rights because he supported a notion of 'differential rationality'. Locke was convinced that exercising reason requires a degree of autonomy and leisure. So, argues Macpherson, Locke must have believed that only the propertied are sufficiently rational to exercise political rights. Only the propertied can be full members of the political community. Thus Macpherson's 'explanatory' theory sees Locke as advancing a position that can be reconstructed as an apology for a conception of the political community, access to which was restricted to the propertied class whose ends government would serve.

Macpherson's development of this interpretation repays serious examination. He focuses on two related and ambiguous aspects of *Two Treatises*: (i) Locke's account of the origins of ownership, and (ii) Locke's line on consent, political obligation and membership of the political community. For Macpherson, these elements of Locke's political philosophy are informed by social presuppositions (for example, the rationality of the propertied and industrious) that led Locke to take the process of capitalist appropriation for granted.

Hence, Macpherson contends that Locke's references to the master–servant relationship presuppose the wage-relation of capitalism. And servants who, on Macpherson's reading can only consent tacitly (by treading the highway), cannot thereby be full members of the political community. They must obey, but cannot influence, political authority.

Macpherson's critics focus particularly upon his contention that Locke did not make his social assumptions explicit because he had no need to do so – the line that Locke's meaning would have been readily understood by contemporaries. Here is a key point of interpretive conflict: are these Locke's social assumptions or is Macpherson imposing his own understanding of the rise of capitalist political economy upon Locke? Miller (1982), Pocock (1985) and Tully (1980, 1993) are to the fore in contending that Macpherson reads into Locke social assumptions not evident until the era of commercialisation of which Adam Smith wrote nearly a century later.

Despite the ferocity of attack upon Macpherson the quasi-Marxist interpretation of Locke has not remained unsupported. Wood (1984), although in certain respects critical of Macpherson, seeks to refine the Macphersonite analysis of Locke's background assumptions by contending that Locke operated within a context of *agrarian* capitalism and Cohen (1995) cites Locke as a proponent of an illegitimate property, and thereby political, regime. Even so, Ryan speaks for many in identifying an essential shortcoming of the 'quasi-Marxist' approach when he accuses Macpherson of erroneously crediting Locke with a degree of coherence that is simply not a feature of *Two Treatises* (1965).

Locke's Political Liberalism in Context

In the words of one prominent advocate of meticulously contextualising Locke 'any interpretation must necessarily place a heavy reliance upon contextual evidence in its portrayal of the development of Locke's political thought' (Ashcraft, 1986, p. 76). The position challenges Macpherson's depiction of Locke as bourgeois. Locke is identified as a political *radical*. Thus *Two Treatises* constitutes the refutation of the 'conservative' Filmer's defence of absolutist and arbitrary government.

The forerunner of this approach is Laslett (1960). Contrary to conventional opinion at the time of writing, Laslett demonstrated that *Two Treatises* was written not as a defence of the Glorious Revolution, nor as a refutation of Hobbesian absolutism. Laslett's detailed reconstruction of the circumstances informing the lengthy gestation of *Two Treatises* focuses on Locke's sympathetic involvement in Whig political circles. Accordingly, and contrary to long-held beliefs (including those of Strauss), *Two Treatises* turns out not to have been written as a defence of the 1688 Whig Revolution, although its publication in 1689 was certainly apposite. Its composition, the bulk of which is seen by Laslett as situated around 1679–80, is a pragmatic justification for Whig opposition to royal prerogative and constitutes 'a demand for a revolution to be brought about, not the rationalization of a revolution in need of defence' (Laslett, 1998, p. 47). Hence Laslett's contention that *Two Treatises* should be regarded purely and simply as a political *tract* rather than as a systematic work of political or social philosophy. Locke was attempting to come up with specific arguments capable of sustaining the Whig position in opposition (for example on the right of resistance), rather than a general theory extended from his broader philosophical position (for example, a natural rights-based theory of ownership). So an essential feature of Laslett's interpretation is that he presupposes distance between *Two Treatises* and Locke's other works.

The historical revisionist approach has been reappraised and developed, particularly by Ashcraft (1986, 1987). Ashcraft also focuses upon the *exact* circumstances of the composition of *Two Treatises* and what this reveals concerning its meaning but, contra Laslett, asserts that, when prompted by circumstance, Locke produced a defining work of liberal political philosophy – the outcome of prolonged intellectual endeavour (for Laslett's response see 1998, pp. 123–6).

Ashcraft attempts to integrate three broad lines of enquiry: (i) a revisionist historical account of Locke's political activism and of why he wrote *Two Treatises*, (ii) an analysis of the implications of natural rights theories for Locke's intellectual development once he had become politically engaged, and (iii) the case for regarding the philosophical position outlined in *Two Treatises* as fulfilling Locke's purpose. Ashcraft advances his position as representing an eclectic sophistication of approach to the interpretation of Locke, not least because, in linking *Two Treatises* to ideas central to Locke's philosophical development, Ashcraft opens the way to analysis, in which he himself engages, of the overall philosophical coherence of Locke's political philosophy.

Ashcraft identifies ideas available to Locke as he constructed his ideological defence of religious and political dissent to argue that Locke's position is similar to the earlier, radical natural rights theories of the Leveller movement active during the English Civil War. The influence of a radical natural law tradition upon Locke meant that he was able to deploy a theory of practical reason in defence of equal natural rights. Thus, in stark contrast to Strauss and Macpherson, and in alignment with Dunn and Tully (below, 'Locke's philosophical liberalism'), Ashcraft argues that Locke's theory of property is formulated within a context of *moral obligations*. So too is his resistance theory. Locke did not underestimate the difficulty of constructing a theory of popular resistance in which the concept of the 'political community', endowed with the right to exercise resistance, is consistent with 'the people'. But, according to Ashcraft, such is Locke's radicalism that Macpherson's contention that Locke represented a narrower class interest is effectively undermined. For Locke, government based on popular consent is essential to the realisation in practice of the natural right to toleration. So, the right of resistance amounts to exercising liberty of conscience. This also entails the sort of political equality that Macpherson's Locke, operating with a view of differential rationality, could not contemplate.

Ashcraft concludes that Locke's credentials as a theoretical under-labourer of political liberalism are well founded. But Ashcraft seeks to demythologise Locke And so Locke's political philosophy is interpreted as encapsulating, in embryonic form, the internal tensions of liberalism – not least problems subsequently encountered by liberals in attempting to reconcile egalitarian political principles with economic inequality.

Locke's Philosophical Liberalism

Although acknowledging that his involvement with the Shaftesbury Whigs prompted Locke to produce *Two Treatises*, certain interpreters dig deeper towards the roots of his political philosophy. Thus it is contended that Locke saw himself as engaged in developing a philosophically coherent theory. *Two Treatises* can be understood only by identifying the 'intellectual equipment' (ideas, language, presuppositions about the nature of the world) used by Locke during the course of its composition. *Two Treatises* is, thereby, not so much the issue of Locke's socio-economic or political context but rather a discernibly theological and philosophical work. Hence Locke is regarded as a thinker, engaged in a long-term philosophical project, who put that project to effect in support of a political cause (see also, Harris, 1994).

Advocates of this approach have contested whether or not, in assimilating the radical potential of natural rights theories, Locke successfully developed a political philosophy consistent with natural law's foundational principles. Once it is recognised that Locke struggled in this respect, the way is then opened to questioning the overall coherence of Locke's project – an enterprise exposed by Hume and often savaged by the techniques of 'analytical philosophy' (see below, 'philosophical pitfalls').

Dunn (1969, 1984) stresses that Locke's political thought is intelligible only in terms of his theological commitments and philosophical premises, each of which turn upon Locke's appreciation of humanity's relationship to God. Emphasis is placed upon Locke's belief that, through natural law, the author of the created universe defines rights and duties. This is to presuppose a divine guarantor of moral knowledge, a precept forming the fulcrum of Locke's broader social theory. Crucially, and contentiously, Locke argues in *An Essay Concerning Human Understanding* that natural law is discernible via the operation of reason. Upon this philosophical edifice Locke's political philosophy stands or falls. Locke's epistemology commits him to a defence of individual autonomy in the religious, moral and social realms. Hence his espousal of natural equality and the toleration of belief and, in politics, hence the sanctity of natural rights. Thus, in his critique of Filmer's view of monarchical rights, it is not difficult to see why Locke advances a theory of property rights originating in natural equality. Dunn argues that Locke the political theorist is motivated by the commitment that only legitimate government can enable men to discharge their duties under natural law – decisively the requirement that men attend to their *self-preservation*. Political obligation becomes, for Locke, a medium for fulfilling a religious duty. The limits of legitimate government, and the right of resistance, are defined in similar terms. Locke's project seeks to reconcile theories of individualism and constitutionalism within the peculiar context of the late seventeenth-century English polity (see also Harris, 1994; Goldie, 1997).

For Dunn, Locke's political philosophy is heavy in terms of ideological enterprise but light in terms of philosophical clout. Locke foreshadows the compelling tragedy of the liberal political project. Witness Locke's fumbling efforts to construct a consent-based theory of political obligation. According to Dunn, Locke's political ideas are fundamentally incoherent because they are insecurely established. Locke's political philosophy stands or falls on the intelligibility of his account of the universal facility of reason to discern 'natural law'. This enterprise is ultimately flawed, as it was destined to be, by Locke's inability to convince us of the possibility of true 'moral knowledge' (and see below, Jolley).

Amongst interpreters who see Locke as essentially a natural law thinker it is not agreed that Locke's project constitutes a philosophical dead-end. Tully (1980, 1993) argues that, assuming Locke's foundational principles (that is to say the coherence of a natural rights-based political theory), *Two Treatises* represents a substantial achievement in which the natural rights theories of the day are brought to fruition. *Two Treatises* is not merely a refutation, through a defence of natural freedom, of Filmer's theory of natural subjugation. It is more a reworking of a well-established position: natural law theory as developed, in particular, by Locke's predecessors Grotius (1925) and Pufendorf (1934).

Tully recognises Locke's need to show that exclusive rights of ownership and political equality can be both reconciled and explained by reference to the natural law. Through a detailed and ingenious analysis of Locke's property theory Tully seeks to establish precisely what Locke sought to have *preserved* by political society: even to the extent of advocating resistance to arbitrary government. Locke's themes (property, toleration, revolution) are consistent extensions of his passionate defence of natural liberty. On this reading Locke emerges as a radical whose theory amounts to a defence of the 'natural right to the means of preservation', who sought the preservation of 'property' in the widest contemporary understanding and who regarded natural law as the basis of the public good to the extent of advocating discernibly 'welfarist principles'. Clearly, all this stands in marked contrast to Macpherson's possessive individualist approach which claims that Locke defended extensive rights of individual ownership. According to Tully, developing a theory of ownership based upon the 'natural right of labour power' enabled Locke to successfully counter Filmer's criticisms of the natural law theorists.

Tully's interpretation of Locke's property theory (especially 1993, chapter 4) is, therefore, diametrically opposed to Macpherson's – which places far greater emphasis upon the positive sanction of ownership within civil society. Drawing upon a tradition of *a priori* natural law, Tully's Locke regards the earth as common to all, prior to its occupation. But there is the problem of individuation, the difficulty of establishing, in order to ensure self-preservation, an exclusive right to the use of sufficient property to which the access of others is restricted. Here natural law prescribes a set of rights and duties or mutual obligations. Amongst the rights is the inclusive right of each to access and use of the earth in pursuit of self-preservation. With respect to duty, individuals are not only obliged to fulfil God's purpose by seeking self-preservation but are also required to do so whilst respecting the inclusive rights of others.

According to Tully, Locke's determination to demonstrate that exclusive property rights can be established without the inclusive rights of others being transgressed means that his conception of fixed property rights in estate, particularly in land, is very much more conditional than Strauss and Macpherson recognise. Locke takes the limitations on appropriation detailed in Chapter V, which Macpherson claims were rendered redundant through the introduction of money, more seriously than Macpherson supposes. Nevertheless, Locke is obliged to admit that a difficulty occurs in that a natural rights account of the foundation of property in land runs into trouble when the common land available for appropriation becomes scarce. At this point, exclusive property rights in land must be sanctioned by consent. Crucially, once civil society is established, property rights become conventional but also *conditional*. So, given the natural rights basis of his property theory, Locke is committed to arguing that property, even that legitimately acquired via the process of natural individuation, cannot be retained exclusively once the conditions for natural individuation can no longer be met. For Tully, Locke is able to reconcile individual ownership with social welfare in several ways. One is his contention that occupation and cultivation enhance fertility and contribute to the general welfare (Locke the utilitarian). Another is more radical and brings to mind Leveller natural rights thinking. Exclusive civil rights, including those of ownership, are conditional upon the fulfilment of social duties derived from *moral obligations*. Here too, according to Tully, Macpherson misses the mark. Locke is not defending unconditional private property. Instead, and here Tully accords with Dunn's interpretation (1968), Locke fully acknowledges the rights of the needy and, thereby, the duty of the propertied to meet those needs through charitable giving.

Given all this, it is not surprising to discover that Tully, in considering controversial passages such as 'the Turfs my Servant has cut' (Locke, 1998, p. 28), is anxious to do further damage to the Macphersonite case by contending that Locke's meaning lies within what was contextually assumed about the social division of labour. On Tully's reading, (and here he follows other of Macpherson's critics), Locke's reference to the master–servant relationship is not to the wage-relation of capitalism. The exchange is instead voluntary: the servant is a free man selling a service rather than his labour. And if this proviso constitutes an obstacle to nascent capitalism then we should not be surprised. Locke's objective is not to defend capitalism but is instead to defend, against the Filmerians, the rights and duties necessary for universal self-preservation.

Analysing the Philosophical Pitfalls of Locke's Political Theory

Some interpreters are less exercised by trying to identify Locke's intentions than by analysing the quality of his broader philosophical project in relation to *Two Treatises*. Locke's position is interrogated conceptually, its coherence is queried and, in certain instances (Nozick, 1974; Sreenivasan, 1995; Kramer, 1997), Locke's arguments are reconstructed. Considering whether *Two Treatises* forms part of a broader philosophical project leads to a concern to demonstrate where these connections hold together and where they do not. Whilst such analysis highlights aspects of Locke's argument that do not hold water (for example, his line on the bases of political obligation), this is not necessarily to rebuke Locke. Instead, such analysis is often undertaken on the understanding that the watertight arguments Locke needed are not actually attainable.

Locke on Consent
The analytical approach often involves taking Locke's text out of its context and subjecting it to critical appraisal in light of issues of continuing

interest (for in-depth analysis see Simmons, 1992, 1993). An accessible version of this method is provided by Lloyd Thomas who professes a self-consciously philosophical approach intended to evaluate the relevance to ourselves of Locke's political theory (1995). In attempting to identify the core of Locke's political ideas, Lloyd Thomas concludes that Locke is primarily concerned to demonstrate that people are morally justified in rebelling against a tyrannical government. Locke is, therefore, most definitely a radical. This evaluation prompts Lloyd Thomas to examine the coherence of Locke's case. His overall conclusion is that Locke's political project is doomed because it is ill-founded. It is not, for Lloyd Thomas, sensible to follow Locke in believing that legitimate political authority rests on the consent of rights-bearers: not least because of the implausibility of Locke's position on tacit consent. Locke's difficulties do, however, help us to see the correct way of perceiving the relationship between the subject and the state which, according to Lloyd Thomas, entails following Hume by taking a consequentialist approach, and focusing on the benefits of belonging to a political community. So, although often flawed, Locke's analysis inadvertently provides important insights into fundamental political problems and their resolution.

Locke on Property

Lloyd Thomas also undertakes an appraisal of 'Of Property'. He brings into further doubt the overall coherence of Locke's project by contending that Locke's property theory is an attempt to justify ownership in the unconditional sense which has little to do with the substance of Locke's political thought. Even as a discreet enterprise Locke's property theory is fallible on a number of grounds. Amongst these are the problem of trying to use the labour theory of value to line up individuals with particular material possessions and the difficulty posed by the rights of successive generations.

From a broadly analytical perspective other critics argue that Locke's property theory is not only central to his overall social theory but also that it constitutes a defining contribution to property theory in general. Nozick's controversial book *Anarchy, State and Utopia* (1974) has spurred much of the analytical reappraisal of Locke's property theory. Heralding 'New Right' thinking, Nozick espouses a bone dry and secular reconstruction of individual and exclusive 'Lockean' property rights to make the case for minimal, unobtrusive government. Although not strictly a contribution to Lockean scholarship, Nozick takes Locke's case on the preservation of 'property', understood in a highly 'traditional' sense, to a logical extreme.

According to Nozick, any form of governmental interference in legitimately acquired property holdings, particularly in support of redistributive systems of social justice, is morally unjustifiable. Hence taxation constitutes the slavery to which Locke is so vehemently opposed.

Waldron's rights-based analysis is prominent not least because it is located more firmly within the mainstream of Lockean scholarship (1988). Waldron provides a secular restatement of Locke's property theory and examines critically whether Locke was successful in what he was attempting to achieve. Waldron contends that *Two Treatises* should not be regarded as one dimension of a wider philosophical project. Instead, the work stands alone and by and large lacks the analytical rigour evident elsewhere in Locke's writings. Thus emphasis is placed upon what Waldron sees as the untenable nature of many of Locke's arguments. In the process of highlighting these shortcomings, Waldron develops an ongoing critique of Tully's 'contextual' reconstruction of Locke's theory of ownership, which Tully takes as integral to Locke's philosophy and through which Tully promotes the thesis that Locke is not defending unconditional private property in land. Waldron attacks Tully's appreciation on several fronts: (i) the 'mixing labour' motif is subjected to analysis to see if it makes sense, and is discovered not to do so (1983); (ii) similarly the 'sufficiency limitation' where, again, Locke is deemed to have committed himself to an implausible position that ties him up in knots (1979); and (iii) in which Tully's position is subjected to particularly vehement criticism, Locke's rendition of 'the Turfs my Servant has cut' is taken apart analytically as Waldron concludes, aligning with Macpherson, that Locke presumes something very much more akin to a potentially exploitative wage relationship (1982).

Waldron's contention is that, just as Locke fails in his attempt to provide the unachievable (a rights-based defence of private property), so too Tully's reconstruction must also be doomed. Crucially, whereas Tully argues that Locke presupposed the conditional and consensual nature of property rights once civil society had been established, for Waldron, Locke is committed to establishing unconditional property rights.

This notwithstanding, two recent contributions (Sreenivasan, 1995; Kramer, 1997) have kept Lockean property theory very much alive by agreeing that important aspects of Locke's position, including his labour theory of value and defence of exclusive rights of ownership, are significantly flawed. But by reconstructing the logic of Locke's argument and by identifying the limits Locke's position places upon rights of ownership what emerges is, it is claimed, not a defence of individualism but rather a persuasively communitarian conception of ownership.

The Philosophical Basis of Locke's Project

Jolley has recently undertaken a systematic assessment of Locke's philosophical project and of the place of his political thought within it. He concludes that 'it is more instructive to see difficulties in Locke as arising from an over-ambitious programme than from a series of gratuitous muddles and mistakes' (Jolley, 1999, p. 178). Through considering Locke's political philosophy in relation to his wider philosophical project, Jolley recognises that Locke attempts to derive social obligations from natural law. *Two Treatises* is, therefore, an essentially theological argument about the proper function of the state which attempts to demonstrate that absolutism is not a morally legitimate option. Nevertheless, Jolley concurs with Dunn in regarding Locke's project as thwarted by serious difficulties. In attempting to maintain consistency between his various works Locke is driven into some impossibly tight corners: for example, the need to reconcile his view that there are no innate ideas with his belief that natural law is a guide to reason. Here there are obvious tensions between Locke's epistemological individualism (through which he holds that (i) our knowledge is limited, but also that (ii) human freedom is a central element of the metaphysics of morals) and his commitment to natural law theory. Does Locke provide an account capable of convincing the sceptical reader that natural law *is* the guide to morals and to political conduct? And is that same sceptical reader, Hume for example, going to be persuaded by Locke's attempts to develop a theory of inalienable natural rights from his doctrine of natural law? As Jolley puts it, 'in the *Second Treatise of Government* Locke suggests that the law of nature is not attended with any epistemological difficulties, but we can see that he is merely whistling in the dark' (*ibid.*, p. 202).

Evaluation

Disagreement concerning Locke's liberalism is inevitable. Locke grappled with problems (the appropriate weighting of individual freedom and social welfare) that still beset liberal political theory.

Regarding Locke's political thought as a straightforward bequest to liberal constitutionalism distorts Locke's intentions by understating his context. Conversely, attempting to contextualise Locke by identifying his 'background assumptions' carries the risk of narrowing the context in pursuit of a definite explanation of what Locke was about. This is the trap into which Strauss, and more especially Macpherson, fall. Macpherson's contention that Locke's politics can be understood through reference to his socio-economic position has prompted subsequent interpreters to focus much needed attention upon the ambiguous aspects of Locke's theory – particularly his account of the origins of ownership and the relationship, if any, that Locke assumes to hold between political and economic rights. But Macpherson's interpretation is coloured by his broader critique of liberal democracy's perceived attachment to capitalism and thereby constitutes an example of contextualising by attribution. Macpherson goes too far in reading into Locke essentially secular beliefs about the commercialisation of society and the unlimited nature of property rights.

The historical revisionist response to the 'Macpherson version' enhances our understanding of the circumstances in which *Two Treatises* was composed. But whereas this approach forms a necessary starting point for discerning Locke's intentions, recognising that Locke was writing for a specific purpose provides an incomplete insight into *Two Treatises*. Historical reconstruction cannot tell us *all* we need to know. Laslett's view that *Two Treatises* is philosophically distant from Locke's other writings is persuasively challenged by those (Dunn, Tully, Ashcraft, Jolley) who believe that *Two Treatises* is an important element of Locke's broader project.

Emphasising the significance of Locke's rationalist theology and his concern with natural law and natural rights allows us to appreciate that, whilst historical contextualism is important, there still remains the need to uncover the essence of Locke's political thought. Regarding Locke as essentially a natural law thinker explains why such a self-contained, devoutly Christian personality grew so animated in defence of a political cause (Harris, 1994). Examining the philosophical basis of Locke's thought enables us to enhance our understanding of Locke in several ways. As Tully and Ashcraft show, it is possible to reconstruct Locke's natural rights and property theory to depict him as a social, economic and political radical. But as Dunn and Jolley show, the foundational beliefs identified by these interpreters as essential to Locke's project are not immune to challenge. So Locke's construction of a moral theory of politics is open to criticism. Here we confront the fundamental problem with Locke's political thought. Whereas Locke's theological rationalism constitutes the essential explanatory context to his political thought it also provides insights into the philosophical and analytical deficiencies of his project. Given these impediments, Ashcraft's attempt to provide the analytical substantiation of Locke's political philosophy in context appears over-ambitious.

The Waldron–Tully debate highlights the difficulty of interpreting Locke. If as Tully insists (along, to a degree, with Dunn) Locke advocates curtailing property rights within civil society the possibility arises that Locke could also have countenanced governmental regulation of property for it to serve a 'social function'. But Waldron responds with two commensurate points: (i) Locke promotes a vigorous, rights-based defence of private property and (ii) Locke fails because his arguments are flawed (see above). Point (i) is particularly intriguing. If Waldron convinces us that the defence of an exclusive and extensive rights-based conception of private property is *essential* to Locke's political philosophy, then Waldron appears to provide credence to *both* the Macphersonite and Nozickian interpretations. So Waldron's robust analytical defence of the view that Locke's political theory is about the preservation of individual property rights against government intervention explains why the interpretation of Locke's political thought has resulted in the sharing of beds by scholars with markedly different values (the radical–socialist Macpherson and the conservative–individualist Nozick).

Any adequate interpretation of Locke's political thought must come to terms with its complexity and, thereby, the recognition that simplifying Locke's position in order to produce a watertight reconstruction of what he meant inevitably results in distortion. A truly convincing interpretation would have to recognise Locke's essential problem – that of deriving his preferred version of a liberal constitutional polity and system of social distribution from a basis in natural equality. Attempts (Tully and Ashcraft) to depict Locke as more socially radical than previously supposed fall short of the mark. Locke is insufficiently radical to be coherent. But had he been more consistent in arguing for conditional ownership Locke would have been forced to address a persistent problem for liberalism – that of how the ongoing social redistribution necessary to secure limited ownership can be managed without sacrificing the desire to limit government.

4

Hume (1711–1776)

JOHN SALTER

Introduction

Hume's political philosophy consists of a theory of justice and property and a theory of political obligation. These theories were not a response to a particular political event or an attempt to solve a single political problem. Moreover, the works in which they appear – the *Treatise on Human Nature* and the *Enquiry Concerning the Principles of Morals* – are comprehensive works of philosophy, and they give us little indication of Hume's practical political concerns. However, Hume also published a series of political essays in which he undertook an analysis of aspects of British politics since the Revolution of 1688, and they provide some insight into the relationship between Hume's political philosophy and the practice of politics.

Hume, a Scot, thought that whether or not the Revolution had been justified at the time, the Hanoverian regime was fulfilling the proper functions of government. England was a country governed by law, and the period since George I took the throne in 1714 had been a period of political stability and commercial progress under the Whig administration of Sir Robert Walpole. However, Hume thought that these achievements were being undermined by different currents of opposition and resistance which were rooted in speculative and dogmatic political theories, and in partisan interests and loyalties. Moreover, in Scotland, which had not participated in England's commercial progress and remained an economically backward country, the problem of the relationship between economic improvement and political institutions was more urgent.

The political theory of the Whigs was the theory of the social contract. This theory occupied a central place in the modern theory of natural law, where it was used to explain how people living in a state of natural liberty and equality voluntarily entered into political society under the common authority of a government. Locke had produced a separate version with the avowed intention of justifying the 1688 Revolution, and the Whigs had used it to portray the Revolution as a restoration of the original contract between rulers and ruled. However, in the first half of the eighteenth century a group of Old Whigs and Tories under the leadership of Bolingbroke, accused the ruling Whigs of betraying the principles of the Revolution and of pursuing policies that were leading the country into corruption and decay. There were two policies in particular that led to the charge that Walpole was corrupting the nation. The first was his use of patronage as a means of extending his influence over parliament, which was seen as undermining the constitutional balance between parliament and the crown. The second was the expansion of public debt, which was enhancing the wealth and political influence of the financiers at the expense of landowners, thus shifting the balance of power away from those who, in Bolingbroke's view, were best able to exercise it in a virtuous and patriotic way.

The most serious threat to political stability in the first half of the eighteenth century, however, was the continuing Jacobite resistance to the Hanoverian government. In England, the Jacobite threat was kept alive, according to Hume, by the irrational attachment of the Tory party to the Stuart dynasty. But in Scotland, Jacobitism was associated with a form of nostalgic nationalism, which Hume thought was damaging to Scotland's prospects for political and economic modernisation, and of its chances of enjoying the commercial benefits of political union with England.

Bolingbroke's opposition and Jacobite resistance demonstrated to Hume that the theory of the social contract was incapable of providing support for the established government. For one thing, it held out the prospect of a further revolution whenever it was thought that the original contract was in need of renewal. It could, in any case, only offer support for the established government by justifying the revolution that had led to it. And the problem with such a defence, Hume thought, irrespective of whether it was convincing, was that it was irrelevant for the same reason that Jacobite ideology was irrelevant: the origins of a government had no bearing on the reasons for obeying it.

In Book III of the *Treatise* Hume presents a detailed critique of the theory of the social contract. He does not object to its conclusions, at least insofar as they justify resistance to tyrants. The problem with it was that it bore no relationship to the way most people understood their political duties. Everyone, Hume says, thinks they have a moral obligation to obey government. But no one, unless their judgement has been 'led astray by too strict adherence to a system of philosophy' imagines that their obedience depends on a contract or promise. The principle that government should be in the interests of the governed could, in any case, be established in a more straightforward way.

The substructure for Hume's theory of political obligation was his account of the conventional origins of justice. Justice, by which Hume means respect for other people's property and the keeping of promises and contracts, is an 'artificial' virtue, which originates in human conventions. People enter the convention on justice before they agree to live under the common authority of a government, and so the laws of justice established by the convention are binding independently of the obligation to obey government. Government was introduced at a later stage to enforce the laws of justice, and thus to force people to follow their 'real and permanent' interests. Justice and government are both, therefore, human inventions to remedy the 'inconveniences' of a life of absolute liberty, and they both acquire their moral sanction 'from their remedying those inconveniences' (Hume, 1978, p. 543). It follows, without the need to invoke any additional 'higher' principle such as a promise, that when a government fails to administer justice and becomes oppressive and tyrannical, 'we are no longer bound to submit to it' (*ibid.*, p. 551). Hume insists, however, that that it is only in cases of 'grievous tyranny and oppression' that resistance is justified. Resistance and revolution are disruptive and costly, so the 'common rule' requires submission (*ibid.*, p. 554).

Now Hume does not think that the majority of people, or the 'vulgar' as he calls them, think about their interests and duties in this philosophical and calculating way. Nevertheless, he thinks that most people have at least an 'implicit notion' of the connection between obedience and the public interest. Moreover, this interest is so urgent and compelling, that the question of *who* should govern assumes far less importance in most people minds. People are born into political societies and most obey the existing government out of habit or custom. Furthermore, Hume thinks there is an 'instinct or tendency' to 'suppose' there is a moral obligation attached to loyalty. So common morality, as well as prudence, requires us to 'submit quietly to the government, which we find establish'd in the country where we happen to live, without enquiring too curiously into its origins and first establishment' (*ibid.*, p. 558).

Hume's analysis of political obligation does not yield a doctrine of resistance, nor does it establish any firm principles for deciding the legitimacy of a ruler. In fact, his whole point seems to be that it is impossible to be precise about such matters, and attempts to theorise about resistance are destabilising. The general principle that resistance is justified when governments cease to provide economic security is supported by common sense and historical practice, but strict adherence to any rules, or a rigid loyalty to any person or family, are 'virtues that hold less of reason, than of bigotry or superstition.' Hume's theory of political obligation is not one that offers practical guidance, but one that determines the boundaries between philosophy and political speculation (*ibid.*, p. 562).

Problems and Issues

The *Treatise* is a difficult book to read and it is generally acknowledged that Hume is not always clear in presenting his arguments. The *Enquiry*, which covers much the same ground, is less difficult, but is not always consistent with the *Treatise*. For both these reasons it is possible to find textual support for quite different interpretations of some of Hume's central ideas.

For example, Hume says that justice 'is not derived from nature, but from *artifice*; or more properly speaking, nature provides a remedy in the judgement and understanding, for what is irregular and incommodious in the affections' (Hume, 1978, p. 489). But he is not always precise about what he means by judgement and understanding. On the one hand, he says that the alteration of the interested affection 'must necessarily take place upon the least reflection; since 'tis evident, that the passion is much better satisfy'd by its restraint, than by its liberty' (*ibid.*, p. 492). And when he explains the particular rules of justice in the *Enquiry*, he says that rules that are most useful and beneficial are obvious from 'vulgar sense and slight experience'. On the other hand, he says we are unable to perceive the benefits of justice 'by study and reflexion alone', but by reflecting on our experience. And he gives the impression that a good deal of experience is necessary. For example, he says that the convention on justice 'arises gradually, and acquires force by slow progression, and by our repeated experience of the inconveniences of transgressing it' (*ibid.*, p. 490). And he likens the development of justice to the development of language, or the development of money as a medium of exchange.

There is also some ambiguity about the extent to which Hume thinks life in family units shapes our early experience of justice. He seems to reject the theory of Shaftesbury, according to which justice is an expression of certain public affections, which have their origin in families. Hume says that justice only becomes necessary when people encounter the selfishness of strangers, and life in the family does not prepare them for this because familial kindness and affection, 'instead of fitting men for large societies, is almost as contrary to them, as the most narrow selfishness' (*ibid.*, p. 487). Elsewhere, however, Hume says that it is within the family that 'the first rudiments of justice' appear: 'nothing can be more simple and obvious than that rule [for the stability of possession] ... every parent, in order to pre-serve peace among his children, must establish it' (*ibid.*, p. 493). It would seem from this that society results from the application and modification of a principle that men have learned from living in families. The convention does not explain the origins of justice but its extension to wider social groups.

A third example of ambiguity in Hume's texts is his account of the par-ticular rules of property. The rules of property that Hume identifies are the standard Roman laws of property, namely: occupation, long possession or prescription, accession and succession. But his explanation of these rules is one of the most controversial features of his whole theory. In the *Enquiry*, he gives a fairly straightforward account of the rules in terms of utility. For example, he thinks it is simply obvious that the things people have pro-duced or improved should be theirs to encourage industry and that property should descend to children and that contracts should be honoured for the same reason (Hume, 1975, p. 195). But elsewhere in the *Enquiry*, Hume says that while it is essential for the interests of society that there are rules of property, what the rules should be 'is generally speaking, pretty indiffer-ent; and is often determined by very frivolous views and considerations' (*ibid.*, pp. 309–10). And in the *Treatise* he says that while public interest is no doubt a motive for most of the rules of property, he thinks that they are 'principally fix'd by the imagination, or the more frivolous properties of our thought and conception' (*ibid.*, p. 504).

A further problem is the difficult question of the relationship between the different elements of Hume's philosophy, and in particular, the relationship between his sceptical attack on reason in Book I of the *Treatise* and the political philosophy, which appears in Book III. What, if any, is the rela-tionship between this scepticism and Hume's criticisms of the traditional theories of natural law and the theory of the social contract? And does it have any bearing on Hume's conservative and sceptical politics? Another aspect of Hume's scepticism is his religious scepticism. In the introduction to the *Treatise*, Hume states his intention of basing all his inquiries on the foundation of observation and experience. This certainly implies an entirely secular political philosophy, which Hume's undoubtedly was, but how important is this in our assessment of the significance of Hume's theory?

Hume's political writings were so wide-ranging, and they displayed such scholarly depth, that interpreters who aim to produce a contextualist reading are confronted by a multiplicity of possible contexts and targets. For exam-ple, Hume's critique of the contract theory was undoubtedly an intervention in contemporary politics, but it would be an attenuated interpretation that ignored the broader context and failed to explore the relationship between

Hume's view of political obligation and that of Hobbes or the natural lawyers. Similarly, the discussion of justice in Book III of the *Treatise* is extremely complex in its relationship to different branches of moral philosophy and natural law, and it would be a mistake to think that Hume had a single intellectual or practical objective.

Why Conflicting Interpretations?

Because Hume's philosophy covers so much ground, and can be located in so many different contexts, it is not surprising that it has generated a wide range of interpretations. Moreover, readers of Hume unavoidably approach his work from different intellectual backgrounds with different interests and research agendas. Philosophers, historians and political theorist have all read Hume in different ways, partly because they have looked for different things, but also because their expertise in a particular discipline has made them more sensitive to particular subtleties, which readers with a different kind of expertise may overlook. In many cases, of course, this leads to different but complementary interpretations, but it can also lead to conflicts.

For example, historians who are primarily concerned to interpret Hume's writings against the background of the different currents of political and social writing in eighteenth-century Britain, have tended to reach different conclusions about Hume's intentions and the nature of his political outlook than political theorists who are more interested in Hume's relationship to a wider spectrum of political philosophy over a longer time period. Hume's critique of the contract theory, when viewed as a critique of Whig doctrine, shows him to be a conservative thinker anxious to stress the dangers of resistance, and to provide a more secure basis for established order. But in granting that there must be exceptions to obedience, and at the same time insisting that resistance is only justified as a last resort in *extremis*, Hume was in the mainstream of European political thought. This illustrates the danger of characterising a past writer's views as conservative, radical or liberal: the judgement depends entirely on the point of comparison.

For some interpreters, however, the key to understanding Hume's moral and political philosophy is the epistemological theory of Book I of the *Treatise*. From this perspective, Hume's moral scepticism, his denial that justice is a natural virtue, and his sceptical and conservative political outlook, can all be 'explained' as a more or less direct result of the sceptical attack on reason. Context is brought in, not to help us understand Hume, but to demonstrate the *implications* of Hume's philosophical conclusions. The danger here is that a desire to portray Hume as a major political thinker, as well as a major philosopher, can lead to the temptation to interpret the context *in the light of* his philosophical achievements.

For example, a long-standing and still common assessment of Hume's principal significance as a political philosopher, is that his attack on reason undermined the basis of traditional theories of natural law, and thereby destroyed the foundations of moral and political certainty. Adherents of this view characterise the whole of natural law as depending on the kind of rationalism that Hume was attacking. However, according to a rival interpretation, which has gained ground in recent years, Hume's attack on reason had a more limited target, namely: the ethical rationalists, such as Samuel Clarke and William Wollaston, whose version of natural law was fundamentally different from the continental tradition of Grotius and Pufendorf. Hume was not, according to this interpretation, trying to destroy natural law but was working within the tradition and trying to modernise it.

Conflicting Interpretations

The Destruction of Natural Law

According to James Moore (1976), Hume's theory of justice and property was directed against all three of the naturalistic traditions – the natural law school, the natural rights school of Locke, and the moral sense theorists, including both Shaftesbury and Hutcheson. Moore says that Hume agreed with Shaftesbury that the family is the earliest nexus of human relations and Hume's own references to the family were intended to counter the extreme individualism implicit in the state of nature model employed by Hobbes and Locke. But Hume thought that Shaftesbury was wrong to think that experience in family units was the source of social affections that were gradually extended to wider social groups. So while man's very first state may have been sociable, this sociability does nothing to prepare the individual for life in the larger society of strangers. Mackie agrees with this assessment, and says that the fact that people had always lived in families 'shows that Hobbes has slightly mis-stated the problem. As Hume rightly puts it, what produces competition is not pure selfishness, but a combination of selfishness and confined generosity' (Mackie, 1980, p. 15).

According to Moore, people become sociable as they learn from their experiences that their interests are best served by restraining and regulating their natural selfish impulses. And this happens in 'an experimental or empirical manner over long periods of time, and after repeated experiences of the inconveniences of behaving otherwise.' The implication of this is that 'many misdirected and poorly contrived attempts to set up appropriate conventions are likely to precede the establishment of judicious and useful arrangements' (Moore, 1976, p. 108). Frederick Whelan interprets Hume in a similar way and says that the artificial virtues generally 'appear to be more the product of local custom and fortuitous evolution than of reasoned choice' (Whelan, 1985, p. 332). And for Moore, this all shows that 'Hume's position stands in direct opposition to the conviction of the natural lawyers that certain eternal and immutable rules of justice are demonstrable from the nature of things' (Moore, 1976, p. 110).

Hume's discussion of the role of the imagination in fixing the rules of property is further evidence for Moore of Hume's opposition to the natural lawyers. This discussion shows that the rules of property are founded on the 'imagination and the fancy' and are merely 'fictions' or 'products of the legal imagination'. What mattered was not that one rule was more or less eligible than any other, but 'the uniform manner of their application'. And the point of this was to show that the natural law claim that the distinctions of ownership have a rational foundation 'in the nature of things' is both unwarranted and unnecessary (*ibid.*, p. 113).

The Modernisation of Natural Law

Hume says, however, that his account of the origins of the laws of justice was, at least, consistent with that given by the natural lawyers: 'Examine the writers on the laws of nature; and you will always find, that, whatever principles they set out with, they are sure to terminate here at last, and to assign, as the ultimate reason for every rule which they establish, the convenience and necessity of mankind' (Hume, 1975, p. 195). Duncan Forbes says that Hume is being disingenuous with this remark because, for the natural law writers, the 'ultimate reason' for the laws they established was God (Forbes, 1975, p. 68). Forbes means that it is one thing to understand the beneficial consequences of following a rule, and have a reason for it in that sense, but quite another to show why it is a law, that is, why there is an obligation to follow it. According to Pufendorf and his followers it is only because we must believe in a benevolent God, who has the power to impose sanctions on those who transgress the rules of morality, and who break their promises, that we have an obligation to follow the rules. Nevertheless, Forbes thinks that Hume is justified in linking his theory to the natural law writers, at least 'if one ignores the "higher", religious dimension in the theorists of natural law', because then 'one gets in Grotius, Pufendorf and their followers a naturalistic, conjectural–historical account of the social origin of justice and the natural laws and their development to meet the progressive needs of men in society, which in general, and often in particular, is very similar to what one finds in Hume' (Forbes, 1982, p. 193).

One of Hume's central aims, according to Forbes, was to provide an exclusively secular and exclusively empirical account of justice. This required an account of the origins of the rules of justice and of the obligation to justice that did not rely on the 'religious hypothesis' that is, on supernatural justifications and sanctions, or on exaggerated claims about people's calculating reason and foresight. According to Forbes, Hume finds the origins of justice in the sex-instinct and the family, which is man's 'first social tutor' (Forbes, 1975, p. 70). The family unit requires elementary rules of mine and thine and it is for this reason that Hume says that man's 'very first state and situation may justly be esteem'd social.' Forbes says that this remark is 'wholly in line with natural law theory' and that the word 'justly' in the sentence implies an agreement with the natural law tradition against the various versions of the 'selfish system' (Forbes, 1975, p. 74), and the neglect of this 'vital social dimension of Hume's philosophy, taken as a whole, has been one reason, no doubt, for the temptation to regard it as "Hobbesian" ' (Forbes, 1982, p. 193).

Hume's most direct contribution to natural law theory, according to Forbes, is his psychological explanation of the laws of property. Hume is concerned to discover whether the rules of property depend on public utility or the imagination or neither. What Hume is doing in all these cases is to examine 'what lies behind legal fiction and conventional usage'; he is trying to show that the rules of property are 'grounded on universal principles of human nature, and whatever the differences between Hume and the natural lawyers may be, they are not adequately summarised in a nature versus convention dichotomy' (*ibid.*, p. 196). Forbes says that if we do not see that Hume is here providing a natural explanation of the rules of property, in the sense that they are the natural products of human imagination and human sentiments, we can go seriously astray 'and see these rules as the wholly arbitrary fictions of lawyers in accordance with conventions and needs of particular historical societies ... thereby drastically diminishing or altogether dissolving the natural law content of his political thought' (*ibid.*, p. 195).

Steven Buckle (1991) has taken a similar view to Forbes of Hume's relationship to the natural law writers, at least to the extent that he sees Hume working within the same tradition. Hume's claim that justice is artificial, meaning that it is the product of reason and understanding, shows, according to Buckle, that 'Hume's account of justice is thoroughly in tune with the natural jurists. In the older vocabulary, his position is simply that justice is a dictate of right reason, because necessary for sociability and self-preservation' (Buckle, 1991, p. 287). Buckle differs from Forbes, however, in his assessment of the significance of Hume's alleged rejection of the religious hypothesis. The fact that God plays no *direct* part in Hume's theory does not set it apart from the natural law *tradition*. It certainly sets Hume apart from Pufendorf and his followers, but Grotius had said that the law of nature has validity even if we deny the existence of God. The source of law for Grotius is human nature: sociability, and the intelligence to see what we *must* do to be sociable. Grotius concedes that God can be considered as *another* source of law 'in a larger sense' for those who believe in Him and who believe that our essential traits were implanted in us by Him (Grotius, 1925, Prolegomena, 12). Hume, similarly, says at one point that our standard of morality 'is ultimately derived from the Supreme Will, which bestowed on each being its peculiar nature, and arranged the several classes and orders of existence' (Hume, 1975, p. 294). But for Hume, as for Grotius, the immediate source of law is human nature. Hume's position, therefore, is 'a commonplace of natural law: that justice arises from, or reflects the requirements of, human sociability. The rules of justice are necessary for the establishment of a social order which, as Grotius puts it, is "consonant with human intelligence"' (Buckle, 1991, p. 262).

Buckle regards Hume as a moderniser of natural law, not just because he provided a secular version of it, but because he was a contributor to the moral sense theory, which was itself an attempt to modernise natural law by providing 'a psychology of action adequate to the requirements of natural law', that is to say, to ground the theory of sociability in human psychology (*ibid.*, p. 235). The significance of this project according to Buckle was that, in attempting to discover a moral motive to justice that is independent of a divine will, it was in effect an attempt to rehabilitate 'the Grotian conception of an obligation to obey the dictates of natural law that is independent of belief in God' (*ibid.*, p. 200).

Mitigated Scepticism

According to David Miller (1981), the key to understanding Hume's political outlook is his attack on rationalism and his stress on custom, habit and the imagination. Miller characterises this as 'mitigated scepticism', a term Hume uses in the *Enquiry* (Hume, 1975, p. 161). The political implications of this scepticism, according to Miller, are that 'it sets limits to the kind of argument that can be produced in politics. It excludes the possibility of advancing normative claims that are either rationally self-evident or capable of empirical demonstration.' It differs, therefore, from traditional natural law, according to which 'certain politically relevant principles could be known to be true' (Miller, 1981, p. 189). The theory of the social contract was Hume's main target. It embodied the rationalism and radicalism that Miller thinks characterised traditional natural law. It was radical, Miller says, because it justified rebellion 'whenever the terms of an imaginary contract were violated' (*ibid.*, p. 93). Hume's alternative theory justified resistance only in exceptional cases. Governments were set up to administer and enforce property rights and they should only be removed when there is a 'serious infringement of property rights' (*ibid.*, p. 92). Miller accepts that this was, more or less, Locke's position but says that 'popular versions' of the social contract theory were more radical.

Phillipson (1993) also thinks that Hume's political philosophy was a 'sceptical assault on reason' which 'destroyed the epistemological foundations on which theories of natural rights and contract depended' (*ibid.*, pp. 302, 311). But he offers a different interpretation of why Hume's theory of government was less radical than the contract theory. 'At one level', he says, Hume's theory of allegiance provided as much scope as the contract theory, by which he means that both theories agree that resistance is justified when governments fail to govern in the interests of their subjects. Phillipson says that Hume's was a theory of resistance that was 'universal and unlimited'. It is only a prudential view of interests that ensures that resistance is limited to extreme cases. The problem is that since different people have different opinions of the public interest, they will reach different conclusions about the respective advantages of liberty and authority. Hume finds, however, that there is a 'natural disposition to submit to established authority' and it is this, rather than a calculating view of interest, that is the foundation of political authority (*ibid.*, p. 315). People are prudent out of custom and habit, not out of reasoned calculation.

Scientific Whiggism

According to Forbes, Hume's objections to the theory of the social contract had less to do with his alleged attack on reason and natural law, than with his attack on its theological premises. In fact, Forbes thinks that the modern natural law tradition of Grotius, Pufendorf and their followers, was Hume's main inspiration for his theory of allegiance. The theories of these writers were theories of limited resistance, allowing much less scope for rebellion than the kind of English theories of popular consent that seemed to be the object of Hume's criticism.

Hume's principle political objective, according to Forbes, was to provide the established Hanoverian regime with 'respectable intellectual foundations', on which moderate and forward looking politicians of all factions and parties could unite. The theory of the social contract was not a respectable theory, for the reason already mentioned, even though its conclusions were 'perfectly just and reasonable'. However, a supporter of the Hanoverian regime is not necessarily a supporter of the Whig administration, and Forbes characterises Hume's politics as scientific or sceptical Whiggism as opposed to vulgar Whiggism. The contrast is primarily that between a cosmopolitan outlook, which takes into account the history and constitutions of the European states, and the parochialism, common to all English parties and factions, which saw liberty as the unique product of English history and the English constitution. For Hume, liberty meant 'liberty and security of the individual under the rule of law' and not the political or public liberty, which was the product of particular political constitutions. It was the latter kind of liberty that was at stake in the comparison between 'English liberty' and 'French slavery', between the balanced British constitution, which preserved the independence of parliament from the crown, and the absolute monarchy of France. Liberty of this kind, Hume says, 'is the perfection of civil society' but liberty and security under the rule of law is provided by the absolute monarchies as well, and so 'for all practical purposes, they answer the purpose of government as such' (Forbes, 1975, p. 153). It was this political outlook that made Hume a moderate. But its implications were favourable to the Whig administration. Political liberty should be preserved as much as possible, but opposition to the government should not be pushed so far that it threatens liberty of the other kind.

Civic Humanism

The contrast between these two different concepts of liberty and their associated political outlooks, is for some interpreters best approached as part of a more general contrast between the natural law or jurisprudential tradition, and the tradition of civic humanism. The latter tradition was concerned with the economic, political, military and moral preconditions of political community, that is, with the liberty and independence required for the active participation of patriotic citizens in public affairs. The kind of society that ideally, and classically, matched the requirements of the civic outlook was the small agrarian republic divided into a class of independent, landowning warrior politicians on the one hand, and a class of dependent producers on the other. A society, in other words, which in eighteenth-century England had long been replaced by a commercial society, in which mobile, financial property was a large proportion of society's wealth, and in which the division of labour extended to politics and warfare. Nevertheless, the characteristic concerns of the civic tradition, in particular, its concern with the danger to the political community of corruption of the public spirit or 'virtue' of the citizens, leading to national decay, were central to the ideology of Bolingbroke and his party in their opposition to the Whig oligarchy under Walpole. Furthermore, Scotland in the eighteenth century was not an advanced commercial society, and so faced a different set of economic and political problems. For some Scots, who were influenced by the civic outlook, Scotland's backwardness presented the opportunity of modernising its economy and political institutions in a way that would avoid the corruption of the advanced European commercial societies.

Following the lead of J. G. A. Pocock (1979, 1983, 1985) a number of historians have interpreted Hume's political writings as a defence of a commercial society in general, and of the tendency of British society and government in particular, which addressed the agenda of the civic humanist tradition. Hume conceded that commerce and luxury may be inimical to political virtue, but argued that commercial societies are more friendly to culture and politeness of manners. Progress in commerce and the arts go hand in hand and both are favourable to government: politics are conducted with greater politeness and moderation, and the useful industrial arts strengthen the nation's martial capabilities. Moreover, the greater equality of commercial societies enhances the authority of 'that middling rank of men, who are the best and finest basis of public liberty' (Robertson, 1983, p. 157). In any case, the design of constitutions should not presuppose the virtuous character of politicians, rather 'every man must be supposed a knave' (*On the independency of parliament*) and the 'natural depravity of mankind' must be checked by constitutional balances (*That politics may be reduced to a science*) (Hume, 1994).

Hume's response to the accusation that Walpole's policies of patronage and public credit were corrupting the nation was, according to Pocock, to accept one and reject the other (Pocock, 1979, p. 333). In *Of the independency of parliament*, Hume argues that without patronage, the executive would have no influence at all over the legislative powers of parliament. So patronage, whether or not it was considered corrupting, was a necessary element in a government like Britain's. Hume accepted, however, that public credit was damaging and raised the prospect that it would destroy the government (*Of civil liberty*). And this shows, according to Pocock, that in his concern that commercial progress would eventually destroy 'both liberty and prosperity', Hume's attitude to commercial progress was ambivalent (*ibid.*, p. 334).

Evaluation

Hume's remark that man's first state can justly be regarded as social indicates, as Forbes says, an important area of agreement with natural law theory, and an important disagreement with Hobbes. But I think there must be serious doubts about the extent to which Hume's references to the sex-instinct and to primitive family-societies supports this contention. Quite apart from Hume's lack of clarity on this point, it would have been no answer to Hobbes to point out that his state of nature was a fiction because he had overlooked the fact that people had always lived together in family-societies. And this is not because Hobbes himself thought that his state of nature was a fiction or a 'methodological device'. Hobbes's state of nature was a state without a common power and he refers to the American tribal societies as an example of what such a state was like. These societies live under the 'government of small families, the concord whereof dependeth on natural lust'. But because they lack a common power they 'live at this day in that brutish manner, as I said before' (Hobbes, 1996, p. 89). As Mackie says, conflict between families is just as destructive as conflict between individuals and nothing Hume says about the family mitigates the force of Hobbes's arguments for the necessity of a common power or supports his own contention that society *without* government is natural.

To the extent that Hume does provide an answer to Hobbes it is because he was more optimistic than Hobbes about the possibility of people agreeing on conventional rules of justice and trusting each other to follow them out of a sense of common interest without the fear of punishment. He was more optimistic because he narrowed down the source of conflict to competition over scarce material goods. People were not, in Hume's account, fundamentally fearful and distrustful of each other as Hobbes thought, nor were they 'continually in competition for Honour and Dignity' (*ibid.*, p. 119). It is only our avidity 'of acquiring goods and possessions for ourselves and our nearest friends' that is 'insatiable, perpetual, universal, and directly destructive of society.' All the other passions are either easily restrained or are not so destructive (Hume, 1978, pp. 491–2). And the potentially destructive tendencies of this avidity are fairly easily avoided once people have enough experience to see that their own interest coincides with the common interest. Hume's human beings are more like the bees and the ants in Hobbes' account, who 'live sociably with one another' because 'the Common good differeth not from the Private' (Hobbes, 1996, p. 119).

Turning to the question of property, when Grotius described the law of nature as a 'dictate of right reason', and when he said that its principles 'are in themselves manifest and clear, almost as evident as are those things which we perceive by the external senses', he did not mean that each of the laws of property are eternal and immutable and demonstrable by reason. He simply meant that it was possible for intelligent human beings to understand how they should behave to others if peace was to be established within and between states (Grotius, 1925: I.I.X.1 and Prolegomena 39). Moreover, since the character of people and their circumstances were much the same everywhere, there was a core of law that was common to all peoples, irrespective of their particular customs and practices. And it was this part of the law that he called the law of nature. The distinction between justice and injustice, therefore, is not just a matter of opinion and custom but is natural, in the sense that it is natural product of human intelligence. Hume seems to be saying much the same when he says in the *Treatise* that in calling justice artificial rather than natural he means that it requires 'the intervention of thought and reflection'. The rules of justice, although artificial, are not arbitrary, and it is not improper, therefore, to call them '*Laws of Nature*' (Hume, 1978, p. 484).

There is certainly no evidence that Hume thought the laws of property were the product of local custom. The three fundamental laws concerning the stability of possessions, their transfer by consent and the keeping of promises, were universal laws, because no kind of society can be maintained without them. As to the particular rules, first possession, occupation and the others, it is true that Hume says that they are determined by 'frivolous views and considerations' but he nevertheless thinks that the standard Roman laws, accepted by the natural lawyers, are the ones to be explained.

Hume's explanation of the particular rules of property, however, is complicated by the fact that he is trying to explain two kinds of problem which he, and some of his interpreters, do not always clearly separate. He is concerned, primarily, to explain the origins of, and reasons for, the basic rules of property acquisition, namely: present possession, occupation, prescription, accession and succession. But he is also concerned to explain how difficult it is to resolve some of the controversies that have arisen in applying these basic rules. Hume here discusses a number of standard natural law problems, such as when occupation begins: is it when the object has been first sighted, that is, when it is discovered, or when physical possession has been taken? And it is here that the 'frivolous' aspects of property rules are

most apparent. It is in this context that he refers to the perplexing nature of
the issues involved and says how some of them cannot be resolved by 'any
reasonable decision' at all (*ibid.*, p. 507). Moore, therefore, is quite right to
say that for Hume '[n]o natural criterion of occupation would enable one to
decide the moment at which an individual has taken possession of a wild
beast, or a plot of land' (Moore, 1976, p. 113). But he is quite wrong when
he goes on to say that the natural lawyers thought otherwise.

Regarding matters of allegiance to government, it is one thing to say that
most people's beliefs and judgements are the result of custom and habit, and
therefore 'incapable of being justified by reason', but quite another to say
that political argument and political theories cannot be justified by reason or
'resolved empirically' (Miller, 1981, p. 191). Hume certainly advanced the
first proposition, and he thought it had profound implications for political
theory and action, but there is little evidence that the second proposition had
any bearing on the way Hume explicated his theories, conducted his political analysis and responded to his adversaries. Furthermore, while there is a
plausible link between the first proposition and a conservative political outlook, there seem to be no political implications of the second. Miller in fact
makes this point himself when he says that Locke's theory, which he regards
as representative of the kind of rational natural law theory that Hume
opposes, was no more radical than Hume's (*ibid.*, p. 93n).

The strength of Phillipson's interpretation is that it makes this last point
clear: when Hume says that resistance should only be a last resort in
extremis, he is not drawing a direct conclusion from his theory of allegiance. He is drawing his own prudent or moderate conclusion after bal-
ancing the advantages of liberty and authority, and he is arguing that
common sense and common morality supports this conclusion. However,
the distinction between reasoned prudence and unreflecting habit should
not be exaggerated. Even our tendency to assign authority to the existing
government can be explained as a form of rational prudence. For example,
Hume says that present possession has greater authority in determining
obedience to governments than in private property 'because of the disorders
which attend all revolutions and changes of government' (*Of the original
contract*). This suggests that people tend to obey the existing government
because they can see that doing so will avoid disorder. This tendency may
be reinforced by the non-rational operations of the imagination, but this
does not render the whole of Hume's theory anti-rationalist.

Hume's own theory of allegiance is a reasoned political theory, based on
empirical judgement about the way people form their political beliefs. He
thought he could demonstrate its truth by careful logical argument and by
appealing to the facts. And when he engages in political debate, he tries to

convince the opposition factions that the benefits of supporting the established government are, on balance, greater than the benefits they can hope for by resisting. When we try to understand the underlying values and polemical strategies Hume brings to these debates, epistemological scepticism offers little guidance, and it is at this point that we must turn to the other interpretive paradigms.

There can be little doubt that the jurisprudential perspective, in which Forbes locates scientific or sceptical Whiggism, and the civic perspective, have both provided valuable insights into eighteenth-century British political discourse, and the challenge they have presented to each other has been an important factor in the development and refinement of both. But to what extent are they alternatives: do they offer competing paradigms or are they mutually reinforcing? Pocock has remarked that rival explanations are not necessarily mutually exclusive, in the sense that 'to strengthen one is necessarily to weaken the other'. But he has also argued that the civic and jurisprudential perspectives are premised on irreconcilable concepts and values: rights and freedom under the law in one case, and virtue and freedom of the active citizen to participate in government in the other (Pocock, 1983, p. 248).

Faced with this dichotomy, Hume's political philosophy taken broadly, that is his theory of the origins of society, his theory of justice and his political preferences, fits squarely in the jurisprudential camp. But that still leaves the question of whether any part of it can usefully be considered a response to the civic humanist critique of commercialisation, and if so, whether the response shows any signs of the ambivalence noted by Pocock. And here I think it can be said of Hume what Donald Winch says of Adam Smith: 'a *defensive* interpretation seems optional' (Winch, 1983, p. 266). In the political essays, Hume certainly covers the ground and discusses the issues of concern, but only in the way that any commentator on eighteenth-century British politics must. As to Hume's ambivalence, the issue is whether his worries about the public debt indicate a concern that commerce 'destroys both liberty and prosperity' (Pocock, 1979, p. 334). Istvan Hont has argued that Hume identified war, rather than commercial progress, as the cause of the public debt (Hont, 1993). And in any case, the fragility of the Walpole regime, or even the British form of government, did not threaten prosperity, or liberty as Hume understood it. Hume's worries, therefore, were not an indictment of commercial progress, or of the economic and jurisprudential arguments that he used to defend it. This is precisely the point conveyed by Forbes in characterising Hume's political perspective as one of 'scientific Whiggism'.

In *Whether the British government inclines more to absolute monarchy, or to a republic*, Hume outlined the commonwealth case purporting to show that the British government under Walpole was undermining the British spirit of liberty and was taking the government towards an absolute monarchy. The growing wealth of the crown, the increasing luxury of the nation and 'our proneness to corruption', the power and prerogatives of the crown and its command of a standing army, are all mentioned. And although Hume thinks that much of this is overstated, he is, nevertheless, prepared to concede that it is a case to be answered. But his answer is that 'though liberty be preferable to slavery, in almost every case', he would rather see an absolute monarchy than a republic in Britain. It may be true, he says, that it is possible to imagine a republic that would be preferable to an absolute monarchy. But there is no reason to expect such a republic would follow the dissolution of the monarchy in Britain. The republican cause is founded on a paradox: if anyone had the power to dismantle the established government and set up a republic, he possesses the power of an absolute monarch, and cannot be expected to establish a free government. So whichever way the British government is tending, the choice is really between the manner in which liberty will be lost. Hume concludes that absolute monarchy 'is the easiest death, the true Euthanasia of the BRITISH constitution.' (Hume, 1994).

What mattered, however – freedom under the law and the conditions for commercial progress – could survive the Whig regime, or at least, they could if the regime was allowed its natural death. The fact that Hume could contemplate this death with such equanimity is surely the best evidence we could have of his political commitments.

5

Rousseau (1712–1778)

ALAN APPERLEY

Introduction

Rousseau's political writings have earned him a reputation as one of the most important and influential of modern political theorists. Yet to describe Rousseau as a *modern* political theorist requires immediate qualification, for although Rousseau – in common with many other Enlightenment thinkers – rejected traditional forms of authority in favour of the individual capacity for self-determination and self-government, he nevertheless remained critical of much that is now associated with Enlightenment thought. For example, the Enlightenment is now usually associated with a belief in progress through the application of science and reason to social and political affairs. Rousseau, however, was sceptical of the idea that science and reason, if applied to social and political affairs, could deliver progress. Rousseau was often more interested in looking backwards to the ancient republics of Sparta and Rome than forwards, with many of his Enlightened contemporaries, to increasingly large-scale, industrialised societies underwritten by the principles of science and reason.

Yet Rousseau's writings were not mere nostalgia for a time long past. Rousseau spent much of his life living and working in monarchical France, and whilst it is true that he drew on ancient models in his critique of absolutist government, he also drew upon his knowledge and experience of an actually-existing republic, for he was, and proudly declared himself to be, a citizen of the republic of Geneva. Similarly, Rousseau's critique of progress was not born out of a nostalgic desire to return to the past, but rather out of a sense that the dogmas and prejudices of pre-modern times were being replaced by new dogmas and prejudices: science and reason. Where many of his contemporaries saw the development of large-scale industrialised societies and the ensuing rise of the market economy as a means for liberating humanity, Rousseau saw instead a danger that such developments would result not in emancipation but in new and more profound forms of slavery. Rousseau may have felt uncomfortable in the face of the optimism of the modern age, but his critical voice nevertheless places him firmly in, and of, that age.

Problems and Issues

In *The Social Contract* Rousseau sets out the 'fundamental problem' to which this work is addressed, and to which it supposedly provides a solution. That problem is

> to find a form of association that will defend and protect the person and goods of each associate with the full common force, and by means of which each, while uniting himself with all, may nevertheless obey only himself alone and remain as free as before (Rousseau, 1997a, pp. 49–50, quotation modified).

It is clear from this statement of the problem that Rousseau places freedom, or independence, at the heart of his political project. Any form of political association for Rousseau must uphold the freedom of the individual, and it must do this by so arranging things that the individual would be enabled to govern himself (there is no doubt that, for Rousseau, self-governing individuals are *male*).

The importance for Rousseau of self-government is tied to his *perfectionist* account of human nature, developed primarily in his *Discourse on the Origin and Foundations of Inequality Amongst Men* (1755) commonly referred to as the *Second Discourse*. Here Rousseau provides a speculative history of the human race from the innocent egalitarian idyll of the state of nature, where human beings, in common with non-human animals, enjoyed independence and natural liberty, to (as Rousseau saw it) the vice-ridden society of his day in which dependence on others had become the norm. From the free and independent individuals of the state of nature, humanity had become enslaved 'to a multitude of new needs, to the whole of Nature, and especially to those of his kind, whose slave he in a sense becomes even by becoming their master' (Rousseau, 1997b, p. 170). In part, Rousseau attributes this loss of independence to the development and subsequent unequal distribution of private property – modern man, obsessed by status, constantly compares himself and his possessions against those of others. Because he is 'capable of living only in the opinions of others' he loses sight of his real or authentic self (Rousseau, 1997b, p. 187). Rousseau maintains that society is a necessary condition of the development of one's moral faculties whether these take the form of vice or virtue. Unfortunately, Rousseau seeks to show, society has developed in such a way that there is a preponderance of vice over virtue. The task he sets himself in *The Social Contract* therefore is to discover a form of political association that will produce the opposite of this – a preponderance of virtue over vice. Thus the social contract and the participatory political association it creates not only enshrines civil freedom, but also allows for the development of *moral* liberty 'which alone makes man truly master of himself' (Rousseau, 1997a, p. 54).

It is at this point that there occurs what Patrick Riley has described as 'the greatest paradox' in all of Rousseau's work – a paradox around which a great deal of interpretative dispute has largely focused. The social contract is supposed to set in train a process of socialisation which will produce the virtuous society envisaged by Rousseau, yet in the pre-contractual condition the motives required by individuals if they are to relinquish the *status quo* are absent. These motives can only be the *result* of the process of socialisation that they are supposed to initiate (Riley, 1982, p. 110). This is a paradox that Rousseau himself acknowledged when he wrote, in *The Social Contract*, that

> [f]or a nascent people to be capable of appreciating sound maxims of politics ... the effect would have to become the cause, the social spirit which is to be the work of the institution would have to preside over the institution itself, and men would have to be prior to laws what they ought to become by means of them (Rousseau, 1997a, p. 71).

This problem also emerges in Rousseau's discussion of the *general will*. According to Rousseau, the ideal state (which *The Social Contract* models) is one in which the entire citizen body participates in the process of governing, which is to say in the process of generating the laws by which the political community will be governed. Each citizen, in his capacity as citizen rather than private person, wills the laws by which he, and every other citizen, will be governed. The general will is therefore the will of the political community as a whole.

However, the *general* will is not to be conflated with the *actual* will of the people for, as Rousseau says, although '[b]y itself the people always wills the good, it does not always see it. The general will is always upright, but the judgement which guides it is not always enlightened' (Rousseau, 1997a, p. 68). Until the process of socialisation has made men virtuous the people are 'a blind multitude' (*ibid.*) and their particular or private interests will get in the way of their attempts to will the general good. It is at this point that

Rousseau introduces two proposals that have led to great controversy amongst his interpreters. The first of these proposals is that, in the act of deciding democratically which policy to adopt, it is the will of the majority that ought to prevail. This does not mean that the majority is necessarily correct in its interpretation of the general will – '[t]here is,' says Rousseau, 'often a considerable difference between the will of all and the general will' (*ibid.*, p. 60) – but he believes that majority-rule is the best available guide to the general will. Rousseau's subsequent assertion that 'whoever refuses to obey the general will shall be constrained to do so by the entire body: which means nothing other than that he shall be forced to be free' (*ibid.*, p. 53) has led to considerable debate amongst interpreters of his work. Some have seen this as merely a background assumption of any democratic community; others have seen in this the potential for a tyranny of the majority; and others have seen in this the roots of totalitarianism.

Rousseau's second proposal is for the introduction of a 'Lawgiver' – a being of 'superior intelligence' whose task is that of 'changing human nature' to fit the requirements of society (*ibid.*, pp. 68–9). Because the citizens are not yet able to see the good, the Lawgiver must find ways to enable them to see it. This cannot be done via rational persuasion because where the multitude is 'blind' they will not see the virtue in rational argument: 'The wise who would speak to the vulgar in their own rather than the vulgar language will not be understood by them' (*ibid.*, p. 70). Therefore the Lawgiver must 'persuade without convincing' – in other words, by means *other* than rational argument. In particular, he must dress his proposals up in the language of divine authority, the better to lead the blind multitude to the truth. Once again, Rousseau the lover of liberty sits uneasily alongside an apparently authoritarian Rousseau – for what, critics ask, is to guarantee that the Lawgiver is not a fraud or – worse – a potential Hitler?

Why Conflicting Interpretations?

Rousseau is a paradoxical figure in the history of political thought. He was a contributor to the central masterpiece of the European Enlightenment – Diderot's *Encyclopédie* – yet he appeared to set himself against many of the key principles associated with the philosophers of the Enlightenment. His political writings are said to have directly influenced the French Revolution, setting in train the discourse of the Rights of Man; yet his political thought has also been held responsible for both the Jacobin Terror, into which the French Revolution ignominiously collapsed, and twentieth-century totalitarianism. He made liberty his central concern, yet in his most important work of political philosophy – *The Social Contract* (1762) – he notoriously asserted that those who disagreed with the collective *general will* should be 'forced to be free'. On the basis of arguments put forward in *The Social Contract* Rousseau is often credited with presenting a novel, even radical form of democracy – a direct participatory model that stands in a critical relation to the indirect, representative model associated with modern liberal democracy (Weale, 1999; Held, 1996; Macpherson, 1966, 1973). Yet Rousseau himself states that democratic government is an unattainable ideal – suitable for Gods but not for men (Rousseau, 1997a, p. 92). As we shall see, a great deal of Rousseau scholarship can be represented as an attempt to come to terms with the allegedly paradoxical character of his work. For his own part, Rousseau was aware of the paradoxical nature of his work remarking that 'you cannot avoid paradox if you think for yourself' and insisting that he 'would rather fall into paradox than into prejudice' (Rousseau, 1974, p. 57). For some writers, this use of paradox is deliberate: Rousseau's 'literary love of paradox' (Cobban, 1964, p. 15) betrays a rhetorical style designed to 'jolt the reader or listener into recognising something he might otherwise overlook' (Plamenatz, 1972, p. 320).

However, for other writers the paradoxical character of Rousseau's writing is the result, not of a conscious decision concerning style, but of a lack of rigour in argument. Rousseau's work has variously been described as absurd, incoherent, inconsistent, unsystematic, and 'a farrago of contradictions' (Canovan, cited in Dent, 1988, p. 2). In spite of Rousseau's own insistence that his work is systematic (for example, Rousseau, 1979) the attempt to demonstrate that it is not has been a dominant theme amongst his less sympathetic critics. One historically important example of the alleged contradictory nature of Rousseau's work lies in the juxtaposition between the *Second Discourse*, which supposedly defends 'a more extreme form of individualism than any previous writer had ventured to set forth' and *The Social Contract* which, it is claimed, defends 'a collectivism as absolute as the mind of man has ever conceived' (Vaughan, 1915, Vol. I, p. 119, p. 39).

Conversely, there are those who insist upon, and seek to demonstrate, the consistency and rigour of Rousseau's work. However, opinions differ as to where the key to the unity of Rousseau's work lies. Some writers have sought to demonstrate the unity of Rousseau's work through a close analysis of Rousseau's texts – often informed by a knowledge of the *context* in which Rousseau lived and wrote (for example, Masters, 1968), or by emphasising the *moral* content of his work – often by seeking to show the close thematic connection between his educational treatise *Emile* and *The Social Contract*, published in the same year (for example, Cassirer, 1989; Dent, 1988; Levine, 1976; Miller, 1984). For others, Rousseau is to be understood primarily as a *political* philosopher rather than a moral philosopher (for example, Crocker, 1968; Melzer, 1983) and *The Social Contract* should be read in conjunction with his practical proposals for constitutions for Corsica and Poland (Fralin, 1978). The alleged inconsistency between the *Second Discourse* and *The Social Contract* has been challenged by writers such as MacAdam who sees merely a division of labour between the two texts, with the former playing a diagnostic role and the latter providing the cure (MacAdam, 1989).

Other interpreters have looked not so much to the texts themselves in order to explain their inconsistencies as to aspects of Rousseau's personality. Rousseau wrote several works of self-analysis – most notably *The Confessions* (1782/1789) and *Reveries of a Solitary Walker* (1780) – and these, as Judith Shklar has argued, are 'of utmost significance' to our understanding of his work (Shklar, 1985, p. 219). Rousseau undoubtedly experienced psychological problems – his paranoia is, for example, evident in the *Reveries* – and for some writers, the paradoxical nature of Rousseau's work is directly traceable to his unstable psychology (for instance, Talmon, 1952; Crocker, 1968). Rousseau's *Social Contract* has been associated with what is surely one of the seismic political events of the modern era – the French Revolution – but this association further illustrates the problematic nature of his work. Rousseau was undoubtedly a critic of the *ancien régime* and of the way inequality had been sanctioned by tradition, stifling the development of moral liberty. His work was cited by the French Revolutionaries in defence of the Rights of Man against hierarchy, privilege and tradition, and liberals and socialists alike have subsequently interpreted the critical element of his work as a defence of individual liberty.

However, Rousseau was by inclination a *republican* and he was as much (perhaps *more*) concerned with republican ideas of duty, civic virtue and the common good (general will) as he was with the notion of rights. Where these republican ideas are interpreted as prioritising the collective – the *res publica* – over the individual, Rousseau's work can be represented as a threat to individual liberty. It is for these reasons that his work been associated with both the emancipatory aspects of the French Revolution and with the Jacobin Terror into which it descended.

Conflicting Interpretations

Rousseau as Totalitarian

As we noticed in the previous section, one of the most important, and contentious, strands of interpretation in the case of Rousseau is that which identifies totalitarian tendencies in his thought. This interpretation has deep roots, stretching back to Rousseau's own time. One of the first to point up the totalitarian potential inherent in Rousseau's *Social Contract* was Edmund Burke. For Burke, it was in the abstract nature of Rousseau's argument that this potential lay; Burke believed that Rousseau's advocacy of the 'inalienable' Rights of Man undermined the concrete customs and traditions that were the source of the *actual* rights of citizens and the guarantee of their actual, as opposed to merely theoretical, freedom (Burke, 1968). The abstract character of Rousseau's writings was to continually trouble his critics throughout the nineteenth century, although by this time Rousseau's work had come to be associated with the spectre of socialist collectivism (Hampsher-Monk, 1995). As one nineteenth-century critic put it, '[t]he fundamental principle of the Rousseauite ... polity is the omnipotence of the State' (Huxley, 1898, p. 395; cf. Bosanquet, 1923; Vaughan, 1915, Vol. I). This latter interpretation was given new impetus by the rise and defeat of fascism and the onset of the Cold War. These events comprised the background against which Rousseau's *Social Contract* was reinterpreted as an incipiently totalitarian tract, and several works published during this period accord Rousseau a key position in the supposed genealogy of totalitarianism (Crocker, 1968; Popper, 1945; Russell, 1946; Talmon, 1952). For these interpreters of Rousseau the concept of 'the Lawgiver' is readily translated into a Hitler, a Stalin, a Robespierre or a Napoleon, bent on turning populist sentiment, dressed up as 'the will of the people' to their own ends. But it is the concept of the general will, as it appears in *The Social Contract*, that allegedly most qualifies Rousseau for his place in the totalitarian tradition.

Rousseau maintains that the citizens of a well-ordered society will have a particular will, which looks to their own interests as private individuals, and a general will, which looks to the interest of the society as a whole. In his role as citizen, the individual is expected to allow the general will to take priority over his particular will. As we saw above, the general will is not simply an aggregate of the particular wills of the individual citizens since it is conceivable that a people can be in unanimous agreement as to what the general will is, and yet be entirely mistaken. The general will is what is *objectively* in the interest of a people, and not what they *believe* to be in their interest. For some critics of Rousseau, it is in the gap between truth and belief that the seeds of totalitarianism lie. To see why, we can look briefly at Isaiah Berlin's influential essay *Two Concepts of Liberty*, originally published in 1958 against the background of the Cold War (Berlin, 1969). It is in this essay that Berlin sets out his important distinction between *negative* and *positive* liberty. Negative liberty consists in freedom from interference in the pursuit of one's goals, whatever these may be.

Positive liberty is much more problematic. Proponents of positive liberty, according to Berlin, posit a gap between the actual, empirical self – an inauthentic or false self – and a 'higher' more rational self which is more authentic, more 'real' than the empirical self. According to Berlin, those who characteristically hold this view believe also that those who have achieved the higher more rational state may legitimately strive to raise those who have not up to their level. 'Once I take this view,' Berlin says, 'I am in a position to ignore the actual wishes of men or societies, to bully, oppress, torture them in the name, and on behalf, of their 'real' selves' (*ibid.*, p. 133). Rousseau's notion of the perfectibility of human beings, combined with his belief that, under present circumstances, they live false or inauthentic lives, may be employed in this way (*ibid.*, pp. 162–6). According to this view, when Rousseau writes that 'whoever refuses to obey the general will ... shall be forced to be free' (Rousseau, 1997a, p. 53) he can be interpreted as advocating the enforced conformity of allegedly misguided or misinformed individuals to a uniform and objective truth. As Talmon, anticipating Berlin, put it: the general will becomes 'a pre-ordained goal, towards which [the citizens] are irresistibly driven' by those who claim to know what this goal, or truth, is (Talmon, 1952, p. 48).

Berlin's influence can also be seen in the work of one of the more persistent defenders of this view of Rousseau – Lester Crocker. 'Liberty', Crocker maintains 'certainly includes the assurance of an unassailable private realm ... a personal sanctuary' (Crocker, 1995, p. 245). This, of course, is Berlin's negative liberty. Rousseau's mistake is to make everything – including morality – subservient to politics, leaving no room for individual expression, and no room for personal morality or conscience since these would pose a threat to the unity of the political community (*ibid.*, pp. 247–8). The politicisation of private life, of which Rousseau thus stands accused, is allegedly a classic trait of totalitarian regimes. The effect of Rousseau's 'staggering, hallucinatory conception' of political life is to eradicate pluralism in favour of 'orthodoxy' and 'conformity' (*ibid.*, pp. 247, 245). More recently still, Charles Taylor has described Rousseau as the 'the origin point' of the idea of 'self-determining freedom' – a central idea in the modern identity and one akin to Berlin's positive liberty (Taylor, 1989, pp. 362–3). This idea, in its political form of 'a social contract state founded on a general will ... has been one of the intellectual sources of modern totalitarianism' (Taylor, 1991, p. 28).

These apparently illiberal aspects of Rousseau's work seem to be supported by other elements of the political theory presented in *The Social Contract*. For example, Rousseau prescribes a civil religion, and proposes banishment for those who do not publicly accept its dogmas and death for those who publicly flout them (Rousseau, 1997a, p. 150). He also argues (following Machiavelli) for the proscription of factions and hence is sometimes accused of advocating a one-party state on fascist or communist lines. He argues for the proscription of public debate in relation to the general will (*ibid.*, p. 60). Finally, he appears to threaten the institution of private property when he suggests that the social contract entails a 'total alienation' of citizens' rights to the State so that 'with regard to its members, the State is master of all their goods' (*ibid.*, p. 54). Critics who interpret Rousseau in this way need not believe that he intended his work to lend comfort to tyrants. Burke, for example, believed both that Rousseau's personality was morally reprehensible and that his work had provided the French Revolutionaries with a justification for their violent excesses, but he did not believe that Rousseau – at least were he in 'one of his lucid moments' – would have approved of the use made of his work (Burke, 1968, p. 284). Of course, Rousseau may not *consciously* have intended his work to be employed in this way, but for those who inhabit a post-Freudian world the idea of an *unconscious* drive for a totalitarian politics cannot be ruled out. For example, summarising his own earlier account of Rousseau's personality, Crocker points to 'alienation and distantiation, resentment, a private phantasy life, especially phantasies of uniqueness and power as the prophet and guide who will be revered in the future for having shown men the true path' as the driving forces behind his political thought (Crocker, 1995, pp. 247; 1968). Similarly, Talmon detects in Rousseau (amongst others) a 'totalitarian Messianic temperament' born of the tension created by a dual personality in which the 'disciplinarian' vied uneasily with the 'tormented paranoiac'. In a clear reference to Hitler, Talmon links Rousseau's psychology to the 'strange combination of psychological ill-adjustment and totalitarian ideology' of the Nazi *Führer* (Talmon, 1952, p. 39). The roots of this lie, inevitably, in Rousseau's troubled childhood as 'a motherless vagabond starved of warmth and affection' (*ibid.*, p. 38).

The Case against Rousseau as Totalitarian

It seems reasonably clear from the previous discussion that all of the key interpreters to which we referred above attribute to Rousseau's ideas a continuing influence stretching well beyond the context in which Rousseau first developed them. In terms then of the 'text *versus* context' debate, this fact alone leaves these writers open to the straightforward criticism that their reading of Rousseau is anachronistic, for the context to which Rousseau's ideas are addressed is not the same as – and is on some accounts

incommensurable with – that of Hitler. Granting this point, it would seem
to follow that placing Rousseau's thought in its context could then have the
effect of insulating it against this particular interpretation. One example of
a contextual defence of Rousseau's thought can be introduced through a critique of Popper's reading of Rousseau. According to Popper, Rousseau is a
proto-Hegelian who, allegedly like Hegel after him, endorses the idea of an
organic state unified around a collective will. The state is thus a 'moral
person' with a single will – the general will – which can brook no opposition
from the particular, private wills of the individual subjects (Popper, 1945,
p. 52). Popper has been widely criticised for his idiosyncratic readings of
thinkers such as Plato, Hegel and Marx, and his account of the affinity
between Rousseau and Hegel ignores the latter's critical stance towards the
former. But when Rousseau says, for example, that the State is 'a moral
person whose life consists in the union of its members' and whose will – the
general will – has 'absolute power over all its members' (Rousseau, 1997a,
p. 61) he appears to bear out Popper's (amongst others) worst fears.
However, the actual phrase used by Rousseau, and translated here as 'moral
person', is *personne morale* and this, as several commentators have pointed
out, is better translated as 'artificial person' (Cobban, 1964; Jones, 1987).
To Rousseau's contemporaries, it is argued, this phrase would not have had
the moral overtones ascribed to it by his post-Hegelian interpreters. Thus by
placing Rousseau's thought in its context, he can be insulated from at least
one aspect of the accusation of totalitarianism. Going back to the context of
Rousseau's work may not conclusively establish that Rousseau's thought
does not have potentially totalitarian implications (and after all, even contemporaries of Rousseau such as Burke believed that his work had this
potential) but at the very least it provides a counterweight to the claims
made by subsequent interpreters.

Turning from *contextual* to *textual* concerns, writers have sought to
defend Rousseau by pointing to constraints on the general will that are internal to the text. As we have already seen, although Rousseau believes that the
will of the majority is the best guide to the general will, it remains the case
that the will of the majority might be mistaken in its judgement. It has been
suggested that those who seek to interpret Rousseau as a nascent totalitarian
fail to take this distinction seriously. As one of Rousseau's defenders has put
it, the general will, understood as 'the people's will' or 'the will of society',
is 'without moral authority'. This is because 'the authority of the general
will is the authority of *just* law and not of society as such' (Chapman, 1956,
p. 82, emphasis added; cf Reiss, 1991, p. 29). In other words, principles of
right ought properly to circumscribe the will of the people, as is suggested
by the full title of the work – *Of the Social Contract, or Principles of*

Political Right. In a similar vein, Robert Derathé has argued that Rousseau subordinates the actions of a sovereign people to a framework of divinely-inspired natural law which sets limits on what the sovereign may rightly do to any of its members (Derathé, 1970, pp. 151–71).

However, Patrick Riley has suggested that it is precisely on the issue of principle that the deepest tensions in Rousseau's *Social Contract* lie. Rousseau, he argues, is caught between the 'voluntarism' of the modern social contract tradition in which subjective will is the source of morality (as it is, for example, with Hobbes) and the 'essentially nonvoluntaristic' ancient tradition with its 'common good' morality (Riley, 1982, pp. 99–100). The general will is, Riley claims, an unsatisfactory notion in Rousseau's *Social Contract* precisely because it is an attempt to fuse these two incompatible traditions. Cohen, on the other hand, has suggested that there need be no necessary incompatibility between voluntarism and the common good morality. According to Cohen, Rousseau's citizens 'want more than an avail-ability of alternatives within a system of laws and institutions that they view as a set of constraints imposed by others on their actions.' But where 'there is a widely shared general will to which the [political] institutions do on the whole conform' then reflective (i.e., autonomous) identification with those arrangements effectively unites autonomy with the common good (Cohen, 1986, p. 286).

There are then constraints of *principle* upon the general will, but there are also – as Cohen and others point out – *institutional* constraints too. Rousseau insists that legislative authority is inalienable and that represen-tative government is a form of slavery. But if sovereignty is inalienable, executive power is not and this, Rousseau insists, ought to be ceded to the government. There is thus a division of responsibilities between the *sover-eign* – which legislates in *general* terms – and the *government* – which applies that legislation in *particular* cases. Although this is not a full-blown theory of the separation of powers such as one finds in Locke or Montesquieu, nevertheless it does provide evidence that Rousseau under-stood the importance of institutional constraints in upholding the freedom of individual citizens. Whether or not these constraints are adequate in this respect is something we shall consider later. The idea of the Lawgiver as Hitlerian demagogue would also appear to be weakened by consideration of the limits Rousseau places upon the office. For example, the Lawgiver may propose legislation but – invoking religious authority apart – the Lawgiver has no power to implement legislation: 'he who drafts the laws … should have no legislative right' (Rousseau, 1997a, p. 70). Moreover, no matter how impressed they may be by his 'superior intelligence', the people may not legitimately cede their legislative right to the Lawgiver even if, as a people, they decide to do so (*ibid.*, p. 70). Again, it is a matter of principle that sovereignty cannot be alienated. Finally, Chapman draws our attention to the fact that for Rousseau the tyrant is distinguished from the Lawgiver in that the former always chooses a moment of social upheaval in which to make his proposals, thus taking advantage of the people he is supposed to be assisting (Chapman, 1956, pp. 76–7; Rousseau, 1997a, p. 77). This suggests that Hitler, Stalin, Robespierre and Napoleon would all be ruled out as Lawgivers by no less an authority than Rousseau himself. There are other considerations that count against the totalitarian reading of Rousseau. In the next section we consider liberal interpretations of his work, which implicitly – and sometimes explicitly – undercut the totalitarian reading.

Rousseau as Liberal

In spite of the totalitarian readings of Rousseau, liberty nevertheless remains central to his concerns, in *The Social Contract* and elsewhere. Emphasising Rousseau's comments on liberty, therefore, may lead one to interpret Rousseau as a liberal of one stripe or another. For his own part, Rousseau's preferred form of government was *republican* – he often identified himself as a citizen of the Genevan republic and explicitly says that 'every legitimate Government is republican' (Rousseau, 1997a, p. 67). His concern for civic virtue and duty (he was a great admirer of Sparta) places him in what Pocock has called the 'Atlantic Republican tradition' alongside writers such as Machiavelli (whom Rousseau greatly admired) and indeed Pocock describes him as 'the Machiavelli of the eighteenth century' (Pocock, 1975, p. 504). Republicanism is sometimes thought to be opposed to liberalism, though this opposition may be overstated, and much recent research into the republican tradition has pointed to the importance of republican ideas to modern liberalism (For an overview of recent debates, see Haakonsen, 1993).

One aspect of Rousseau's republicanism that contributes to his liberal credentials is his emphasis on the importance of the rule of law. According to Levine, the concept of law is the key 'ordering concept' in Rousseau's work, and Chapter 6 of Book II ('Of Law') is, he claims, the heart of the entire *Social Contract* 'for which all the rest is just commentary' (Levine, 1976, p. 46). Rousseau himself says – in the *Discourse on Political Economy* – that 'it is to law alone that men owe justice and freedom' (Rousseau, 1997a, p. 10). Moreover, Rousseau devised constitutions for Corsica and Poland, seemingly anticipating the modern constitutional state.

As Norman Barry has pointed out, Rousseau's insistence upon the 'generality, equality and impersonality' of law would find favour with liberals everywhere (Barry, 1995, p. 50).

However, Rousseau had argued in the *Second Discourse* that good laws contribute to the moralisation of citizens whilst bad laws corrupt them, and the idea that good laws can have this positive effect on citizens clearly grows out of Rousseau's perfectionist account of human nature. This sets Rousseau apart from those liberals, such as Hayek and Nozick, for whom the system of law ought not to be construed as a positive instrument for moralising the citizenry, but rather as a negative instrument for the maintenance of order and the regulation of conflict. The system of law for these writers is straightforwardly a means by which private interests can most efficiently be satisfied. For his part, Rousseau believes that a society based on private interest will always breed corruption rather than virtue. Rousseau may also be set apart from utilitarian liberals such as Bentham for whom laws are a means to maximising the greatest happiness of the greatest number. For Bentham, the greatest happiness of the greatest number is an aggregative concept, but as we have already noticed Rousseau insists that the general will is not the same as 'the will of all', which is 'a sum of particular wills' (Rousseau, 1997a, p. 60). Rousseau in fact has been read as a Benthamite utilitarian (Allen, 1962) but this, as Jones has pointed out, is anachronistic and says more about the interests of the interpreter than it does about Rousseau (Jones, 1987, p. 118). According to Jones, attentiveness to the problems with which Rousseau was concerned, and to the context within which they appeared as problems for him, avoids such anachronism.

If Rousseau is to be interpreted as a liberal, then in current post-Rawlsian terminology he is a *perfectionist* liberal or, as Richard Dagger has recently argued, a *republican* liberal (Dagger, 1997). His work is to be placed in the same tradition as communitarian liberals such as T. H. Green (though Green himself thought that Rousseau's general will was 'unprincipled' – see Harris and Morrow, 1986, p. 57), and Bosanquet (1923), or it is to be placed in the tradition of *developmental* liberalism alongside such liberals as J. S. Mill, rather than the classical or neo-liberal traditions with their static view of human nature. For example, Chapman argues that those who interpret Rousseau as a proto-totalitarian fail to see that the general will is a *dynamic* concept; it is a *process* of continual striving – not merely a *product* of that striving. Since the general will is, so to speak, always 'in question' it cannot readily be used as a stick with which to beat dissidents. After all, it is surely possible that they may be right in *their* interpretation of it and the majority wrong. Thus if it is accepted that the general will is a dynamic process, then the maintenance of civil liberties is required if it is not to ossify. As Chapman puts it: 'Freedom, both moral and political, is essential to the very existence of a general will' (Chapman, 1956, p. 78). Levine – who offers a Kantian reading of Rousseau – also emphasises the dynamic aspects of his theory when he points out that the social contract is not an historically fixed moment located in the past but one that is constantly renewed in the ongoing act of legislation (Levine, 1976, p. 51). Whilst acknowledging that there are manifestly illiberal aspects of his political philosophy – most notably in its practical aspects – Levine nevertheless points out that in presenting the social contract as a dynamic rather than a static phenomenon Rousseau provides a 'theoretical motivation for some of the central liberal doctrines: freedom of speech, freedom of inquiry, and the freedom – indeed, the obligation – to publish and disseminate information' (*ibid.*, p. 79).

How can the idea of 'forcing people to be free' be given a liberal interpretation? One way in which this can be done is to argue, as many liberals have done, that freedom can only be achieved within a framework of law. Outside of such a framework, there is not liberty, but licence – a Hobbesian 'state of nature'. There is then a *prima facie* reason for each individual to endorse a system of law. But a system of law requires also a system of coercive sanctions, and any individual who breaks a law can expect to have those sanctions applied in his or her case. When those sanctions are applied in any particular instance, they can in part be justified in the name of the larger freedom which the system of law guarantees to all, including the recalcitrant: 'Since we benefit from the existence of laws in general, we should obey those laws we have opposed; if we break them, we should recognise the punishment as just' (Hope Mason, 1995, p. 125; also Barry, 1965, p. 198). Such an idea 'is not dangerous to liberty' (Plamenatz, 1972, p. 318).

A Kantian Rousseau

The affinity between Kant and Rousseau is widely acknowledged (not least by Kant himself) and reading Rousseau through Kantian spectacles can have the effect of rendering his thought more liberal. For Kant, rational individuals are morally autonomous when they will the rational moral law (the *categorical imperative*). Because willing is a *subjective* notion, Kantian moral agents are effectively self-legislating when they will the moral law, but the moral law itself is an *objective* notion, accessible to all rational agents. Thus Kantian moral agents can be said to achieve moral autonomy in much the same way that Rousseau's citizens achieve moral liberty – by placing themselves under a system of general (strictly speaking, for Kant, *universal*) law so that 'each obeys only himself'. Dagger, for example, has described Rousseau's general will as 'a principle akin to Kant's categorical imperative' (Dagger, 1997, p. 88). For Cassirer too, Rousseau is primarily a moral philosopher whose concern for the 'unconditional universal validity' of law 'runs through all of his political writings' (Cassirer, 1989, p. 58). Indeed, for Cassirer, the affinity between these two thinkers' work was such that Kant was the only eighteenth-century writer to fully understand Rousseau's political thought (*ibid.*, p. 70). For Cassirer (following Kant's judgement of Rousseau's moral theory) it is important to stress the foundational role of *reason* over that of feeling in Rousseau's moral theory (*ibid.*, p. 99). Rousseau is often held up as someone who disparages reason in favour of feeling – it is on this basis that Rousseau is often seen as the father of Romanticism and Nationalism – but this is too crude for Cassirer. Rousseau, he contends, was much more sophisticated in his realisation that feeling had to be tutored by reason.

Other Kantian readings of Rousseau's general will are more indirect. For example, Rawls has described elements of his influential theory of justice as 'Kantian' (Rawls, 1980; but cf. Rawls, 1993, pp. 99–107). Rousseau's general will has, in turn, been interpreted as performing a similar function to Rawls's 'veil of ignorance'. The purpose of this hypothetical device is to identify principles of justice for a constitutional regime that all citizens could endorse. It does this by excluding particularistic information – such as class, status, religion, and (more controversially) race and gender – the better to reveal the general interests which 'free and equal' citizens have in common. Rawls believes that if principles of justice are chosen on the basis of these general interests then they cannot be skewed in favour of the interests of one person, group, class, and so forth, against all others (Rawls, 1972, pp. 17–22). Since for Rousseau the general will 'must issue from all in order to apply to all' (Rousseau, 1997a, p. 62) attending to it 'leads the parties to promote their common interest as citizens rather than their private interests as men' (Dagger, 1981, p. 361). Rousseau's terms are different from Rawls's, 'but the point is much the same' (*ibid.*, p. 361).

Problems with the Liberal and Kantian Rousseau

Clearly there are many liberal elements to Rousseau's political thought and even ideas such as the general will can be given an interpretation that is not obviously authoritarian. Yet there are problems with the attempt to read Rousseau as a liberal. As a child of the Enlightenment, liberalism has tended to view human beings as primarily rational creatures whose chief concern is the satisfaction of their own individual interests. Moreover, the social contract tradition of which Locke is perhaps the exemplary liberal has tended to treat such individuals as logically prior to, and unencumbered by, any particular social, political or moral context. Custom and tradition, which for many conservative writers embody a notion of the common good, are undermined by the liberal prioritising of individualistic reason. For his own part – and anticipating Hegel's later critique of Kant – Rousseau clearly understood the importance of custom and tradition to the political community. As Viroli has pointed out, Rousseau, like Kant, believes in 'an objective moral order and the existence of an objective truth' (Viroli, 1988, p. 23). As Rousseau himself put it: 'What is good and conformable to order is so by the nature of things and independently of human conventions' (Rousseau, 1997a, p. 66). But so abstract is this conception of justice that it can have no purchase on the hearts of men: 'Reason alone is not a sufficient foundation for virtue' (Rousseau, 1974, p. 255). Therefore: 'Conventions and laws are necessary to combine rights with duties and to bring justice back to its object' (Rousseau, 1997a, p. 66). It is for this reason that custom and tradition form 'the State's genuine constitution' (*ibid.*, p. 81). Despite Burke's strictures against Rousseau he is, in this respect at least, much closer to Burkean conservatism than to Enlightenment liberalism.

As Levine has argued, despite the liberal inclination of Rousseau's theory of sovereignty and law, it is (*contra* Cassirer) in his insistence that custom and opinion are fundamental that his illiberalism ultimately occurs (Levine, 1976, p. 79). Liberalism generally is disinclined to grant such pre-rational, even irrational, elements a foundational role in its political and moral theory, though as one commentator points out it is a failing of liberalism that it cannot adequately account for what binds a people together as a people: 'Liberalism is perpetually embarrassed by the often non-rational preconditions that make the appeal to reason in public affairs possible, and sometimes effective. Rousseau is not so shame-faced' (Dent, 1992, p. 147). It is Rousseau's emphasis on the fundamental importance of custom and opinion that makes some Kantian readings so problematic. Whereas for Kant the moral law which is willed by autonomous moral agents is properly speaking *universal* in that it applies to the entire universe of rational beings – it is, as Hans Reiss has pointed out, the 'will of reason' as such (Reiss, 1991, p. 28) – the general will is the will of a *particular* people. The general will does not therefore apply to the entire universe of rational beings, but only to the members of the discrete political community. The political community will have customs and traditions – in short, a history – that is unique to it and that will have shaped its members in a way that marks them off from other political communities.

The Case for Rousseau as Radical

Rousseau's appeal to radicals and revolutionaries is long-standing – we have, for example, already remarked upon the impact of his writing on the French Revolutionaries, and the Cuban revolutionary leader Fidel Castro is reported to have said that 'Jean-Jacques had been his teacher and that he had fought Batista with the *Social Contract* in his pocket' (cited in Colletti, 1972, pp. 143–4). Liberal critics of Rousseau such as Plamenatz have recognised the affinity between Rousseau's ideal state as it is set out in *The Social Contract* and the revolutionary Paris Commune of 1871, much admired by Marx (Plamenatz, 1952, p. xi). Marx himself, it must be said, had little time for Rousseau, dismissing him as an unhistorical, *petit bourgeois* social contract theorist (Marx, 1973b, p. 83). Marx apart, radicals have often found much to admire in Rousseau, both in his account of the corrupting effects of the unequal distribution of property, and in his support for direct participatory democracy as a means to the development of a collective moral consciousness exemplified by the general will. According to Pateman, for example, it is a mistake to read Rousseau's *Social Contract* through 'liberal democratic spectacles' for Rousseau is critical of the liberal contractual tradition exemplified by Hobbes, Locke and, more recently, Rawls (Pateman, 1985, p. 142). Ironically, Pateman's Rousseau is presented as a fierce critic of the kind of abstract, unhistorical, and individualistic thinking of which Marx accused Rousseau. Whereas the liberal social contract is concerned with the most efficient means of satisfying the self-interest of the parties to the contract, Rousseau's social contract is concerned with the transformation of self-interest in a more communal direction. For Pateman, Rousseau is a thoroughgoing egalitarian for whom social, political and economic equality is a 'central' concern (*ibid.*, p. 155). Pateman's Rousseau has no truck with the liberal belief that the political sphere can be understood independently of the sphere of civil society, and that formal political equality alone is therefore adequate. For Rousseau 'the private and political spheres of life cannot be separated' in the way that liberal contract theorists assume (*ibid.*, p. 149). If liberals fear that collapsing the private and political spheres opens the way to totalitarianism (see, for example, the discussion of Crocker above) Pateman pins her hopes to the moralising effects of participation. For example, whereas liberals see the potential for tyranny in Rousseau's claim that those who disagree with the general will must be 'forced to be free', Pateman (following Ellenburg, 1976) argues that the actual phrase used by Rousseau – '*forcer d'être libre*' – can be translated as '*strengthened* to be free' rather than the more controversial '*forced* to be free' (Pateman, 1985, p. 156). Here, it is the educative effects of participation that are brought to the fore. Moreover, as a fellow 'New Left' writer pointed out, if we take the context in which Rousseau was writing into account then the idea of 'forcing people to be free' is mitigated by the consideration that 'before he wrote men were already being forced to be free' and Rousseau's proposals, for all their problems, were 'offered as an antidote' to this (Macpherson, 1966, p. 7).

Despite Marx's dismissal of Rousseau as a bourgeois theorist, many Marxists have sought to point up the affinity between the two theorists. For example, Engels, Marx's close collaborator and political ally, described the *Second Discourse* as a 'masterpiece of dialectic' in which Rousseau's account of the rise of bourgeois society and the place of property in this story anticipates Hegel by twenty years and whose sequence of ideas 'corresponds exactly with the sequence developed in Marx's *Capital*' but without 'the Hegelian jargon' (Engels, 1935, p. 26, pp. 156–7). Nevertheless, even for Engels Rousseau was primarily a theorist of bourgeois democracy who, in common with many other eighteenth-century philosophers, could not pass beyond the limits of his own time. However, for the Italian Marxist, Galvano della Volpa, Rousseau's 'anti-levelling egalitarianism' especially as it is set out in the *Second Discourse* 'should be numbered among the essential historical and intellectual premisses' of Marxism (della Volpa, 1978, p. 150). It is, claims della Volpa, 'embarrassing' to later Marxists that Marx and Engels failed to recognise the radical implications of Rousseau's work (*ibid.*, p. 147).

Colletti, for his part, argues that whilst Rousseau was indeed constrained by the 'objective historical limitation inevitable in his time' he nevertheless 'sketched the first and basic chapters of "a critique of bourgeois society"' (Colletti, 1972, p. 174). Indeed, whilst acknowledging 'the backwardness of [Rousseau's] economic thought' Colletti nevertheless argues that '[i]n an age in which all the most advanced thinkers were interpreters of the rights and reasons of rising bourgeois society, its prosperity and industry', the critique of that society mounted by Rousseau in the *Second Discourse* 'made his thought appear absurd and paradoxical' to his contemporaries (*ibid.*, pp. 169–70). Reading Rousseau as critical thinker thus removes the illusion of paradox from his work. His critique of the emerging bourgeois order – civil society, driven by competitiveness and private interest – set him apart from Enlightenment thinkers such as Adam Smith and David Hume, as did his claim, in the *Second Discourse*, that private property – 'the real foundation of civil society' – was the source of corruption and vice (Rousseau, 1997b, p. 161). But it also set him apart from Kant in whom 'we find praise of competition, of mutual unsociability and the resulting desire for "honour, power and wealth"' (Colletti, 1972, p. 161). Whereas for Levine 'Kant is the link between Rousseau and the early Marx', (Levine, 1976, p. vii; but see

Levine, 1993 in which the link between Marx and Rousseau is made more directly) for Colletti, Marx makes a direct if 'unconscious' return to Rousseau in the *Economic and Philosophical Manuscripts* of 1844 (Colletti, 1972, p. 161). Colletti's thesis, explicitly stated, is that 'so far as "political" theory in the strict sense is concerned, Marx and Lenin have added nothing to Rousseau, except for the analysis (which is of course rather important) of the "economic bases" for the withering away of the state' (*ibid.*, p. 185). The key to this reading of Rousseau, Colletti argues, lies in *The Social Contract*'s insistence that 'popular sovereignty is inalienable and indivisible' which amounts to a radical critique of parliamentary or representative government. Thus 'the ultimate development to which all the theory of *The Social Contract* tends' is nothing less than 'the abolition or "withering away of the State" ', where 'the State' is understood as an instrument of sectional (that is, class) interests (*ibid.*, p. 184).

Problems with Rousseau as Radical

The attempt to interpret Rousseau as a radical runs up against a number of criticisms. For example, Rousseau's model of participatory democracy is presented as progressive – even revolutionary – in its implications, but it is well known that Rousseau was deeply sceptical about the idea of progress (for example, Rousseau, 1997a, p. 106, pp. 109–10, p. 269; Dent, 1992, pp. 197–8) and was no lover of revolution (Rousseau, 1997b, pp. 185–6; 1997a, pp. 244–7). It is true, of course, that Rousseau endorses direct participation in legislative matters and this is undoubtedly an idea with radical potential. But it is also true that Rousseau's model state is small-scale – a Geneva or a Sparta – and he is aware of the difficulties in applying his theory to modern, mass societies (Rousseau, 1997a, p. 4). Moreover, even in the small-scale, face-to-face polity favoured by Rousseau, not everyone qualifies as a citizen. Women, for example, are excluded and in this regard Pateman is a scathing *critic* of Rousseau (Pateman, 1988, pp. 96–102).

It has also been suggested that Rousseau's principled commitment in *The Social Contract* to direct participatory democracy is not as strong as it might appear to be. Fralin (1978) has pointed out that despite Rousseau's strictures against representative democracy in that work, he elsewhere – notably in his *Considerations on the Government of Poland* – proposes a representative system (Rousseau, 1997a, pp. 200–1) whilst in the *Discourse on Political Economy* Rousseau appears to argue *against* direct democracy (Rousseau, 1997a, pp. 24–5). Fralin's argument has been criticised in some detail (Miller, 1984; Cohen, 1986) but at the very least these aspects of

Rousseau's work might suggest a realism concerning practical politics that more utopian interpretations miss (Melzer, 1983). Concerning Pateman's point that Rousseau undermines the liberal distinction between the political realm and the realm of civil society, we have already noticed that the scope of the general will is restricted to those areas that all citizens have in common. Rousseau seeks to keep private interests *out* of politics because he associates their entry into the political sphere with the tyranny of one class (the rich) over another. Finally, for those who seek to make Rousseau into a Marxist of sorts it remains the case that Rousseau defends the institution of private property, even if he does acknowledge the pernicious effects of too wide a disparity in its distribution.

Evaluation

What are we to make of these various interpretations of Rousseau? There is no doubt some merit in all of these interpretations since they all, in various ways, draw attention to aspects of Rousseau's thought. I think, however, there are reasons for finding some accounts of Rousseau more plausible than others. As we saw above, Rousseau's work has since his own time been thought to provide a philosophical justification for tyranny, including twentieth-century totalitarianism. Is this a credible interpretation of Rousseau's work? There are undoubtedly elements of Rousseau's political theory that can have authoritarian implications and even writers who are generally sympathetic to Rousseau's concerns recognise that, on the whole, Rousseau's political proposals provide inadequate safeguards for the individual against the collective (for instance, Masters, 1968, pp. 421–5). For example, even if the 'will of all' is constrained by *right* it remains the case that what is right is determined for all intents and purposes by the will of all, or at least of the majority.

Rousseau may therefore justifiably be criticised for failing to provide adequate constraints on the exercise of sovereignty, yet he is not alone in this failing and there are authoritarian elements to be found even in the work of some of the greatest of liberal thinkers. What then is it that leads a generally measured philosopher such as Bertrand Russell to claim that 'Hitler is an outcome of Rousseau' (Russell, 1946, p. 660)? Here the explanation probably lies less in Rousseau than in his critics and the needs of their time. As we noticed earlier, the totalitarian interpretation of Rousseau came to the fore against the background of the rise of fascism and against the ideologically-driven Cold War. The desire to construct a tradition of thought in which to locate and explain these phenomena is perhaps understandable as part of the effort to ensure their containment. This is laudable and it reminds us that the activity of interpreting political theory is not merely an 'ivory tower' exercise, but can be a matter of directly *political* importance (though, of course, much remains to be said about exactly *how* ideas impact upon the world).

The problem is that writers such as Rousseau only fit the supposed tradition of thought if their work is suitably edited, and much that would mitigate their inclusion must be left on the cutting-room floor. Thus Rousseau's totalitarian interpreters largely dismiss the principled and institutional constraints devised by Rousseau in their efforts to represent him as a philosopher of tyranny. Such a practice may certainly perform the useful function of alerting us to the danger inherent in certain of the ideas presented by Rousseau, but as an approach to the interpretation of his work it simply does not do justice to its complexity or indeed to Rousseau's own awareness concerning the problems which he identified and which he sought to resolve. In this respect the attempt to read Rousseau as a liberal fares much better – not least because the totalitarian reading has for a long time achieved such dominance that any attempt to emphasise the liberal aspects of Rousseau's thought must inevitably address the concerns raised by the totalitarian interpretation. The problem for liberals who seek to enlist Rousseau as a fellow liberal, is that Rousseau is himself critical of the dominant liberal paradigm, characterised by subjectivism and the insistence upon private interest as the foundation of the political order. As we saw earlier, Rousseau was a self-declared *republican* and liberalism has not always found it easy to accommodate itself to republican notions of duty, civic virtue and the common good since these often seem to cut across the liberal insistence upon the primacy of *rights*.

Yet as the recent history of political theory shows, many liberals are themselves now concerned that the exclusive focus on rights leaves out much that is of value in civic and political life. Liberals such as Stephen Macedo – who emphasises the important role that virtue plays in a liberal polity – and Joseph Raz – who defends a non-individualist perfectionist liberalism – do not explicitly draw upon Rousseau in support of their positions, but they do show that liberalism itself is not necessarily to be associated solely with the defence of individual rights and private interest (Macedo, 1990; Raz, 1986).

We should probably not ask 'was Rousseau a liberal?' but rather 'what kind of liberal was he?' Was he a *Kantian* liberal? What Rousseau's Kantian interpreters are surely right to insist upon is the important role that the faculty of reason plays in grasping the requirements of justice. As with Kant, Rousseau believes that there is an objective moral order to which rational people can gain access – the equivalent of Kant's moral law. Rousseau may, of course, be wrong concerning the existence of an objective moral order, but nevertheless, the important point about this moral order for Rousseau is its *generality*. The good man, says Rousseau 'orders his life with regard to all men: the wicked orders it for self alone' (Rousseau, 1974, p. 255). The problem with reading Rousseau through Kantian spectacles is that it leads interpreters to *over*-emphasise the role of reason in his work whereas, as we noticed earlier, Rousseau was clearly aware that any viable political society could not be based on an appeal to reason alone.

It remains the case, however, that reason is instrumental in moving the individual away from the absorption with self (*amour propre*) and towards generality. 'Reason alone is not a *sufficient* foundation for virtue' (*ibid.*, p. 255, emphasis added), but neither can virtue be attained *without* reason. Rousseau can clearly be criticised for failing to give an adequate account of the relationship between reason and sentiment – who has? – but it seems clear that he does not make reason merely the slave of the passions. To accuse Rousseau of irrationalism, as the totalitarian critique tends to do, is once again to overlook Rousseau's many attempts to think through these complex issues.

If the totalitarian critique plays down liberal and radical elements of Rousseau's work, the radical interpretation tends to ignore the conservative elements of his political theory. As we saw earlier, Rousseau defends convention in a way that is reminiscent of Burke. He does not seek to eradicate the institution of private property – indeed his ideal state would consist of self-sufficient property-holding peasants – and he blames many of the ills of modern society on advances in technology. Rousseau looks backward, rather than forward. Yet he also realises the impossibility of going back in time so that he does not even, on the whole, share the optimism of his radical interpreters. The undoubtedly radical elements of Rousseau's work – his critique of the assumptions of natural law liberalism (or, as Colletti puts it, his 'critique of civil society'); his insistence on direct participation – are radical only *in spite* of Rousseau, when the conservative elements of his thought have been trimmed away. Once these elements are brought back in, Rousseau loses much of his radical edge. The Rousseau that finally emerges from the plethora of interpretations is ultimately a complex thinker, both personally and politically. He cannot easily be co-opted into any ideological tradition – elements of his work are at home in all such traditions whilst other elements are ill at ease. At a time when the easy construal of political matters into a 'left *versus* right' dichotomy has been challenged, Rousseau's work is likely to continue to provide a fertile ground both for those who wish to understand and defend these traditional categories, and also for those who seek to think beyond them.

6

Burke (1729–1797)

DAVID P. SHUGARMAN

Introduction

Edmund Burke is especially remembered for his counterrevolutionary *Reflections on the Revolution in France*, which he published in 1790. That work is widely regarded as the classic conservative statement in defence of the traditions and institutional framework of a hierarchical society. In his *Reflections* Burke argued that customary constitutional practices, inherited liberties, an established monarchy, an established church, and a privileged aristocracy were all integral to a society's prosperity and ordered civility. In England, said Burke, 'We fear God; we look up with awe to kings; with affection to Parliaments; with duty to magistrates; with reverence to priests and with respect to nobility' (Burke, 1968, p. 182). To Burke these were all 'natural' sentiments, which were in keeping with the features of social life, the *manners* characterising and informing communication and morality, which, in turn, reflected and kept vibrant the ancient wisdom that made Britain a great society. To Burke these sentiments and manners were what the French revolutionaries were rejecting. Furthermore, Burke proclaimed, 'all the good things' conveyed by these manners rested upon 'two princi-ples': 'the spirit of a gentleman, and the spirit of religion' (*ibid.*, p. 173). These two, he believed, the revolutionaries could not abide. He saw the French Revolution and its proponents both in France and in England dan-gerously, outrageously, threatening these principles, achievements and commitments. He worried that if the revolutionaries, whom he referred to as Jacobins, could wreck the foundations of French society then their move-ment might be exported to the rest of Europe and make its way across the Channel. It is his response to that Revolution and his re-articulation of that response over the last seven years of his life that has led to his canonisation in many quarters as the founding father of modern conservatism.

As an icon of conservatism, however, Burke is intriguingly complex and somewhat puzzling. He was not a member of the Tory Party of his day but rather a key member of the Whigs who opposed them. While major studies of conservatism treat him, as mentioned earlier, as one of its 'founding fathers' (O'Gorman, 1986, p. 12; Eccleshall, 1990, p. 39), he is also described by one of his most recent biographers and champions as a 'liberal and pluralist' (O'Brien, 1992, p. 608). A leading American conservative thinker and great admirer of Burke maintains that, 'Burke the conservative was also Burke the liberal' (Kirk, 1960, p. 13). In marking the bicentenary of his death, just a few years ago, Burke was praised not only by conservatives, but also by liberals, and by a devotee of New Labour (Crowe, 1997). Early in the last century even the left-wing historian of political thought Harold Laski had approving things to say about Burke's contributions (Laski, 1920). Conservative, socialist and liberal theorists have also criticised him (Strauss, 1953; Macpherson, 1980; Herzog, 1998). He seems to have said and meant different things to different minds. There is no question that in his own mind throughout his life he consistently held to the principles and subscribed to the positions he associated with the Whig parliamentary party that he joined in the mid-1760s. His *An Appeal from the New to the Old Whigs* (Burke, 1962), which appeared a year after the *Reflections*, was written in large part to underscore that point. Yet many of his interpreters, whether of an admiring or critical bent, have had trouble over the years both locating the most central features of Burke's Whiggism and discerning the underpinnings of his political thinking.

While political theorists over the years have sought to grapple with Burke's ideas, his contemporaries knew him best as a practising, party politician. He entered British politics and the House largely through the patronage of Lord Rockingham, who led a wing of the Whig party and briefly served as prime minister. As a spokesperson for the Rockingham Whigs, Burke often opposed a variety of policies both domestic and foreign that were initiated either by the crown or by Tory government leaders close to the crown. He defended the new role of parties and their legitimacy in British politics, and questioned official English policies towards Irish Catholics, India and America. In the 1770s he took the side of those seeking to challenge official government policy when he expressed sympathy for the interests and concerns of a rebellious America. In all these endeavours Burke's contemporaries saw him as a reformer. Later political historians and commentators generally agreed and have tended to regard him prior to his *Reflections* as a 'liberal' for his times, though neither 'liberal' nor 'conservative' had yet emerged as terms to describe parties or policies. Then came his reaction to the revolution in France and the break with his party and from his reputation as a reformer.

As a thinker who actively engaged in, and was at times highly influential in, public life he resembles many other major figures in the history of western political thought. Yet unlike them, with the possible exceptions of Machiavelli and Marx (with both of whom he is diametrically opposed on a wide range of matters), Burke was dismissive of the role that philosophy might play in contributing to a better understanding of politics. In addition, as a partisan, impassioned critic and activist he adopted a speechmaking and writing style which much of the time was less that of the philosopher or theorist and more that of someone who seems part newspaper columnist, part political rhetorician, part dramatist, and part preacher. As a result, there are those who caution against reading too much of any philosophy into Burke and instead focus on his skills as a rhetorician and political actor. His self-consciously philosophical writings were largely confined to his earliest endeavours. One of those early titles began with the words '*A Philosophical Enquiry*'. Yet throughout the rest of his life he responded to concrete political issues as they arose and resisted any inclination to set out a treatise on the nature of politics. He argued or asserted repeatedly that the attempt to apply philosophical inquiry to politics was dangerously inappropriate. It meant digging up what should be left to flourish. Combined with his eclectic use of metaphors, examples and rationales, Burke's counsel to resist resorting to philosophy when addressing practical issues makes the place and meaning of theory in his own approach to politics difficult to characterise and appreciate.

Over the past thirty years or so several new, important reassessments of Burke have appeared which try to account for different Burkes or different interpretations of him. Some of these reassessments have assumed or 'read in' to Burke's writings and actions a hidden, repressed or implicit side to him. These readings consider contending inclinations or tensions in his sensibilities in the hope of explaining his thought more fully. Others, including significant reinterpretations by C. B. Macpherson and Conor Cruise O'Brien, have found less contradiction or ambivalence in Burke. They have suggested ways of resolving what have long been seen as problems in comprehending Burke.

Problems and Issues

The problems in interpreting Burke have to do both with his political positions taken over the course of his parliamentary career, and his philosophical orientations and principles. For most of Burke's commentators there has always been a question of how or whether the 'liberal' politics he is associated with championing for much of his life can be reconciled with his attack on the French Revolution. In addition, his interpreters have differed on what is foundational to his political thought and even whether he had a coherent political theory.

There seem to be at least two very different political Burkes. One Burke who for most of his life is a reform-minded spokesperson for the Whigs under Lord Rockingham, and another who dons the uniform of a highly conservative, almost reactionary, counterrevolutionary warrior. The first is a representative of the party that championed the Glorious Revolution of 1688 and supported a major change in the governance of Great Britain a century prior to the French Revolution. This Burke sought a strong parliamentary voice to rein in the prerogatives and power of the crown and saw the need to protect and encourage the activities of newly influential groups of profit-seekers in the cities and country. He also urged conciliation rather than confrontation with America's rebels. The later Burke railed against those who called for social change – people he called atheists and 'monied' men and their intellectual supporters – and defended the monarchy and all its trappings. This move from sympathy for not one, but two, revolutions to outright condemnation of a third startled many of his contemporaries who had seen him as a fellow reformer. To many of Burke's friends and long-time political associates his reaction to the French Revolution meant, as William Hazlitt wrote just a few years after Burke's death, that he had 'abandoned not only all his practical conclusions, but all the principles on which they were founded' (Hazlitt, 1819, p. 264).

So one of the first problems in understanding Burke has to do with accounting for what appear to be his dramatically different responses to political events (Macpherson, 1980; Winch, 1985, p. 231; Canavan, 1995, p. x; Furniss, 1993). Arising out of his apparent political shifts and what seem to be very contradictory theoretical orientations a second major 'Burke problem' has been to explain how he could maintain his economic views that were associated with the new political economy alongside his commitment to ancient manners and institutions. This second question or problem has to do with reconciling his clearly articulated economic liberalism with his emphatic social and political conservatism.

Yet another serious problem for any attempt to clarify Burke's contributions is that he adopted a number of different styles to express himself *and* frequently moved from one set of considerations or rationale for this or that proposition to another (Cameron, 1973, p. 15). For example, when we turn to his theoretical propositions about the nature of government, he says, in the same work, both that the state is willed by God (Burke, 1968, p. 196) and that it is 'the offspring of convention, a contrivance of human wisdom to provide for human wants' (*ibid.*, pp. 150–1). While there is little doubt from reading his speeches or perusing his writings about *where* he actually stood on most issues that he addressed, there is considerable disagreement and controversy among commentators as to *why* he took the political positions he did and on *how* or *what* he grounded those positions.

Complicating the difficulties of fully comprehending Burke's thought is the fact that he composed most of his speeches and writings as a political actor addressing events of his day rather than as a political theorist issuing a treatise. His frequently expressed impatience with metaphysics and the applicability of philosophy to political action and the fact that almost all his writings and speeches after he took his seat in the House were directed to particular issues and circumstances have made it difficult for students of Burke to agree on whether he really is a theorist of politics and whether there is a coherence in his ideas. In some respects there does not seem to be enough theorising by Burke for him to be treated as a theorist. In others he can be seen as having said so much on so may different issues that his work provides ample room for a variety of interpretations as to its major themes and character.

Why Conflicting Interpretations?

As if to try the patience of later historians of ideas and political theorists trying to fathom his thought Burke offers his readers a number of options. To some he bases his analysis of what is to be done or what is worth preserving on the utility of public policies and/or historical practices; to others he appeals to natural law; then to deeply religious belief and sensibilities. He also presents himself as a bourgeois theorist convinced by and seeking to convince others of the benefits and objectivity of the new political economy. At times he appears unsystematic, and purposely anti-theoretical, stressing the importance of addressing circumstances pragmatically. At times he seems inclined to use polemics and rhetoric rather than philosophical argument to press his concerns.

In addition to concerns about the nature of Burke's thought there are also questions of Burke's enduring appeal, whether he made unique contributions to political thought, and his relevance today. Some interpreters, for instance, Michael Freeman (1980) and Don Herzog (1998), draw attention to Burke's dismissive remarks about democracy, his scorn for tradesmen and his denigration of the people generally as a 'swinish multitude' and see him as the paradigmatic counterrevolutionary, and anti-democratic thinker. But one can also read him, like Conor Cruise O'Brien (1992), as someone decidedly upset about the oppression of Irish Catholics and the manipulative machinations of the East India Company and thus as someone dedicated to conserving liberties and traditions of civility against usurpation and the abuse of power by those in authority. He has modern admirers (like O'Brien and Stanlis) who profoundly disagree on how to characterise the philosophical principles that ground and motivated his reactions and pronouncements, but who largely share the judgement that his political sensibilities were brilliantly attuned to the dangers of tyranny and the importance of liberty.

Commentaries on Burke have had to deal both with the difficulties involved in understanding his context as he understood it and those presented by his propensity to use a wide variety of what appear to be disparate, if not antithetical, arguments to support the policies he advocated. Furthermore, various interpreters of Burke have often reflected and woven the ideologies and concerns of their different historical periods into their versions of Burke and his time (Wilkins, 1967, p. 10). How texts are read, 'classic' or otherwise, depends very much not only on understanding the context in which they were written but also on the context in which they are read.

Historians of ideas have brought to the study of Burke and his era their own efforts to legitimise contemporary political positions by identifying Burke as providing wise counsel from a past which has much to teach us about the present (and future). Late nineteenth-century and early twentieth-century commentary by thinkers sympathetic to the development of liberal democracy saw Burke as an important contributor to the utilitarian liberal tradition. In the 1950s and early 1960s American conservatives drew attention to the natural law component in Burke and, reflecting their concerns over the Cold War between communism and 'the free world', saw his treatment of the dangers of Jacobinism as prophetic in regard to what they deemed as parallel dangers of Marxism. In this – the penchant for finding precursors in the past to shore up one side of an ideological and policy dispute – commentators on Burke are not unique as historians of political figures and controversies. But interpretations of Burke have not been the preserve of historians of ideas or political theorists.

It may be surprising that a long list of articles and books on Burke are now coming out of English departments rather than Philosophy or Political Science (Whale, 2000; Blakemore, 1992). It is not surprising that professors of literature should find in Burke a master rhetorician who has much to teach us about the role of language in culture and communication (Eagleton, 1998). Since the situation in many scholarly circles since the 1980s has been one consumed by reassessment of the ideas, achievements, and problems of 'modernity' and its alleged supercession by 'postmodernity', it is also not surprising that many new studies are intent on revealing Burke as a thinker who wrestled with modernity and even had postmodernist sensibilities (White, 1993; Furniss, 1993). Again, those moved by interpretive paradigms influenced by psychoanalysis have found Burke a psychologically conflicted and repressed figure (Kramnick, 1977).

Conflicting Interpretations

Inconsistent Dualism: The Conservative and the Liberal

To some analysts Burke was 'one of the first social theorists to base his economic and political ideas on entirely opposed principles' (Shklar, 1957, p. 225). With his argument that there were 'two Burkes ... struggling with each other' Isaac Kramnick introduced a new version of the dualism at the core of Burke's contributions. Calling Burke a father of conservatism 'tells but half the story' (Kramnick, 1977, p. 4). According to Kramnick, radical bourgeois sympathies and inclinations often moved Burke. But his values conflicted. He both admired and feared the drive of industrious, self-made men. He both admired and held in contempt men with inherited wealth and position.

To Kramnick, Burke's ideological and social shifts reflect confusion and ambivalence about his personal identity concerning both his sexuality and his sense of place in English society. Burke had to wrestle with his own homosexual tendencies and an 'unresolved ambivalence between his identification [as an] aristocratic personality and [a] bourgeois one' which, to Burke, were gendered categories (*ibid.*, p. 10). Kramnick holds that Burke was obsessed by his own longings and guilt and was concerned that the masculine characteristics he identified as sublime and dominating in his early philosophical work on aesthetics would destroy the loveliness and orderliness of life. But he both identified with and recoiled from feminine, aristocratic attributes. He was in awe of and disgusted by aggressive, thrusting masculine characteristics. The argument here is that Burke's rage against the revolution in France reflected his own pent-up hostilities having to do with his troubled ambivalence over the changing nature of his own society, his place in it and who he was.

Kramnick's return to Burke's early aesthetics and the relationship of his aesthetics to his later politics has been taken up in several other studies, most often through post-modernist readings which emphasise the inconsistencies and tensions not only in Burke's work but in the intellectual and social climate of the eighteenth century. Tom Furniss (1993), for instance, builds on Kramnick (and Macpherson, 1980) but is concerned to explore Burke's texts through his 'revolutionary aesthetics' without trying to resolve inconsistencies. He sees Burke's key aesthetic categories of the sublime and the beautiful somewhat differently than Kramnick (Kramnick, p. 11). Rather, Furniss sees the texts as 'fissured', 'unmade even in their making' (*ibid.*, p. 9). Furniss's aim is to reveal tensions and what he calls 'instabilities' in Burke's work and his ideological context.

Michael Freeman is another who catches the dualistic Burke. In his time Burke was a

> 'progressive' [i.e., liberal] in that 'he championed the advance of science and the increase of wealth ... If ... Newton and Adam Smith represent 'the Enlightenment' he was for it. If Voltaire does, he was against it ... Burke was a man of two worlds: the world of deference and discipline and the world of free thought and free enterprise' (Freeman, 1980, p. 150).

The principles of the reforming liberal 'and those of his conservative *alter ego*' cannot be fully reconciled according to Freeman (*ibid.*, p. 161). Burke at times 'distinguished sharply' realms of economics and politics (*ibid.*, p. 42). He 'believed in both laissez faire and firm government' (*ibid.*, p. 193). In other words, Burke was a liberal in economics, a conservative in politics.

Burke as a Sceptic

In his earlier treatment of Burke's rage, Kramnick argued that scepticism, especially in relation to the utility of abstract reason, was an important ingredient of Burke's conservatism from his earliest writings. And in the Introduction to his recently revised edition of Burke's writings Kramnick claims that scepticism is 'Burke's most enduring legacy' (Kramnick, 1999, p. 4).

Here what is alleged is that Burke's distrust of the role of reason in social affairs, his 'revolt against the eighteenth century', in Cobban's words (Cobban, 1960), was a revolt against enlightenment faith in the powers of reason, and the role of philosophy and theory. Burke's preferred reliance on custom and his emphasis on the great skills of aristocratic political leadership show him to be a doubter concerning claims of reason to uncover social foundations and, therefore, a conservative with respect to proposals for political and social change.

Several other commentators have addressed Burke's alleged scepticism either directly or indirectly and find the characterisation problematic.

As Freeman points out, if we credit Burke's metaphysical assumptions, he believed that nature was regular and governed by laws which could be appreciated and followed (Freeman, 1980, p. 237ff). And as Hampsher-Monk puts it, Burke actually had an antipathy towards scepticism, which started early and remained a theme in his writings over the course of his life (Hampsher-Monk, 1987, p. 44). Hampsher-Monk, like Freeman, shows that Burke saw scepticism as one of the chief threats to established order (Freeman, 1980, p. 77; Hampsher-Monk, 1987, 1988).

Natural Law Conservative

Burke has also been placed in a conservative historical tradition dating back through St Thomas Aquinas to Aristotle. A number of interpreters (for example, Stanlis, Parkin, Kirk and most recently, Pappin) maintain that natural law, man's fixed nature and a belief in Providence ground all of Burke's political thought.

For those of the Natural Law school Burke was masterfully insightful on the importance of moral leadership. They argue that Burke's articulation of experience, prudence and attention to the particularities of circumstance as paramount characteristics of leadership all went along coherently with his reliance on natural law as the moral basis of politics. In this view Burke wove together religion, natural law and European history not because he thought them useful rhetorical symbols but rather because he believed these were the crucial components of the fabric that made up a decent society. According to this line of thought Burke's teachings remind us that decent societies were – and still are – in danger of being ripped apart by agitators among the intelligentsia and uncultured materialists intent on whipping up the 'swinish multitude' to support subversion.

One of the most recent attempts to set out the Natural Law argument has been presented by Joseph Pappin. Pappin claims that though Burke was 'not a systematic philosopher and certainly not a speculative' one, he was moved by an 'implicit' metaphysics of Natural Law' (Pappin, 1993, p. 44, p. 73). Burke, according to Pappin, is a 'moderate realist' in the Aristotelian–Thomist tradition. The place of Aquinas is crucial to Pappin and other members of the Natural Law school of Burkean interpreters because it is Aquinas they believe who best makes the argument that the informing presence that provides us with natural laws and everything else that is valuable is God. Burke, they believe, is acutely aware of, and fundamentally moved by, the importance of divine providence and the existence of natural law. Pappin's argument is not meant to 'deny compatibility' with treatments of Burke as an empirical, utilitarian or pragmatic (*ibid.*, p. 53); but it is a mistake, says Pappin, to treat Burke as an anti-metaphysician, despite his often derogatory remarks about metaphysics and metaphysicians. His invective is aimed against a 'false metaphysics' (*ibid.*, p. xvi). So it is not philosophy or metaphysical argumentation in general that Burke has in mind as not being useful when confronting practical political questions; it is rather *bogus* philosophy. Pappin refers to this false metaphysic as a 'metaphysical nihilism' which is another name for radical atheism which, he maintains, is at the core of Burke's understanding of, and antipathy towards, Jacobinism. Pappin also says that when Burke speaks of metaphysicians he 'generally has in mind the French philosophers of the Enlightenment' (*ibid.*, p. 19).

Not a Natural Law Theorist

Several major studies have taken issue with the Natural Law school. Leo Strauss's (and Harvey Mansfield Jr.'s) Burke is an intriguing figure. His practical political judgements and activities were consistently 'conservative,' but his theoretical contributions were far from conservative with respect to maintaining the tradition of classical political thought. According to Strauss, Burke's approach to theory and its relationship to practice is radically opposite to Aristotle's. Burke's notion of what makes a polity great is that it develops spontaneously over time, 'the unintended outcome of accidental causation' (Strauss, 1953, pp. 314–15) which is quite at odds with classical political thought since the Greeks were concerned with the good in civil society not as it had become but as it ought to be. Burke's treatment of what is natural in regard to the development of an estimable constitution is also at odds with the classics. For him a sound practice or institution such as a constitution is one that develops as a natural process, and a natural process for Burke is something that takes place without planning, over time; but for Plato and Aristotle, maintains Strauss, to say that something is 'in accordance with nature' means that it fulfils the highest expectations of what humans are capable, in terms of the ideas and 'conscious making' of what is best, not, as Burke would have it, because it has grown up imperceptibly or in his words from 'time out of mind' (Strauss, 1965, p. 314).

From the Straussian perspective, Burke holds a number of key positions that are at odds with classical (Greek) political science. He was anti-theoretical, the Greeks were not. For Greek thought 'the best constitution was a contrivance of reason', a result of conscious design by leaders striving for the optimum achievement for men (*ibid.*, p. 314). In contrast,

Burke's admired constitution is a result of largely unplanned, unsystematic prudential responses over time to local problems and developments. Strauss also notes the importance of Burke's political economy and states that treating the 'love of lucre' as a 'natural, reasonable ... principle', and 'as part of the providential order' as Burke does, 'is diametrically opposed' to classical understandings (Strauss, 1953, pp. 315–16). Though Burke's conservative practical judgements are often sound, according to Strauss, his theoretical understandings and legacy are not, since they have more to do with Hegel than with Aristotle or Aquinas.

For Mansfield, the 'one recurrent theme' in all of Burke's public and private writings is 'his emphasis on the moral and political evils that follow upon the intrusion of theory into political practice' (Mansfield, 1984, p. 4). This, says Mansfield, makes it all the more difficult to accept a version of the importance of natural law in Burke's approach to the exercise of viable politics. Mansfield notes that as a political thinker Burke's focus and trust were on leadership and the class of people and their qualities that afforded them the possibilities of dealing with situations without having to draw on theory. In contrast to a motivation to bring out the best in our souls through politics, or a concern to pursue the best course which brings out the best in ourselves, it is upon 'gentlemanly virtue' that Burke would have us rely, claims Mansfield. And that means that Burke is neither a Thomist nor an Aristotelian (*ibid.*, pp. 18, 25).

According to those like Conniff (1994) and O'Gorman (1973), Burke was much more a pragmatic politician than he was a natural law thinker (Conniff, p. 13). In this regard Conniff is joined by Hampsher-Monk, who says it is a mistake to claim that Burke's theorising is that of a natural law or natural rights advocate 'since he does not see either ... as constituting the irreducible moral reality of political life' (Hampsher-Monk, 1987, p. 40). O'Gorman's Burke is not a philosopher but a skilful politician who reacts to events the way any partisan of Whig interests in mid-eighteenth century England would have.

To Dreyer, Burke was indeed a Whig but a reasonably systematic one, 'in the main remarkably coherent and persistent' (Dreyer, 1979, p. 4). Dreyer claims that Burke's Whig perspectives and actions were largely derived from Lockean principles. It is 'a preoccupation' with alleged, speculated motives and beliefs and the 'neglect of his literal statement which have served more than anything else to confound the study of Burke's political thought' (*ibid.*, p. 5). This puts Dreyer at odds with Pocock's (1985) treatment of Whig departures from Locke, but both share the view that the material and practical interests of the new men of commerce were never far from Burke's attention.

Fasel emphasises the importance of utility for Burke and its connection to Burke's concentration on defence of a good constitution: 'Explicitly or implicitly, nearly all of Burke's political writings and speeches hinged on the supremacy and inviolability of the constitution' (Fasel, 1983, p. 126), He 'wove together his utilitarian and prescriptive arguments' (*ibid.*, p. 126). Fasel makes a case for Burke's consistency by showing that 'like so many men in the eighteenth century, his highest criterion for public acts was social utility, which for all intents and purposes he equated with preservation of the English constitution' (*ibid.*, p. 129). What makes Fasel's approach to the role of utility in Burke's thought especially interesting is that he acknowledges that Burke believed that the constitution and society he valued so highly 'were justified by divine sanction' and that he also believed in the superiority of the new urban commerce. So Burke interlaced what was socially useful, ideas of natural law and the developing market society. In maintaining this stance 'he was consistently conservative' (*ibid.*, p. 129).

Dinwiddy has presented one of the most persuasive and subtle recent re-articulations of the importance of utility in Burke's thought. To Dinwiddy 'an interpretation which treats utility as crucial ... must come to terms not only with [Burke's] references to natural rights but also with the appeals which he certainly did make to natural law' (Dinwiddy, 1974–5, p. 114). Dinwiddy claims that Burke 'clearly believed that the rules of justice and natural law almost invariably did coincide with utility' (*ibid.*, p. 123).

Like most others who have treated Burke as someone who was chiefly disposed to measure the worth of policies by their utility, Dinwiddy sees Burke as 'an unsystematic thinker' who 'certainly appealed on occasions to other criteria' (*ibid.*, p. 110). Since, according to Dinwiddy, there are good reasons to believe that Burke believed that natural law and utility almost always overlapped, in order to make the case for utility as Burke's governing principle 'it is necessary to show that it was only so far as such laws coincided with utility that he regarded them as binding' (*ibid.*, p. 123; Dinwiddy, 1992, p. 247). Dinwiddy cites several passages from Burke as crucial to his case. One of the clearest and most troublesome ones for the natural law advocates comes from Burke's *Appeal From the New to the Old Whigs*. In that work, which is perhaps Burke's most philosophical rendering and defence of the position he set out in the *Reflections*, Burke stated that 'nothing universal can be rationally affirmed on any moral or any political subject'. Dinwiddy also cites a letter Burke wrote to a French colleague about the same time. In that letter Burke said he was not a fanatic about kings, and that his support depended *'par l'utilité de leurs functions'*. And in several other writings he finds Burke saying: 'Old establishments are tried by their effects' and, 'as no moral questions are ever abstract questions ... what it is politically right to grant depends upon ... its effects' (Dinwiddy, 1974–5, p. 126, p. 127; Dinwiddy, 1992, p. 250). To Dinwiddy the evidence is overwhelming that 'utility played a more fundamental part in [Burke's] political thought than did natural law' and the latter 'cannot be rightly regarded as the basis of his political philosophy' (Dinwiddy, 1992, pp. 251–2).

Political Economist

In 1980 C. B. Macpherson set out a forcefully concise argument, replete with textual support, demonstrating that Burke both understood and shared a good deal of the assumptions and arguments of the new political economy associated with the reflections of Adam Smith and the economic liberalism of the eighteenth century. Burke accepted the developing agrarian capitalism as well as the emergence of merchandising entrepreneurship in eighteenth century England and treated both as reflective of laws of commerce that required non-interference by the state. But what was remarkable about Burke's articulation of laissez-faire, bourgeois economic principles, Macpherson stresses, is that he allied those principles with God's providence and natural law. In this regard he treated bourgeois interests and Scottish enlightenment ideas as customary and revered notions of civil life. Macpherson's approach is also an attempt to explain how Burke *could* castigate 'sophisters, economists, calculators' and 'monied men', among others as destructive in France at one point in the *Reflections*, laud landed capitalists at another, and just a few years later write approvingly of 'monied men', with avarice and their 'love of lucre', as 'the grand cause of prosperity to all states' (as quoted by Macpherson, 1980, p. 54). Macpherson suggests that for Burke the subversive monied men having an impact in France were not the gentlemanly sort that had grown up alongside the nobility in Britain but rather 'a *petite-bourgeoisie*, who could not be relied on to uphold established property' (*ibid.*, p. 64). According to Macpherson, if we are to appreciate the connection of Burke's liberal political economy and his conservative support for the manners and institutions of the old order we need to see that for Burke orderly accumulation and its legitimacy required that the ruling class (of aristocrats, gentry and new men of commerce) appreciate the importance of having the common people accept their subordinate place in economics, politics and society generally (*ibid.*, p. 60). Macpherson also argues that while Burke owed a good deal to Locke, he differs from him not only in style but very substantively at times; so that, for instance, where Locke's political philosophy was grounded on natural rights, Burke's was 'grounded on the divinely-ordained *duties* of persons born into submission' (*ibid.*, p. 34).

Macpherson claims that there was no real contradiction between Burke's defence of a hierarchical establishment and his market liberalism because Burke saw that 'his traditional order was already a capitalist one' (*ibid.*, pp. 5–7). What this means is that Burke was a consistent thinker whose theoretical as well as political forays reflected his understanding of the successful marriage in England of aspects of a traditional aristocratic society with the newly developing capitalist market economy (*ibid.*, p. 63). The *Reflections* was an attempt to persuade the English ruling class that the French Revolution 'was an immediate threat to their whole way of life, that is to their property' (*ibid.*, p. 37). Macpherson is not saying that Burke supported a hierarchical society or referred to natural law and religion simply because he regarded them as props for capitalism; although 'he believed that the latter needed the former', he also 'believed in both' (*ibid.*, p. 63).

Almost all serious students of Burke now acknowledge the importance of Macpherson's study, especially in stressing the foundational role that property plays in Burke's thought, though, as we have seen, there are a number of elements or factors that have been advanced as foundational for Burke. Interestingly, several major political theorists holding disparate philosophical and ideological perspectives have come to see Burke very similarly to Macpherson. Pocock, who at one stage in his studies of Burke focused on the common law and notions of an ancient constitution as keys to understanding Burke, has recently written that, despite differences he has had with Macpherson over other interpretative matters, he shares the view that Burke was a 'defender of an aristocratic and commercial order' (Pocock, 1985, p. 209). And Canavan, one of the leading Burke scholars associated with the natural law reading, acknowledges Macpherson's finding that for Burke the political economy of England was not only becoming accommodated to traditional society, the features of two worlds were not only overlapping, they had become one and the same. As Canavan puts it, Burke 'wanted to maintain a traditional order that was already a market economy' (Canavan, 1995, p. 130).

Canavan (1995) emphasises the point that for Burke property is seen as a bulwark of an ordered, civil society led by men of discernment and prudence. As a result, suggests Canavan, Burke favoured paternalistic government by a gentlemanly propertied class whose holdings and background would be sufficiently extensive and virtuous that they would be immune from the vulgar selfishness of those who sought power for fame and fortune. Canavan notes that he and other scholars have long wrestled with the problem of whether Burke's economic theory, closely resembling Adam Smith's, could be properly reconciled with his political thought.

Liberal Opponent of Tyranny and the Abuse of Authority

O'Brien's recent study (1992) is a major attempt to resuscitate a liberal appreciation of a liberal Burke. There is resonance with O'Brien's earlier 'Introduction' (Burke, 1968) to a version of *Reflections* but also an important difference of emphasis. In the 1968 essay O'Brien counselled the left to read Burke as a brilliant *adversary* to understand how reactionaries can think *based* on the *Reflections* and also to learn from his practical, intuitively prescient political responses to abuses of power. O'Brien felt the left was making a huge mistake in not reading Burke. O'Brien also was keen to argue that American conservatives were distorting Burke's legacy when they seconded him as a source for Cold War arguments against the Soviet Union and Marxism. In his latest study, however, O'Brien takes no account of C. B. Macpherson's major interpretation of Burke from a left wing perspective and has come round to an appreciation of Burke's legacy strikingly similar to the Cold War version he earlier rejected. There is 'continuity between French Revolutionary practice and Marxism', now says O'Brien and it is from Burke that we can learn much about the dangers lurking in the background as well as in the practices of both, and about Nazism and the Chinese revolution as well (O'Brien, 1992, p. 598, p. 599). To O'Brien, 'the course and consequences of the three great revolutions of the twentieth century constitute confirmation' of Burke's warnings about trying to build societies according to idealistic theories (*ibid.*, p. 602). But it is a mistake, claims O'Brien, to emphasise a more prescient 'conservative' Burke from the *Reflections* in contrast to an earlier 'liberal' politician. The Burke of the *Reflections* 'is the same as "Burke on the American Revolution," "Burke on India" and "Burke on Ireland"' (*ibid.*, p. 602). Burke's principles and his concerns remained the same, but they were applied to changing, different circumstances where different priorities were required, depending on the circumstances (*ibid.*, p. 602). What moved him in all these instances was the abuse of power (*ibid.*, p. 321).

O'Brien's Burke is no reactionary; he is rather a sensitive, prudent liberal concerned to conserve liberal canons of civility and decency, and a balanced constitution. O'Brien's central theme is that from the time Burke moved to England as a young man Ireland continued to pre-occupy Burke – to haunt him would not be too much to say – throughout his life. It was his awareness and humiliation about English Protestant oppression of the Catholic Irish that explains much of Burke's rage against what he saw as unconscionably unjust in Britain's dealings with America, Warren Hasting's management of the East India Company in India and the attack on aristocratic institutions and conventional arrangements in France. For O'Brien, Burke's rage and sometimes (repressed) revolutionary sentiments stem from his sensitivities to the plight of the disenfranchised Catholic majority in Ireland, his anger at the Popery Laws and his own latent Roman Catholicism. These sensitivities in conjunction with remarkable abilities to measure policy and circumstance are, according to O'Brien, what explain Burke's consistent opposition to political authoritarianism wherever he found it, *not* as Kramnick would have it, because of some repressed homosexuality or bourgeois frustrations, or as the natural law interpreters would have it, because of theoretical commitments to classical philosophy. O'Brien treats Burke as an outsider who had to conceal his true convictions. For O'Brien the deceptive Burke is nevertheless a noble and liberal politician, one who was consistent in addressing major issues from a liberal's practical sensibilities about the importance of defending liberty and speaking out against the abuse of power.

Another attempt to reclaim Burke as a solid, practically-minded eighteenth-century Whig moved by 'the interests and well-being of the people as a whole' has been recently discussed in an essay by Eagleton (Eagleton, 1998, p. 137). To Eagleton, though Burke was 'no radical, no democrat... he never ceased to campaign against sleaze-ridden elites, out of touch with the sentiments of the common people' and he would probably have delighted in the recent downfall of the Tory Government (Eagleton, 1997, p. 33). Modern day conservatives may share his respect for tradition but not 'his passion for social justice' (*ibid.*, p. 33). Eagleton argues that a defence of customary rights rather than abstract ones can sometimes be politically radical and he claims that Burke 'magnificently urged' respect for 'local cultural conditions'. Burke's work, says Eagleton, 'has been a major influence in what has been called the "Culture and Society" tradition in England and much of his writing can be seen as a powerful critique of industrial capitalism' (*ibid.*, p. 32). According to Eagleton 'nothing could be more of an affront to [Burke's] values than the neo-liberalism of our own time' and 'modern-day market forces represent, in Burkean terms, a virulent new strain of Jacobinism, even if the abstract dogmas in question are now those of Brussels bankers rather than French philosophers' (*ibid.*, p. 33). Burke's principal opposition to the French Revolution was 'not so much because he disagreed with their political views, though he certainly did, but because he thought those views spelt the death of political society as such' (*ibid.*, p. 33; 1998, p. 135).

Burke No Liberal

To Herzog (1998) it is a serious mistake to treat Burke as a liberal who might have things to teach us today or as a thinker concerned about the common people. Herzog is concerned to explore the claims and appeal of English social conservatism, and Burke's place in it. Herzog's Burke is very different from the heroic figure depicted by O'Brien and Eagleton. Herzog draws our attention to Burke's opposition to extending political liberties and the franchise to the majority. He emphasises Burke's contempt for hair-dressers and candle-makers and his anxieties about the potential politicisation of those in 'the lower orders', the uppity 'swinish multitude', and the implications of their becoming 'citizens' instead of 'subjects'. For Herzog, Burke is best understood as an anti-democrat for his times and ours. He used an assortment of arguments as it suited him to defend the practices and principles of an inegalitarian society. Burke had 'capacious sleeves' (Herzog, 1998, p. 23). When it suited him and his party's purpose, he could toss tradition and ancient principles to the wind. Herzog quotes Burke's comment (as does Freeman, 1980), that 'with regard to America, policy based on abstract principles of government or even upon those of our own ancient constitution will often be misled ... the object is wholly new in the world' (Herzog, 1998, p. 21).

Herzog's Burke opposed democracy, democratic debate, and transparency on principle. Herzog also directs attention to the thinness of Burke's cele-brated defence of religious toleration when he shows that Burke's writings were replete with derogatory remarks about Jews (*ibid.*, p. 516). Herzog brings out Burke's contempt for Jews, labourers and atheists, which collides with notions (such as, Williams, 1996) that Burke can instruct us about the need to accommodate marginalised groups. To Herzog, Burke's defence of prejudice and privilege and his actual prejudices are indications of both his illiberalism and his anti-democratic convictions.

Rhetorician and Dramatist

A number of recent studies (such as, Blakemore, 1992; White, 1993, 1994; Furniss, 1993; Hindson and Gray, 1988; Reid, 1985; De Bruyn, 1996, and to some extent Hampsher-Monk, 1987), draw attention to Burke's style, his reliance on rhetoric and his fascination with aesthetic qualities. To Browning, Burke's 'greatest contribution' was 'the garbing of a body of received doctrine in the dress of imaginative language. It is his rhetorical talent that accounts for his achievements. And his achievements were largely to extend Walpole's Court Whiggery with the aid of an artful adap-tation of Cicero' (Browning, 1984, p. 71). To De Bruyn, Burke can be more fully comprehended if we take account of the 'persistent weaving of literary forms into his political discourse', especially his adoption of

Scriblerian satire from writers like Swift and Pope and his reliance on the 'discourse of improvement prevalent in eighteenth-century English society', which 'can be traced back to Virgil's *Georgics*' (De Bruyn, 1996, p. 6, p. 7, p. 65). Burke's 'literary accomplishment' was 'in appropriating the formal literary tradition of the georgic' in ways that melded 'the ideology of improvement' with the country's traditional political and social structures' (*ibid.*, p. 110).

Hindson and Gray (1988) treat Burke as a dramatist who sees the world as a stage. Neither Kramnick nor Macpherson, according to Hindson and Gray, provide a comprehensive enough framework for understanding the fullness of Burke's work; and the pragmatic and natural law interpretations make the mistake of treating Burke as consistently articulating a political doctrine. So a new interpretation is required, one that bridges Burke's political and literary aspirations and that appreciates his rhetorical style without ignoring the political message. Burke's political theorising then, is best understood as a 'dramatic understanding of the moral and political organisation of society': he saw politics as a performance and 'parliament the place for drama, the theatre ... the place for politics' (*ibid.*, p. 28, p. 29). In contrast to a natural law theorist, Burke should be understood as seeing the world and depicting it through the eyes of a writer of tragedies. 'He had the constant worry that God had abandoned the human world and was now embarked upon its destruction' (*ibid.*, p. 124). In this view, Burke saw Britain as 'a tragic society in the classical mould ... [where] man was taught there [is] no alternative to the misery of his existence. This was genuine or true tragedy' in contrast to France's 'vulgar tragedy or tragicomedy ... the dramatic version of the creed of solipsism' propelled by 'fanatic energy' (*ibid.*, p. 131). Drama allowed Burke 'to challenge the basic orthodoxy of the social contract and to replace it with a belief in the purpose of human life, as dictated by the divine plot of the world' (*ibid.*, p. 80).

Somewhat like Hindson and Gray, Reid holds that for Burke the House of Commons was a stage for oratorical showmanship (Reid, 1985, p. 98). Reid argues that 'it is the dominance of a specifically agrarian form of capitalism, and the social and cultural life which arises from it, that Burke is concerned to uphold' (*ibid.*, p. 221). It is the remarkable style of that defence, Burke's rhetoric, which, Reid believes, needs greater appreciation than has been the case. Burke believed, according to Reid, that developing arguments and describing political scenarios with rhetorical flourish was the best way of bringing out the complexities of British and human history and his political discourse was shaped by rhetorical skill. Reid shows that Burke was conscious of the importance of using different styles and different idioms of rhetoric to make his points: to quote Burke, 'One style to a gracious benefactor, another to a proud and insulting foe'. At one point Reid goes so far as to say that Burke, 'perceives the French Revolution in aesthetic terms' (*ibid.*, p. 38), that the *Reflections* is mainly about a critique of language, an argument also made by Blakemore (1988). Blakemore tries to argue that the jumble and disaster of the Tower of Babylon provides a motif for the book, despite the fact that Burke hardly ever uses the term.

In noting Burke's accusation that the French revolutionaries were bent on dismantling a politics which incorporated 'sentiments which beautify and soften private society' and 'all the pleasing illusions which make power gentle and obedience liberal' Reid holds that Burke drew upon 'the psychological and aesthetic vocabulary of the *Philosophical Enquiry*'. He did so, according to Reid, to produce a style of writing and a political response that would elicit a challenge to the spread of the revolutionary movement (*ibid.*, p. 41).

Evaluation

Burke's effect on his interpreters shows that he is a thinker who provides an enormous scope for diverse appreciations. Burke can be seen as holding liberal and conservative, progressive and reactionary views, as differing interpretations have brought out. He can be turned to for cautions about the results we might expect of efforts to bring about wide-sweeping change, for reminders about the need to respect limits to power and for reminders about the variety of arguments that can be marshalled in support of privilege and inequality. He attempted to show the importance of combining the old with the new, aristocratic ways and capitalism, that men of ability can manage an accommodation with class deference and privilege – and that it was all ordained by God. Whether he is better understood as a conservative liberal or liberal conservative will continue to divide both his admirers and critics. Perhaps the closer we come to understanding Burke the more we will see that for him there would be little to distinguish one from the other: Old Whiggery encapsulated both.

For all the reasons we have drawn attention to – and we could have added more – Burke has been both an interpreter's dream and nightmare. What should be clear is that, depending on what aspects of his activities and writings one chooses to emphasise, Burke's various reflections will continue to have an appeal to a wide variety of movements and theorists. Despite some very persuasive recent attempts to unravel the obstacles to understanding him, he will remain a fascinating and frustrating political thinker to fully comprehend. In terms of the elasticity of interpretations of Burke there are also limits that need to be remembered.

Burke's alleged scepticism has to have room for – or has to be explained
as reconcilable with – his view that 'we must suppose' that people are in a
'state of habitual social discipline' (*Appeal*, as cited by Macpherson, 1980,
p. 44) and that 'no discoveries are to be made in morality; nor many in the
great principles of government' (Burke, 1968, p. 182). Scepticism about the
description of Burke as a sceptic is supported by Burke's own words about
the importance of prejudice. Reliance on prejudice, he maintained, means
that the individual is not left 'hesitating in the moment of decision, sceptical, puzzled, and unresolved' (*ibid.*, p. 183); through prejudice virtue
becomes a habit, 'duty becomes a part of [our] nature' (*ibid.*, p. 182). For
Burke this means that 'Instead of casting away all our old prejudices, we
cherish them because they are prejudices' (*ibid.*, p. 183). But all of this,
including Burke's confidence that he has discovered God's laws animating
and governing the pursuit of profit, means that instead of being a doubter,
Burke is *sure* about a number of things socially, politically, morally and
economically.

Furthermore, if we understand scepticism as doubt, doubt about origins,
foundations, and claims to knowledge concerning, or flowing from, religion, and a sceptic as an agnostic or atheist – and these are the meanings
the words had for Burke and his contemporaries – then Burke is no sceptic.
To Burke scepticism is at odds with religious belief and is a weapon in the
arsenal of the Jacobins. The Irish devotion to Roman Catholicism is
defended as 'the most effectual barrier, if not the sole barrier, against
Jacobinism' because devotion to religion keeps the 'the great body of the
lower ranks' protected from the 'seduction' of the radicals. 'Let them grow
lax, sceptical, careless, and indifferent with regard to religion,' says Burke,
'and so sure as we have an existence, it is not a zealous Anglican or Scottish
Church principle, but direct Jacobinism, which will enter into that breach'
(cited in Kramnick, 1999, p. 358).

While acknowledging the importance of Burke's appeal to feelings along
with prejudice in support of his generalisations about acceptable 'English'
ways of seeing the world, there are significant problems in accepting claims
about the importance his earlier sensationist philosophy (or psychology)
and aesthetic vocabulary have in relation to the *Reflections*. First, the text
that is so important to literary, psychological and postmodernist readings of
Burke's meaning, his *Philosophical Enquiry into the Origin of our Ideas of
the Sublime and Beautiful* (1958), was written in his twenties, long before
he entered political life and there is scant evidence that Burke referred to it
in his later political speeches or writings. Second, when he uses words like
'sublime' and 'beautiful' in the *Reflections* he does so in a very conventional, not philosophical manner, occasionally ironically or sarcastically

(there is a good deal of both in the work) but almost never in a manner reminiscent of the psychological renderings set out in the *Enquiry*. What studies such as Kramnick's, Reid's and Furniss's provide (and this is also true of recent work by Eagleton, 1998; White, 1993, 1994; Zerilli, 1994) are suggestive ways of enriching our understandings of both the social and ideological contexts and the role that sexual assumptions and tensions may have played in the lives of major thinkers. Unfortunately, these explorations depend on a great deal of 'reading into' texts and situations, and much speculation about what is between the lines, hidden or 'haunted' but implicated. We get imaginatively creative interpretative leaps and psychological assumptions about connections between texts and motivations, but it is not clear that we get a better hold on Burke.

There are also problems with attempts to reinterpret Burke as essentially a dramatist, in Shakespearean terms, as someone seeing all the world as a stage. The words 'drama', 'theatre' and 'tragedy' are found in the *Reflections* but their frequency certainly cannot be compared with the myriad occasions Burke uses the word 'property' and its referents, or 'God', 'religion' and 'providence'. It is salient that when Burke specifically refers to the theatre, it is to point out the difference between the real tragedy taking place in France that is mystifying to many and what an audience would see as shockingly outrageous were it to be acted out on stage: 'No theatric audience in Athens would bear what has been borne in the midst of the real tragedy of this triumphal day' (Burke, 1968, p. 176).

Similar difficulties attend efforts to depict Burke as a theorist mainly concerned to lament the abuse of language. Contentions that the *Reflections* is an outcry against the killing of language (logocide), and that the Tower of Babel is a central metaphor of Burke's have little textual support and are distorting. There is one specific reference to Babylon in the *Reflections*. Burke does indeed on occasion refer to the abuse and manipulative use of language on the part of the 'literary cabal' of *philosophes*, but most often his references to language abuse have to do with the English supporters of the revolutionaries. That should hardly come as a surprise: Burke would have been on shaky ground trying to comment on, let alone correct, the language use of persons whose language was not his own.

What mainly provokes Burke is neither the language nor the rhetoric of the Jacobins but rather their attack on religion, property, traditional authority and established place. Treating Burke as a theorist principally motivated by engagement with rhetoric and language use elevates his own considerable rhetorical talents, his sometimes eloquent language, sometimes purple prose, past the substantive social and cultural concerns he sought to address, and has the effect of diminishing the importance of his attempt to delineate the differences between what he took to be legitimate and illegitimate politics.

Despite the fact that Burke often makes reference to the importance of religion, nature and the moral law there are difficulties with the case for Burke belonging to the Aristotelian–Thomistic tradition (Pappin, 1993, p. 53). The case against his being understood in that way has been strongly advanced by Strauss and Mansfield. It is difficult to reconcile Burke's advocacy of the importance of accumulation and his defence of the love of lucre with either Aristotle's view that a life devoted to accumulation was unnatural or Thomas's Catholic condemnation of greed. And the trouble with Pappin's assertion that when Burke was dismissive of metaphysics he had in mind the *philosophes* is that it is unsustainable. As Macpherson notes, with pertinent supporting quotations, Burke denigrated any resort to metaphysics and abstract theorising well before he came to consider the appeal of the *philosophes* (Macpherson, 1980, p. 15).

To the extent that one branch of Whiggery is a liberal legacy which in turn has a branch associated with 'affirmative government' and the importance of moderating support for individual acquisition by a commitment to governmental initiatives, regulations and standards, Burke's Whig views are outside that tradition. They are also some distance away from contemporary neo-liberalism which, while in agreement with much of Burke's political economy, is emphatically secular in its approach to political affairs. Given his own terms and time he is much more an Old Whig than a modern liberal, whether of the welfare or 'neo' variety. To the extent that the liberal legacy since John Stuart Mill has been associated with support for the expansion of a democratic franchise and of democracy generally, Burke again is not part of that trajectory. He is no liberal democrat.

Because of his affinities for unwritten constitutions, his discomfort with abstract notions of rights and his anti-republicanism he will always be difficult for American conservatives to embrace unhesitatingly. His belief in keeping economic activity independent of governmental scrutiny, his view that governments have no obligations to improve the conditions of the least advantaged and that individuals have no social obligations where the exercise of their property rights are concerned, mean that the left cannot find his recommendations or brand of political economy attractive. However conservative his liberalism, or liberal his conservatism, Burke was no democrat and cannot be made into one without neglecting much that is central to his political thinking and activities, and making him turn in his grave. For that reason, and because we live at a time when democracy has come to have clearly positive connotations, as well it should, there are limits to the pull of Burkean insights and the utility of his thought to the practical politics of our day.

7

Kant (1724–1804)

KATRIN FLIKSCHUH

Introduction

Until recently Kant's political philosophy was little known and often badly understood. His principal political works – the *Metaphysical Elements of Justice* (*MEJ*), which forms the first part of his *Metaphysics of Morals* (*MM*), as well as shorter political essays such as *On Perpetual Peace* – were seriously studied by only a handful of Kant scholars. Most political theorists did not think Kant's political writings sufficiently distinctive to warrant their inclusion on courses in the history of modern political thought. This assessment changed radically with the publication of John Rawls' *A Theory of Justice* (1972). In what has become the most important work in contemporary liberalism, Rawls developed a theory of justice which claimed to be inspired by a specifically *Kantian* understanding of liberalism. Rawls's contention raised the question as to what it is about Kant's political thinking that justifies its characterisation as a distinctive conception of liberalism. The attempt to answer this question in relation to Rawls's work led to a revival of interest in Kant's own political writings.

A second reason for the revival of interest in Kant has to do with a growing minority among contemporary political theorists who believe the heyday of the single nation state to be over. In the face of increasing globalisation, political theory needs to re-orient itself, so these thinkers urge, by paying greater attention to global rather than domestic political developments and their theoretical implications. The fact that Kant is virtually the only one among Western political thinkers in the liberal tradition explicitly to adopt a cosmopolitan position makes him a natural ally of current proponents of global justice.

Although it has not always been so in the past, current interpreters appreciate the importance of assessing Kant's political thinking within the context of his wider epistemological and moral concerns. In his *Critique of Pure Reason* (*CPR*), Kant defends a theory of knowledge that constitutes a critique of rationalist and empiricist philosophical traditions alike. Central to this critique is his conception of human beings as finite rational beings. In *CPR* Kant argues against the rationalist philosophers that human knowledge cannot extend beyond objects of sensible experience; it cannot, for example, extend to rational knowledge of the existence of God. However, he simultaneously argues against empiricism that human knowledge of the sensible world is not simply a matter of passive sensory perception. For Kant, our capacity to conceptualise *as* objects the sensibly given 'manifold' which we perceive is a prerequisite to our having any knowledge of the empirical world at all. We do not simply and passively perceive the world as it is independently of our rational and perceptual capacities; rather, we impose a conceptual framework upon our sensory perceptions and in so doing 'make' the world into what, for us, it is. From the present perspective, the important point in all this is that although Kant thinks of human powers of rational knowledge as limited or 'finite', he nonetheless regards their rational capacities as both an active and a creative power within human beings.

The significance of this conception of the creativity of human reason is evident in Kant's moral philosophy, of which his political thought forms a part. While rational knowledge of objects beyond sensible experience is ruled out, Kant argues that since human reasoning is an active power, we are able to form concepts or ideas which, although they have no corresponding *object* in sensible experience, nonetheless are of practical relevance to us. The concept of duty, for example, has no corresponding object in the world. Nonetheless, we can form the concept of duty, not least because it is indispensable to our practical reasoning about action. Likewise, there is no *object* in the world, to which the concept of justice refers. Yet we can form a conception of justice and give it practical reality. Kant's famous categorical imperative, that is, his supreme principle of morality, is not an object of knowledge. It is an action-guiding principle of moral self-legislation, which is generated from within the resources of creative human reasoning itself, and which enjoins agents to 'act only on that maxim through which [they] can at the same time will that it should become a universal law' (Kant, 1964, p. 88). How precisely the categorical imperative is to be interpreted need not concern us here (Ebbinghaus, 1967). But it is important to be aware that Kant's universal principle of justice, as set out in *MEJ*, is a derivative of the categorical imperative, indicating the systematic connections between Kant's epistemology and his moral and political thinking.

Let us summarise some of the themes in Kant's political thinking that have made him particularly relevant for problems that beset contemporary political philosophy. At the more abstract level we have the question concerning the status of human reason and its role in political justification – an issue taken up most famously by Rawls, mentioned above. At a more substantive level, many perceive Kant's enduring legacy to lie in his cosmopolitan commitments. However, these two distinctively Kantian areas of philosophical and political concern should not detract from some of the more conventional issues of liberal political theory, which we can also find in Kant. The question of political obligation, and closely connected to this the problem of individual property rights, greatly preoccupied him, as did the problem of the right, or otherwise, to legitimate political resistance – an issue which became especially topical in the wake of the French Revolution. All of these seemingly diverse and wide-ranging issues find their unity in Kant's enduring struggle to reconcile the often seemingly contradictory claims of justice and individual freedom.

Problems and Issues

I suggested that the two aspects from his epistemology and his moral philosophy which influence Kant's political thought are his conception of individuals as finite rational beings and his account of agents as moral self-legislators. For Kant, human freedom consists in agents' capacity for self-legislation. Finitude and freedom are related. We have seen that for Kant, human knowledge is finite: it cannot go beyond knowledge of objects in this world. Yet human finitude is not something to be regretted. If we were omniscient, such that we had knowledge of everything in and beyond sensible experience, we would know the complete course of events as it extends backwards and forwards in time. Being in a state of complete certainty, there would be no point to entertaining the notion of alternate possibilities, of how things *could* be. It would be futile to hope that human beings are able to determine their fate in the world. Yet human beings do entertain hopes about the future; they do entertain the notion of alternate possibilities. For Kant, the practical capacity to form a conception of a possible (that is, not pre-determined) future, the capacity to act on that conception, and the capacity to take responsibility for having so acted *is* the capacity for freedom. Lack of complete knowledge, or human finitude, makes possible the idea of freedom.

This is not incompatible with the characterisation of freedom as moral self-legislation. Consider the fact of our co-existence with others. If it is to be morally defensible, the exercise of my freedom must not conflict with the exercise of everyone else's freedom. A person's freedom lies in their capacity for future-oriented action *within* the constraints of the categorical imperative as the supreme principle of morality. This conception of freedom as self-constrained agency differs from the Hobbesian view, according to which individual freedom consists in the 'absence of external impediments': a person is free when nothing and no one prevents that person from carrying out a desired course of action. There is no notion of moral self-restraint built into the Hobbesian account. Kant's idea of freedom is closer to that of Rousseau. Rousseau, too, draws a strong connection between human freedom and responsibility for action. According to Rousseau, the moral depravity of 'civilised man' is entirely the responsibility of civilised man himself. But, the possibility for moral reform also lies within civilised man. Man is as capable of bettering himself as he is capable of depraving himself: freedom consists in choosing either the one historical possibility or the other. Kant parts company with Rousseau concerning the *political implications* of such a conception of freedom. For Rousseau, individual freedom is truly achievable only within the collective. The individual will dissolves itself with all others in the General Will. By contrast, Kant's conception of freedom affirms the separateness of persons; he shies away from Rousseau's suggestion that individuals can be 'forced to be free'.

Here we come to a crucial juncture in Kant's practical philosophy, namely the separation between ethics and politics. Ethics teaches virtue; politics is concerned with principles of justice. Thus, ethics and politics form two distinct branches of morality. Ethics relates to the *moral purity* of a person's will, that is, to a person's internal disposition towards herself and others. Precisely for this reason the state cannot legislate with respect to virtue. Many interpreters have concluded that, because Kant does not regard politics as part of ethics, he does not view it as part of morality. They have further inferred that, for Kant, political agency is amoral. Others argue that Kant's distinction between politics and ethics does not mean that political agency is amoral: Kant merely distinguishes between ethical duties and juridical duties. However, both types of duty are grounded in morality. The disagreement over motivational incentives in relation to political agency is one of the issues of interpretation to be considered below.

But on what is the distinction between ethical duties and juridical duties based? Let us return to Kant's conception of freedom. Two of its components are the capacity for future-oriented deliberation about action and the capacity for moral self-legislation. Yet freedom does not merely consist in the freedom to *deliberate* within the constraints of the categorical imperative. An equally important component of freedom is the notion of *choice*. We must be able to choose to do one thing rather than another. In translating our practical deliberations into actions, we have to make use of objects by means of which to realise our intentions. Freedom of choice implies the use of external objects of one's choice. This gives rise to the problem of property rights and to the further problem of the co-existence of a multitude of individuals, each of whom claims the right to freedom of choice and action. Whether Kant construes the ensuing obligations of justice in contractarian terms, or whether he is closer to the natural law tradition is a further issue of interpretation to be considered below.

However he resolves the problem of political obligation, the crucial question is whether Kant goes further than those liberals, such as Locke, and to some degree Hume, who tend to regard the protection of private property under the institutions of the state as the ultimate end of just politics. Is the establishment of individual states that secure justice between individuals at the national level an end in itself, or is it merely one step towards a higher political end, one that is expressed in Kant's cosmopolitan idea of the world citizen? Again, views differ as to how Kant conceives the relation between individual (property) rights, state sovereignty, and cosmopolitan justice.

Why Conflicting Interpretations?

While the problem of interpretation is often regarded as peculiar to the study of historical texts, we are always constrained to interpret the meaning of each other's propositions. True, in contrast to our contemporaries, we cannot ask past thinkers for clarification of their arguments. Still, semantic ambiguity is built into language use and communication: not everyone is struck by the same passages in a given text, and virtually no one interprets their significance in exactly the same way. A second source for differences in interpretation stems from interpreters' political perspectives, and the way in which these colour conflicting readings of a text. Thus, Rawls, whom I mentioned above, interprets Kant by the lights of twentieth-century liberalism in the United States. His reading differs from those more interested in the historical context of Kant's political writings as well as from those who seek in Kant not so much an ally of, as an alternative to, contemporary liberalism. Thirdly, we can speak of dominant theoretical paradigms in terms of which historical texts tend to be interpreted. Contemporary liberalism overwhelmingly adopts the contractarian framework, inviting a presumption in favour of Kant as a contractarian thinker. Yet dominant paradigms encourage the emergence of dissenting voices, which urge, for example, a natural law interpretation of Kant as a plausible alternative.

Aside from these general reasons for differences of interpretation, there are differences relating to Kant interpretation more specifically.

I mention three, though there are more. First, Kant's epistemology is radical and controversial. Not everyone accepts his view of human beings' limited knowledge of the world. Many also reject Kant's metaphysical conception of freedom as an idea of reason. Such fundamental epistemological and metaphysical disagreements influence a reader's interpretation of Kant's political thought: past interpreters, for example, often interpreted Kant from an empiricist perspective. Second, *MEJ* is beset by text-internal problems of organisation and cohesion, which make its systematic interpretation a forbidding task. What is more, Kant's political writings span a period of more than three decades. He changed his views on some issues, without always explicitly acknowledging these changes. One example is his early view on property rights, which was close to Locke's labour theory of property, compared to his mature view in *MEJ* where he repudiates the Lockean view. A second example concerns Kant's views regarding the possibility or desirability of a world state. In some essays Kant endorses the idea of a world state, in others he advocates a confederation of free republics instead. It is a matter of interpretation which of these conflicting arguments represents Kant's considered view. Third, there is the problem of terminological clarification, or the lack thereof. In several of his writings, Kant mentions the 'idea of a social contract', for example. The term 'social contract' has a well-established meaning in the history of political thought. Kant's characterisation of it as an 'idea of reason' is unusual and unexplained. Is his *'idea* of a social contract' in keeping with the standard assumptions of contractarian thinking, or does it diverge from those standard assumptions? Again, this is a matter of (conflicting) interpretation.

Conflicting Interpretations

This section surveys different interpretations of some of the problems and issues outlined above. The focus will be on the three related issues briefly discussed above in the context of Kant's general conception of freedom. Recapitulating, they include: (i) Kant's conception of political agency; (ii) his account of political obligation; (iii) his view of the scope of duties of justice.

The Self-Interest Interpretation

Kant's separation of politics from ethics has given him the reputation of being a 'Hobbesian' in relation to political agency. According to this view, Kant advocates dutiful action in his ethical writings but endorses acting from self-interest in politics. Note that if Kant does hold this view, this may expose him to the charge of inconsistency. If individuals' capacity for freedom as moral self-legislation consists in their ability to act from duty, the view that in politics individuals act from self-interest implies that they are *not* self-legislators with respect to politics. The need for a Hobbesian sovereign as one who legislates *for* everyone then becomes evident. Yet Kant is also widely regarded as an advocate of republicanism. The latter is inconsistent with appeals to an absolute sovereign. What accounts for this seemingly problematic Hobbesian interpretation of Kant?

Kant says conflicting things about political motivation. In *Perpetual Peace* he famously remarks that, 'the problem of setting up a state can be solved even by a nation of devils (so long as they possess understanding)' (Kant, 1970, p. 112). This could be interpreted as saying that individuals need not be moral to enter the civil condition: they only require a good understanding of their self-interest. The most sophisticated Hobbesian interpreter of Kant is Otfried Höffe (Höffe, 1989, 1992). Höffe recognises that the attribution to Kant of self-interest as the principal source of political motivation has its difficulties. Kant's 'universal principle of justice' is derived from the categorical imperative: 'any action is right if it can coexist with everyone's freedom in accordance with a universal law' (Kant, 1991, p. 56). Consistent with the categorical imperative, the universal principle of justice rules out as non-universalisable, hence as unjust, all actions the commission of which by any one agent would violate the conditions of others' freedom of choice. But if the categorical imperative is the supreme principle of morality, how can its derivative principle be prudential? Höffe points to a passage in *MM* in which Kant says that

> [a]ll lawgiving can be distinguished with respect to the incentive. That lawgiving which makes an action a duty and also makes the duty the incentive is ethical. But that action which ... admits an incentive other than the idea of duty is juridical. It is clear that in the latter case the incentive ... must be drawn from aversions, for it is a lawgiving, which constrains, not an allurement, which invites (Kant, 1991, p. 46).

Kant appears to be saying that in contrast to ethical action, where the incentive is the idea of duty, the incentive of political action is individuals' prudential self-interest – their aversion against suffering the sanctions of the state in cases of non-compliance with the universal principle of Right. This sounds Hobbesian: in so far as they fear the state's sanctions, it is in individuals' rational self-interest to abide by the universal principle of justice. While Hobbes holds that whatever the sovereign decrees as just must be acknowledged as such by the subjects, Kant derives his conception of justice from the principle of morality. In contrast to Hobbes's voluntarism,

Kant proffers objectively valid criteria of justice. Nonetheless, by Höffe's interpretation, individuals act in accordance with the moral requirements of justice on the basis of their rational self-interest, that is, because they fear the sanctions of the state.

Höffe's prudential interpretation of Kant's conception of political agency leads him to a contractualist reading of Kant's account of political obligation. Again some textual evidence supports this reading. Thus Kant declares that

> [n]o one is bound to refrain from encroaching on what another possesses if the other gives him no equal assurance that he will observe the same restraint towards him. ... [W]hat should bind him to wait till he has suffered a loss before he becomes prudent, when he can quite well perceive within himself the inclination of men generally to lord it over others as their master (not to respect the superiority of the rights of others when they feel superior to them in strength or cunning)? (Kant, 1991, p. 122)

The passage is reminiscent of Hobbes's remark that 'one man is another man's wolf'. Mutual distrust and the resulting need to 'bind the other' lead to entrance into civil society. However, Höffe acknowledges that Kantian individuals do not, as in Hobbes, give up their individual rights to an all-powerful sovereign. Rather, they contract with one another because they each recognise that the requirements of mutual restraint are a logical implication of the situation they find themselves. Under conditions of social coexistence and the claims to freedom of each,

> the result is not that there must be a restriction, still less that there must be a law. These would be normative statements, perhaps moral statements, which have no place in a pre-moral duty [sic] of obeying the law. The result is, rather simply, [that] restriction ... is unavoidable from the social perspective (Höffe, 1989, p. 164).

Rational self-interested Kantians contract with one another not because they acknowledge that they owe each other duties of justice, but because they recognise that the logic of their situation rationally requires mutual assurances concerning each other's freedom.

Höffe's views on Kant's cosmopolitanism are Hobbesian to an extent. He asks why Kant initially favoured the idea of a 'world republic' but eventually settled on the idea of a 'federation of free republics' (1995, pp. 109–32). Kant's change of heart, Höffe argues, was based on pragmatic considerations. Although the later Kant claims that his erstwhile idea of a world republic is a contradiction in terms, Höffe believes him to be mistaken about this. Kant argues that the idea of a world republic requires free republics to restrict their sovereignty and to submit to the superior legislative power of a world government. But this is a form of despotism, not republicanism. Kant concludes that the idea of a world *republic* is self-contradictory. But, counters Höffe, Kant does not regard it as self-contradictory that individuals should give up part of their freedom to submit to the government of their state. Since Kant draws an explicit analogy between individuals and states as moral agents, he is inconsistent in detecting a self-contradiction in the one case but not in the other. Höffe concludes that Kant's real reasons for rejecting the idea of a world republic lie not so much in thinking the idea contradictory as believing its practical realisation to be non-feasible. Since states love to wield power, and since they do not trust one another, they will never agree to cede their sovereignty to a higher authority. Given individual states' self-interest, a world republic is not realisable. Kant therefore settles on the pragmatic solution of a federation of republics. Höffe thus offers a thoroughgoing prudentialist interpretation of Kant. Not only individuals at the domestic level, but also states at the international level are fundamentally motivated by rational self-interest.

The Consensus Interpretation

In a series of recent essays Paul Guyer (Guyer, 2000) offers a different contractarian interpretation of Kant's political philosophy. Although Guyer acknowledges Kant's distinction between ethics and politics, he emphasises that it is internal to morality. Hence juridical duties cannot be grounded in self-interest. True, the state has authority to enforce the demands of justice where individuals do not freely act in accordance with them. But the normative grounds of the state's juridical authority lie in individuals' capacity to acknowledge the moral authority of the universal principle of justice as a principle of self-legislation.

Guyer, too, can offer textual support for his interpretation. Kant affirms that

> [I]n contrast to the laws of nature, the laws of freedom are called moral laws. As directed merely to external actions and their conformity to law they are called juridical laws; but if they also require that they (the laws) themselves be the determining grounds of actions, they are ethical laws, and then one says that conformity with juridical laws is the legality of an action and conformity with ethical laws is its morality (Kant, 1991, p. 42).

Here Kant distinguishes not between different motivational incentives, but between different spheres of moral competence. While juridical duties are indeed externally enforceable in a way in which ethical duties are not, it does not follow that we honour duties of justice merely because we fear the sanctions of the state. According to Guyer's interpretation, we recognise that juridical duties are one particular type of moral duty, distinct from ethics, which we owe each other.

As suggested earlier, juridical duties are intimately connected with property rights. The problem of property rights arises for Kant in connection with the idea of external freedom. The right to freedom of choice and action implies a right to external objects of our choice – property rights. Unlike Locke, Kant does not think that we have a *natural* right to property. According to Locke, our natural right to property is an extension of our natural right in our own person: we acquire property by mixing our labour with objects. Kant, and Guyer with him, disagree: 'property rights consist not in an immediate relation between a person and an object, but in a relation among persons' (Guyer, 2000, p. 245). In order for me to claim rightful ownership of an object, mere acquisition of the object is not sufficient. Rightful ownership requires others' consent to my claiming the object as mine: while the *claim* to property arises from the innate right to freedom of each, the *right* to property depends on others' consent. The mutual acknowledgement of the rightful claim of each to external objects of their choice leads to the formation of civil society. Individuals agree to acknowledge the legitimacy of each other's claims to property. The function of civil society is not, as in Locke, the guarantee and protection of natural property rights. For Kant, there are no property rights prior to civil society: there is only the legitimate claim to such rights. Thus, 'the right of the state to control the distribution of property or wealth is a consequence of the fact that the possibility of the rational consent of all to the distribution of property is a necessary condition of the existence of property at all' (*ibid.*, p. 258).

While Guyer's account of the entrance into civil society is contractual, it is non-prudential. Contractual agreement is based on consensus regarding the moral requirements of justice as implied by the legitimate claim of each to external freedom. Turning to Kant's cosmopolitanism, Guyer's position is consistent with his initial assumption that individuals act justly on moral rather than prudential grounds. The achievement of global peace is not possible in the absence of a firm moral intention to work towards peace. Prudential motives cannot stand in for morally good intentions. Only the latter can secure a lasting peace among nations. In some of his political essays Kant makes much of the 'mechanism of nature' compelling men to peace 'even against their will', implying a prudential view regarding the reasons for peace among nations. Yet even granting that institutions of peace can be *established* on the basis of merely prudential motives, Guyer argues that 'these institutions can be *maintained* only as a result of an explicitly moral intention to establish world peace' (*ibid.*, p. 418).

Kant's contrast, in *Perpetual Peace*, between the 'political moralist' and the 'moral politician' illustrates this. The political moralist will use morality to serve her own prudential ends. The moral politician will acknowledge that the highest goal of politics is to realise the moral ends of global peace, and she will adjust her political actions in accordance with this moral aim.

The Teleological Interpretation

Different again is Patrick Riley's (Riley, 1983) teleological interpretation. Like Höffe and Guyer, so Riley accepts Kant's distinction between ethics and politics. However, in contrast to both, Riley views Kantian politics as the helpmate of Kantian ethics. While the state cannot compel individuals to be virtuous, it can create the conditions that make it possible for individuals to be virtuous. The Kantian state has a moral end. Riley's interpretation relies on Kant's teleological conception of man and history (see also Arendt, 1981). According to Kantian teleology, individuals exist as 'ends in themselves'. While everything else in nature exists not only for itself but also as a means to something else, man is not a means to anything else but is an end in himself. This is because man exists as a 'purposive being'. In contrast to other creatures, man can set himself ends. Indeed, man's purpose is to realise himself as a purposive being. Although 'purposiveness' is closely related to Kant's idea of freedom, the teleological conception of *mankind's* purposiveness transcends his account of each individual's innate right to freedom, giving it an historical dimension which envisages the developmental capacities, over time, of the human race as a whole. Hence the close connection between man as a purposive being and the development of culture or civilisation. From this perspective, the historical role of the (moral) state is to enable the culturalisation of the human species. The state sets up the conditions which are necessary to man's realisation of himself as a 'purposive being', that is, as a free being who is capable of setting himself ends that are distinct from nature and that find expression in cultural activities, such as art.

Despite superficial similarities with Rousseau's advocacy of a 'virtuous Republic', Riley does not attribute to Kant a moral revolution of Rousseauean dimensions. The state does not seek the moral transformation of individuals directly; it merely seeks to provide the background conditions that make it possible for individuals to improve themselves. Riley interprets the conditions in question primarily in terms of the state's guarantee and protection of individuals' rights to freedom. His is a Kantian version of liberal perfectionism, where the state provides a legal framework that makes possible the individual realisation of moral ends which the state deems worthy of protection but the realisation of which it does not prescribe directly. For the same reason, Riley believes a contractarian interpretation of Kant to be inconsistent with his political teleology. This is because the grounds of political obligation are given by the objectively valid ends (the realisation of mankind as an end in itself). Kant's references to a 'general united will' do not, therefore, evoke a social contract argument:

> When Kant says that the state laws must be conceived as the product of a (hypothetical) general will of the whole people as sovereign, this must be understood within the natural law context: indeed, he defines natural laws as 'those to which an obligation can be recognised a priori by reason without external legislation' (Riley, 1973, p. 454).

According to Riley, Kant is closer to the natural law tradition than to social contract theory. The state's historical role as 'civiliser' of man is grounded in a teleological conception of man as a 'purposive being'. Man's objectively given capacity for self-realisation, not voluntary agreement, is the ground of individuals' civic obligations. Nonetheless, the objectively given end identified by Riley differs from more conventional natural law arguments about the grounds of political obligation, remaining close to the liberal tradition.

Given his teleological perspective, Riley interprets 'nature's mechanism' for peace differently from Guyer. According to Riley, Kant's advocacy of international federalism is based on two claims: first, establishing such a federation as a means to peace is a moral duty; second, it is also an historical inevitability (Riley, 1983, p. 119). Crucial to this is Riley's reading of Kant's famous remark concerning man's 'unsocial sociability', according to which human beings can neither live without others nor live with them in a natural harmony. Peaceful coexistence is an achievement of freedom, and this achievement can be measured only from an historical perspective, not from the perspective of the individual. The claim is that although working towards peace is the moral duty of each individual considered separately, individual attempts bear fruit only after many generations. The achievement of peace is the result of a 'learning curve' involving all of humanity. Here 'the mechanisms of nature' assists men in working towards what they should be working towards of their own free will. In spreading discord among people, in forcing them to war and competition, nature compels people to try out new, more rational ways in which to settle their differences. It educates them in their reasoning powers until they are able to settle their differences through dialogue rather than war:

> Kant relied on his historical view that nature's purpose for man was the extension of reason and reasonable conduct in the species as a whole

through conflict, and that a series of clashes would ultimately bring states to new and more rational relations in which international good would be voluntarily accepted (*ibid.*, p. 120).

The Natural Law Interpretation

If Riley cautiously moves Kant towards the natural law tradition, Leslie Mulholland (Mulholland, 1990) argues that Kant embraces a thoroughly natural law account of political obligation. Like Guyer, Mulholland locates the basis of juridical duties in Kant's property argument. However, Mulholland interprets Kant's references to the 'united general will' differently from Guyer. Instead of giving it a contractualist gloss, Mulholland views it as a natural law principle of 'consistent willing'. The tendency to read Kant as a contractualist is a consequence, Mulholland believes, of initial indecisiveness on Kant's part:

> Kant is confusing two distinct accounts of the justification to the submission to civil authority. He has the consent theory and the natural law theory. However, in his discussion of the ground of civil authority, Kant ... in fact develops a doctrine of natural law ... , and abandons the notion of the social contract as unnecessary for the justification of civil authority (*ibid.*, p. 293).

Kant's emphasis on individual freedom initially leads him to assume that persons cannot incur duties of justice unless they have voluntarily performed a deed, which allows others to obligate them. Mulholland calls this the 'deed principle', the implication of which is that duties of justice are incurred voluntarily through contract. No one has any obligations of justice towards others unless they have voluntarily incurred such obligations as a result of some deed to that effect. Yet when it comes to the problem of property rights, Kant cannot sustain this account of voluntarily incurred obligations. As physically embodied creatures with basic needs, we cannot avoid taking into possession external objects: survival dictates that we appropriate. Such necessary deeds of appropriation are not voluntary. Since the deed principle holds that we can be obligated only on the basis of our voluntary actions, it appears that we cannot be obligated on the basis of our unavoidable acquisition of objects. But individual appropriation from the common stock inevitably leads to conflict and stands in need of justification. Since the contractualist model of voluntary obligation breaks down at this point, Mulholland concludes that Kant opts for a natural law justification:

> the solution to the problem lies in the move Kant makes from the use of the deed principle to the use of the law of nature principle to establish the

basis of the general will. The unavoidable conflict of wills concerning [property] leads to the *need* of everyone to have rights to [property]. Through this idea, Kant develops the notion of a *natural will* on which the general will is based (*ibid.*, p. 278).

In short, Mulholland argues that the recognition by each of their need for property commits individuals to acknowledge the equal needs of everyone else: 'in claiming the title to [property] everyone is rationally committed by the universality of a law of reason to allow everyone else the same title' (*ibid.*, 279). Individuals' reflections on the needs of human nature lead them to the accept the immutable laws of nature grounded in those needs, the observance of which makes possible peaceful co-existence among men.

Mulholland emphasises Kant's view of the interrelation between domestic justice, the rights of states, and cosmopolitan rights: 'If the principle of outer freedom limited by law is lacking in any one of these three possible forms of rightful condition, the framework of all others is unavoidably undermined and must finally collapse' (Kant, 1991, p. 123). The principles of justice, derived from the need of each for life-sustaining property, obtain equally at all three 'levels of justice'. Just as individual property rights must not be violated at the domestic level, so states' territorial rights must be respected in relations between states. Moreover, states must respect the rights to their possessions of foreign individuals who pass through their territories. However, in contrast to the domestic level, international law cannot be institutionalised: states' rightful claims to sovereignty forbid this. The international level requires non-institutionalised abidance by principles of justice. The only states that are capable of such free acknowledgement of the requirements of natural law are republics:

> only in a republic does the general will and the concomitant element of the rights of man have priority as the principle of political action. Only in the case of a republic, then, is there any reason to trust that the authorities will abide by their commitments' at the international as well as the domestic level of justice (Mulholland, 1990, pp. 369–70).

The Constructivist Interpretation

The final interpretive perspective to be considered is constructivism. Originally introduced by Rawls, constructivism aims to construct a theory of justice, which is the outcome of a reasoning procedure between free and equal individuals. It is designed to yield a 'freestanding' theory of justice, one that is not based on controversial metaphysical presuppositions, but that supports itself in virtue of the reflective consensus among free and equal individuals regarding its objective validity. This approach places a lot of weight on human beings' capacity to reason – to that extent Rawls rightly claims special allegiance between Kant and himself. Nonetheless, Rawls's theory of justice confines itself to justice within liberal societies, ignoring the global context. In this respect, Rawls's theory falls short of Kantian constructivism.

The best known global 'Kantian constructivist' is Onora O'Neill (O'Neill, 1991, 1996). Two aspects are distinctive about O'Neill's approach. First, she derives her Kantian conception of justice primarily from Kant's moral writings, avoiding, like Rawls, his more explicitly political works. Second, she emphasises Kant's conception of humans as finite rational beings. Human finitude comprises their physical and their intellectual limitations alike. Physical finitude refers not just to the fact that we all have to die some time. It draws attention to our vulnerability as embodied beings to others' acts of violence against us. Humans are finite in the sense of not being impervious to physical and psychological violence. Intellectual finitude refers to the fact that human beings cannot adopt the 'God's eye' view when reasoning about justice. They cannot know everything, but must rely on the limited reasoning resources available to them. On O'Neill's strictly Kantian conception of agents as finite rational beings we do not, as with Rawls, need to predicate any particular liberal values of individuals engaged in reasoning about justice. As such, the Kantian conception of agency is, on O'Neill's interpretation, better suited than most liberal accounts for considering principles of cosmopolitan justice.

Following the specification of agency, O'Neill identifies two principles of justice consistent with that specification. These are the principles of non-coercion and of non-deception. She (O'Neill, 1996, pp. 154–83) develops these from Kant's discussion of perfect duties – that is, duties which require strict abidance and application (Kant, 1964, pp. 89–91). Kant's own example of a perfect duty is the example of not lying. The maxim 'I will lie whenever doing so is convenient to me' is morally impermissible because it is not universalisable. The benefits to be derived from lying depend on a general practice of truth telling. Hence, if everyone were to adopt the maxim of lying, this would remove the general condition of truth telling presupposed by this maxim. Liars thus make an exception of themselves when they adopt a principle of action which not everyone possibly could adopt. According to O'Neill, the (cosmopolitan) principle of non-deception is a formalisation of the principle of not lying: not to deceive others is not to lie to them. Analogously, the principle of non-coercion repudiates the maxim, 'I will impose my will on others whenever it suits me'. As with the maxims of lying and deception, this maxim is not universalisable: two persons, X and Y, cannot simultaneously adopt the maxim of coercion. X can dominate Y only in so far as Y fails to dominate X, and vice versa. The maxim of coercion cannot be 'willed as a universal law' on the basis of which everyone could act, indicating the maxim's unjustness. By inference, the principle of non-coercion qualifies as a (necessary) principle of justice.

In so far as the principles of non-coercion and non-deceit are derived from individuals' reflective understanding of themselves as finite rational beings, O'Neill's interpretation avoids resorting to contractarian and natural law arguments alike. Whether her constructivist position avoids, as she claims, metaphysical commitments altogether is a separate question, which lack of space prevents us from considering here. Much of O'Neill's interpretation of Kantian cosmopolitan justice is motivated by a concern to reform international practice. Contemporary global political and economic agency is characterised by routine adoption of maxims of coercion and deception: states and persons gain advantages over others because they deceive and coerce them in a variety of ways. If such practices were ruled out as unjust, it would change the nature of global political and economic relations. O'Neill thus presents us with an elaboration of Kant's discussion, in *Perpetual Peace*, of the 'moral politician' who, in contrast to the 'political moralist', acknowledges the absolute constraints imposed by morality (as distinct from virtue) on political agency.

Evaluation

How best is Kant's political philosophy to be understood today? None of the alternative interpretations of Kant's political philosophy considered above are implausible. Each can offer textual support for the view it advocates; each strives for an interpretation that is internally consistent. The variety of plausible alternative readings is testimony to the complexity of Kant's political thought, especially when placed, as it ought to be, within the wider framework of Kant's philosophy. All of the commentators surveyed approach Kant's political thinking by drawing on related aspects of his epistemology, his moral theory, or his philosophy of history. Riley takes Kant's account of teleological judgement in the *Critique of Judgement* as his point of departure, while O'Neill and Mulholland focus on Kant's moral philosophy. Again, both Guyer and O'Neill draw on their respective readings of *CPR*. By contrast, Höffe does perhaps most to situate Kant within the dominant tradition of modern political thought – attributing to him an essentially Hobbesian understanding of the problem of politics. This is by no means implausible: there is much that Kant appreciated about Hobbes politically (Kant, 1970, pp. 73–87). Nonetheless, the presumption that political agency must be based on self-interest tends to elide the distinction between what is the case and what ought to be the case. Although a number of passages in Kant's political writings can be interpreted in prudential terms, given that he viewed politics as a branch of morality one must judge how well the prudential interpretation fits with Kant's moral philosophy more generally. Höffe encounters difficulties in making his prudential interpretation of the universal principle of justice consistent with the categorical imperative as a principle of self-legislation (Höffe, 1989). Even an exclusive focus on his political writings suggests that Kant's contrast between the political moralist and the moral politician led him, ultimately, to reject the prudential conception of political agency. While many politicians *do* abuse morality for their own purposes, this is not what they *ought* to do. They ought to conduct their political affairs in accordance with the principles of morality. Since ought implies can, the claim is disingenuous that politics provides an exception from the constraints of morality. Recall Kant's Hobbesian remark that 'no one is bound to refrain from encroaching on what another possesses if the other gives him no equal assurance that he will observe the same restraint towards him'. Kant goes on to assert that '[g]iven the intention to be and to remain in this state of externally lawless freedom, men do one another no wrong at all when they feud among themselves ... as if by mutual consent. But in general they do wrong in the highest degree by wanting to be and to remain in a condition that is not rightful' (Kant, 1991, p. 122). In fact, Kant here repudiates the Hobbesian view. If they do treat each other, 'as if by mutual consent', with distrust and hostility, they are doing wrong 'in the highest degree': they should not so treat each other.

The passage also casts some doubt on non-prudential contractualist interpretations of Kant, such as that of Guyer. Even if men were to agree, 'as if by mutual consent', that is, contractually, to treat one another with hostility, the mere fact that of their agreement says nothing at all about the justice of such mutual treatment. While they may then be doing *one another* no wrong, 'in general they do wrong in the highest degree'. The reference to 'wrong in the highest degree' implies a conception of justice and of political obligation the normative grounds of which are valid independently of any contractual agreement among men. What makes a principle of justice just is not the fact that men have agreed to regard it as such. The demands of justice are valid independently of such agreement, and would remain valid even if men were to contract to the contrary.

Does the rejection of a (conventional) contractualist interpretation of Kant's account of political obligation mean that Mulholland is right in casting Kant as a natural law thinker? Guyer offers a fine interpretation of Kant on property rights; he rightly emphasises that in contrast to Locke, Kantian property rights are non-natural rights whose legitimacy depends on others' acknowledgement of their rightfulness. On the other hand, Kant does not mention the social contract as the means through which to resolve the problem of property rights. He mentions instead the idea of a general united will. The two should not be conflated. When Kant does refer to the idea of a social contract he usually has in mind the relation between the sovereign and his subjects (Weinstock, 1996). When passing laws, the sovereign should do so in accordance with the idea of the social contract as an 'idea of reason': he should only pass laws which it would have been possible for individuals to consent to had they been consulted. To conceive of the idea of the social contract as a guiding idea of reason for the moral sovereign is different from thinking of the contract as the ground of political obligation. Political obligation, for Kant, is grounded in the *a priori* idea of the general united will as it emerges from the analysis of property claims. But are Kant's *a priori* grounds of political obligation most plausibly interpreted with reference to the natural law principle of human needs? The problem is that the substantive principle of human needs conflicts with Kant's formal conception of justice, as concerning the form of the external relations between the choice of one and that of another. The principle of justice regulates the external freedom of each in accordance with the equal right to freedom of all others: it is not, at least not directly, a substantive principle of distributive justice. Here Riley's emphasis on individuals as 'purposive beings' who can set themselves ends better draws out the importance which Kant attaches to individual freedom, and which distances him from the natural law tradition. Nonetheless, in his attempt to offer an account of political obligation that is both non-contractarian and distinct from natural law theory, Riley tends to run together Kant's emphasis on external freedom with his teleological conception of history. Whereas freedom pertains to individual human beings, the teleological conception of history pertains to the human race as a whole. In re-interpreting Kant's teleological conception of history in terms of individual freedom understood as purposiveness, Riley arguably ends up with a conception of the political good – the realisation of individuals as purposive beings within the state – that is more Hegelian than Kantian in its basic orientation.

O'Neill's constructivist interpretation has the advantage of breaking free from the urge to assimilate Kant into either of the two dominant political traditions. Her focus on Kant's distinctive conception of human reasoning offers the perhaps most persuasive account of how we are to understand Kant's views regarding the *a priori* obligations of justice. These obligations are *a priori* not in the natural law sense of being grounded in some higher legislative authority (such as God). They are *a priori* in being grounded in the structure of practical human reasoning itself: it is their very capacity to form a conception of the necessity of just relations among them which obliges finite rational beings to justice. A crucial weakness of O'Neill's account is her neglect of Kant's property argument and how the latter connects up with his account of political obligation. Instead of her predominant focus on Kant's moral writings, a more decisive turn towards *MEJ* is required. Nonetheless, on the whole, O'Neill's approach remains the most consistent with the cosmopolitan spirit of Kant's philosophy taken as a whole. Indeed, it seems to me that it is in his commitment to cosmopolitanism that we discover both the heart of Kant's own political thinking considered in itself, as well as its practical relevance for our own reflections as political agents today. Quite how Kant articulates, in detail, this cosmopolitan commitment and quite how we can place our own, current position in relation to his must remain a matter of interpretation, partly for reasons spelled out in the previous discussion. Nevertheless, it seems to me that, in so far as present day political realities are confronting us with a shift away from the paradigm of the single sovereign state and towards an as yet largely untheorised form of global politics, Kant is very much a political thinker of our future.

8

Hegel (1770–1831)

ANTHONY BURNS

Introduction

Georg Wilhelm Friedrich Hegel was a German philosopher whose life
spanned the last third of the eighteenth and the first third of the nineteenth
centuries. For Western Europe this was a period of great commercial expansion combined, especially in England, with industrial revolution. Politically,
European history at this time was dominated by the French Revolution of
1789. Hegel was greatly interested in the significance of the Revolution for
the German states and especially for Prussia where, at the end of his life, he
taught philosophy at the University of Berlin. In this chapter I shall consider some of the different interpretations that have been given of the
mature Hegel's political thought as expounded in the *Philosophy of Right*
(Hegel, 1979), which Hegel published in 1821.

For many years Hegel was only considered to be important because of his
influence on Karl Marx (Burns and Fraser, 2000a). Nowadays, however,
Hegel is a major figure in his own right, someone whose views have a significance, not simply for the study of German history and politics at the time
of the French Revolution, but for anyone who wishes to develop an understanding of European or even world history and politics from the time of the
ancient Greeks to the present. One of Hegel's principal concerns is that of
understanding the causes and significance of great turning points in history,
such as the transition from a pre-modern to a modern society which occurred
in Europe from about the sixteenth century onwards. There are many who
feel that at the start of a new millennium we are again at such a nodal point
in historical development. World history is once more undergoing a major
process of transition, only this time from a modern to an allegedly postmodern society. Because of his historical approach to questions of philosophy and
politics, Hegel's ideas, perhaps more than those of any other philosopher, are

relevant to our efforts to situate ourselves in such a rapidly changing world. As the work of Jean François Lyotard and more recently Francis Fukuyama shows, whether one agrees or disagrees with Hegel one cannot afford to ignore him. Despite the limitations imposed by the immediate historical context within which they were produced, Hegel's views continue to possess a wider relevance even today (Fukuyama, 1992; Lyotard, 1984; see also Browning, 1999; Chitty, 1994; Williams, Sullivan and Matthews, 1997).

Problems and Issues

There are four interrelated questions concerning Hegel's later political thought about which there is considerable disagreement amongst commentators. They are: (i) how are Hegel's politics related to his metaphysics? (ii) What is Hegel's understanding of the relationship which ought to exist between the individual and the state? (iii) What is Hegel's attitude towards the French Revolution and the democratic political ideal with which the Revolution was associated? (iv) Did Hegel think that 'the end of history' had actually arrived when he published the *Philosophy of Right* in 1821? These questions have been answered in opposite ways by Hegel scholars. As a consequence, there are two completely different interpretations of Hegel's political thought as a whole. We may refer to these as the *traditional* and the *radical* interpretations respectively.

Why Conflicting Interpretations?

There are a number of reasons for the disagreement between Hegel's interpreters. First, the language which Hegel uses is often ambiguous and obscure. Take, for example, Hegel's notorious claim (made in the Preface to the *Philosophy of Right*) that 'what is rational is actual and what is actual, is rational' (Hegel, 1979, p. 10). The meaning of this remark, commonly referred to as the *Doppelsatz* (literally 'double saying'), has been the subject of heated debate amongst Hegel's interpreters ever since Hegel first made it (Fackenheim, 1970; Hardimon, 1994, pp. 52–83; McCarney, 2000, pp. 96–9). Second, different people tend to interpret texts differently, according to their own values and ideological beliefs (Gadamer, 1975, pp. 235–42, pp. 245–6, pp. 249–51, p. 258). Hegel's interpreters often write as if their intention is not to understand Hegel's views as he himself understood them, but rather to engage in a moral or political crusade either for or against Hegel. Third, Hegel's instincts usually lead him in the direction of an attempt to think 'dialectically', or to synthesise any two contrasting points of view relating to a particular subject. As a result, Hegel rarely praises or rejects anything outright. If one group of commentators focuses on just one aspect of Hegel's dialectical position with respect to a specific issue, whilst a second group focuses exclusively on the opposite aspect, it is inevitable that diametrically opposed interpretations of Hegel's thought as a whole will result. Finally, as MacGregor points out, some of Hegel's interpreters are methodologically naive (MacGregor, 1998, pp. 33–4, p. 100). They assume that we can take what Hegel says in his writings at its face value. They do not consider the historical and political context within which Hegel wrote the *Philosophy of Right*. They do not allow for the possibility that Hegel may have *said* one thing about a particular issue but actually meant another, or that he may have deliberately employed what Quentin Skinner has referred to as 'oblique strategies' in order to disguise his real meaning or communicate it to his readers in a coded form (Skinner, 1969; see also Strauss, 1952).

Conflicting Interpretations

Metaphysics and Politics in Hegel's Thought

The Traditional Interpretation: Hegel as a Philosophical Idealist

Here there are two key issues. First, how can we best characterise Hegel's metaphysical position? Is he an idealist or is he a materialist? Second, is there a necessary connection between Hegel's metaphysical position and his political thought? Regarding the first of these issues, the traditional view of Hegel presents him as a philosophical idealist. On this reading, like Plato and Aristotle, Hegel subscribes to the doctrine that it is ideas or concepts which constitute reality and not material, physical or existent things. It is the world of mind which is truly real and not the world of matter. Hegel believes that everything which exists in time and space is an appearance of some underlying conceptual reality. For Hegel it is not the case, as materialists argue, that ideas or concepts are the products of the material world and therefore somehow reflect the nature of the physical objects to which they correspond. Rather, the opposite is true. According to Hegel, physical, material or existent things are in some way the products of the world of mind. They correspond to or reflect the nature of the reality of which they are the appearances, namely the ideas and concepts which underpin them, and not *vice versa* (Burns, 2000, pp. 3–7). This interpretation of Hegelian metaphysics is probably best exemplified by Marx's judgement that Hegel's philosophy needs inverting if we are to find the rational kernel (materialism) which lies beneath its mystical shell (idealism) (Marx, 1974,

p. 29; also Engels, 1958, pp. 370–1). As for the second issue, the traditional reading of Hegel maintains that there is a close link between Hegel's metaphysics and his politics. For example, in the young Marx's opinion it is precisely because Hegel is a philosophical idealist that his understanding of existing social and political conditions is completely 'uncritical' and conservative (Marx, 1967, p. 139). The view that one cannot understand Hegel's views on history and politics without first understanding his metaphysics is also shared by a number of more recent commentators on Hegel's politics (Kelly, 1978, p. 8; Plant, 1973, p. 9; see also Dallmayr, 1993, p. 28; Riedel, 1984, pp. 31–2; Wood, 1990, p. xiii, p. 6).

The Radical Interpretation: Hegel as a Materialist

A number of commentators have maintained that Hegel is a materialist. This is the view of Lenin, Lukács and Marcuse (see Burns and Fraser, 2000a, pp. 10–13, pp. 20–3; Fraser, 1998, pp. 1–2, pp. 27–8, pp. 40–1; McCarney, 2000, pp. 60–3). Most recently it has been advocated by David MacGregor (MacGregor, 1984). According to MacGregor, the belief that Hegel is an 'idealist who had everything turned upside down' is a 'myth' which Marx 'helped create' (MacGregor, 1984, p. 3). It is true that when one unpacks this claim, very few people are prepared to argue explicitly that Hegel is a materialist so far as questions of metaphysics are concerned – although Lenin does come close to this on occasion (Lenin, 1961a, p. 98, p. 106, p. 131, p. 148, p. 151, p. 158, p. 189, p. 190, p. 234; Lenin, 1961b, p. 278). They usually concede that Hegel is a philosophical idealist. Rather, what these commentators mean is that Hegel's views on history (as opposed to his views on the fundamental nature of reality) are, at times, strikingly similar to those of Marx. In short, they mean that Hegel (especially the young Hegel in the Jena *Realphilosophie* produced in 1801–3) sometimes writes as if he was an 'historical materialist'. For in these early writings Hegel emphasises the importance of economics for understanding social affairs (Avineri, 1972, pp. 87–109; Lukács, 1975, pp. 319–37; Marcuse, 1973, pp. 77–80). By implication, therefore, these commentators take the view that we *can* make a clear distinction between Hegel's metaphysics (which are idealist) and his views on history and politics (which are materialist), and hence that we do not need to understand the former in order to understand the latter. Indeed, adherents of this view would argue that excessive concern with Hegel's metaphysics (as in the case of Marx) actually prevents us from properly understanding Hegel's views on history and politics. The claim that it is possible (even desirable) for us to separate Hegel's metaphysics and his social and political theory is also made by a number of other Hegel scholars (Germino, 1969, p. 885; Plamenatz, 1958, p. 177; Plamenatz, 1963, pp. 129–32; see also Cairns, 1949, p. 504; Pelczynski, 1964, p. 37; Pelczynski, 1971, pp. 1–2).

Hegel on the Relationship Between the Individual and the State

The Traditional Interpretation: Hegel as a Reactionary

For many years the mature Hegel was presented as a political reactionary in the paid service of the absolutist Prussian state and supporting its repressive policies in the aftermath of the French Revolution (Avineri, 1972, p. 115, p. 123; Cassirer, 1967, pp. 250–1, pp. 266–7; Hook, 1971, p. 19; Plamenatz, 1963, pp. 262–3; Wood, 1991, p. xxx). In the twentieth century the claim that Hegel was a reactionary defender of monarchical absolutism (the doctrine that the sovereign can do no wrong) came to be associated with the claim that he is a totalitarian thinker (Popper, 1966 [1945], p. 66, p.78). Karl Popper maintains that Hegel was 'the first official philosopher of Prussianism' and an 'apologist for Prussian absolutism' (*ibid.*, p. 34), appointed to meet the demands of the 'reactionary' party in Prussia, which after 1815 was in dire need of an ideology in its political struggle against 'the open society', as represented by the French Revolution and the 'ideas of 1789' (*ibid.*, pp. 29–30). According to Popper, Hegel is completely opposed to the political ideals associated with liberalism. For example, he endorses the principle of organicism rather than individualism (*ibid.*, p. 37). He rejects the idea of natural law and embraces the standpoint of moral and juridical positivism – the doctrine that 'might is right' or that 'what is, is good, since there can be no standards but existing standards' (*ibid.*, p. 41; also p. 49, pp. 57–8, p. 66, p. 308). By implication, therefore, Hegel rejects the social contract theory of the origins of the state central to classical liberalism, together with the idea that individuals possess certain natural or human rights which the state ought to respect. Instead, he insists on 'the absolute moral authority of the state', which overrules 'all personal morality and 'all conscience' (*ibid.*, p. 31). Hence, Popper maintains, Hegel is devoted to the 'worship of the state' generally, and of the Prussian state in particular, which in his view can do no wrong (*ibid.*, p. 31). In short, Hegel completely subordinates the individual to the state. It is true, Popper acknowledges, that Hegel claims to want a 'free society' and that he pays lip-service to the value of liberty, but he defines this concept in such a way that liberty amounts to nothing more than performing one's duty to obey the state (*ibid.*, pp. 44–5, p. 305). In Popper's opinion, Hegel's philosophy generally, and in particular the view expressed in the Preface to the *Philosophy of Right* that what is actual is rational, merely serves 'to justify the existing order' (*ibid.*, p. 41).

The Radical Interpretation: Hegel as a Liberal Thinker
There is a more recent and quite different reading of the *Philosophy of Right*, represented by Z. A. Pelczynski, which presents Hegel as a proponent of constitutional government and the rule of law (a *Rechtstaat*) (Pelczynski, 1964; Pelczynski, 1970; also Smith, 1991, pp. 132–64). In Pelczynski's opinion Hegel is far from being a vulgar moral or legal positivist. On the contrary, he is a natural law theorist. Consequently he recognises the validity of ethical principles which constitute 'a rational ideal, serving as a measuring rod of actual laws' (p. 49; also pp. 28–31, p. 37, p. 40, pp. 45–6). According to Pelczynski, such 'belief in rational law as the only legitimate and tenable criterion of laws, institutions and constitutions is the first basic article of Hegel's political faith' (Pelczynski, 1964, p. 29). In his view, therefore, Hegel also recognises the existence of certain natural rights which all states ought to respect. For Pelczynski, it is Hegel's opinion that no constitution can 'be considered rational unless it is substantially based on those rights' (*ibid.*, p. 51). The rational principles associated with these rights 'can and ought to be the basis for the transformation of all established law' (*ibid.*, p. 52). These rights, especially property rights, delimit a private sphere upon which the state cannot legitimately encroach. Pelczyznski insists that the view that Hegel *rejected* the idea of 'absolute human rights' is 'one-sided' and that Hegel never disparaged the French *Declaration of the Rights of Man* (Pelczynski, 1970, p. 83). Hence, according to Pelczynski, Hegel's political thought represents a defence of constitutional government. It is, indeed, very similar to that of John Locke and the classical liberal tradition. As Pelczynski himself puts it, Hegel 'belonged to a constitutionalist or Whig–liberal current of political thought' which is 'the source of modern liberalism' (Pelczynski, 1970, p. 82; also Pelczynski, 1964, p. 135). It is clear that this more recent interpretation of Hegel is fundamentally opposed to the traditional one. As Hook wryly observed at the time, 'not since the baptism of Aristotle' by the Christian thinkers of the middle ages has 'anything as bold as this transfiguration been attempted' (Hook, 1970a, p. 65).

Hegel and the French Revolution

The Traditional Interpretation: Hegel Against the French Revolution
What is the mature Hegel's attitude towards the French Revolution? (Hyppolite, 1973; Ritter, 1982; Suter, 1971). The traditional view, based on what Hegel says about the Revolution in the *Philosophy of Right*, is that he was opposed to it (Hegel, 1979, p. 22, p. 33, p. 79, p. 157, p. 175, pp. 185–6, p. 286). In particular, he objected to it because of its commitment to democracy (Hegel, 1979, p. 130, p. 157, pp. 176–8, p. 183,

pp. 195–6). This assessment of Hegel's attitude is a corollary of the view that he is a defender of Prussian absolutism. On this reading Hegel's main concern is to preserve the existing social and political order in Prussia and especially the institution of private property. Like so many living at the time of the French Revolution, he saw democracy as a threat to these things.

According to the traditional interpretation, Hegel argues that a commitment to democracy is one of the main failings of liberalism. It is the 'outlook of the rabble' and a 'folly' of the understanding with its commitment to 'abstract reasoning' (Hegel, 1979, p. 130, p. 157, p. 175; Hegel, 1975, p. 115, p. 198). In Hegel's view, democracy is based on the principle that it is 'the people' who 'know best what is in their best interest' and who therefore will it, or make laws accordingly. For Hegel, however, the truth is that to 'know what one wills' in this sense 'is the fruit of profound apprehension and insight, precisely the things which are *not* popular' (Hegel, 1979, pp. 195–6). Hegel points out that the French Revolution is the only attempt so far in world history to implement the democratic ideal in practice. But this attempt was a decisive failure. Under Robespierre and the Jacobins in 1793 it 'ended in the maximum of frightfulness and terror' (*ibid.*, p. 157). In the ideal state outlined in the *Philosophy of Right*, therefore, it is not 'the people' who are responsible for legislation but the bureaucracy. In Hegel's opinion this bureaucracy can be relied upon to rule paternalistically in the universal interest (*ibid.*, p. 189, p. 193, pp. 195–8).

Adherents of the traditional view also point out that the *Philosophy of Right* contains a defence of private property. For Hegel a constitutional state, or *Rechtstaat*, is significantly different from an absolutist state. For in a constitutional state (unlike France before 1789, but like England after 1689) liberty is respected. A constitutional state respects the rule of law and hence also the historically inherited right to private property. This is one reason why Hegel associates constitutional rule with the idea of a free society. For, in his opinion, the institution of private property 'is the first embodiment of freedom' and 'personality', whereas communism, for example, especially as we find it advocated in Plato's *Republic*, 'violates the right of personality by forbidding the holding of private property' (*ibid.*, p. 42, p. 45; also p. 41, p. 44, pp. 52–3). This traditional interpretation of Hegel's attitude towards the French Revolution is one which has been held by many of Hegel's interpreters (Avineri, 1972, p. 125, p. 162, p. 184; Brod, 1992, p. 142; Brudner, 1981, pp. 122–3; Cristi, 1983, p. 603; Hardimon, 1994, p. 219; Hook, 1970a, pp. 60–1; Levin and Williams, 1987, pp. 105–6, p. 108, p. 114; Mehta, 1968, p. 77, p. 111, p. 118; Plamenatz, 1976, pp. 211–13, p. 264; Singer, 1983, p. 41; Smith, 1991, p. 129, p. 238; Taylor, 1989a, pp. 444–6; Westphal, 1993, pp. 261–2).

The Radical Interpretation: Hegel for the French Revolution
Some claim that it is highly significant that the young Hegel was very enthusiastic about the Revolution and that even the mature Hegel celebrated its
occurrence each year on Bastille Day (Avineri, 1972, p. 3; Engels, 1958,
p. 361; Harris, 1972, p. 62; Lukács, 1975, p. 10; MacGregor, 1998, p. 53; Plant,
1973, p. 51). They maintain that it is not just the young Hegel, but also the
mature Hegel who embraces the political ideals of 1789. According to them,
the mature Hegel is not only in favour of the liberal values associated with the
French *Declaration of the Rights of Man*, but also shares the French revolutionaries' commitment to democracy. This claim that Hegel was consistently
a democrat, even in his later years, evidently goes further than the claim that
he is a constitutionalist or a classical liberal. It represents an even more radical reinterpretation of Hegel than that of Pelczynski. In the recent literature,
this reading of Hegel has been advocated by David MacGregor (MacGregor,
1998, pp. 63–88). MacGregor argues that Hegel's attitude towards democracy
is similar to that of Tom Paine. He maintains that for Hegel a democratic political system 'forms the core of the rational state' (*ibid.*, p. 144). In his view, the
interpretation of Hegel as an anti-democrat is based on a misinterpretation of
what Hegel says about democracy in the *Philosophy of Right.*
    In MacGregor's work, this claim that even the mature Hegel was a demo-
crat is associated with the stronger claim that Hegel was also a communist
(MacGregor, 1984). MacGregor takes a fresh look at the intellectual relationship between Hegel and Marx and maintains that this relationship has
often been misunderstood. He argues that Hegel's views are often the same
as those of Marx. For example, according to MacGregor both Hegel and
Marx are of the opinion that bourgeois property relations are fundamentally
exploitative in character. Consequently, the ideal state which Hegel
describes in the *Philosophy of Right* closely resembles what Marx calls communist society. MacGregor acknowledges, however, that Hegel's radical
critique of capitalist private property 'has gone virtually unrecognised by all
commentators' – 'not least', he allows, 'by Marx himself' (MacGregor, 1984,
p. 193). MacGregor's assessment of Hegel's attitude towards the French
Revolution, and indeed of Hegel's political thought as a whole, is the most
radical interpretation currently to be found in the literature on Hegel.

Hegel and the End of History

The Traditional Interpretation: The End of History has Arrived
When discussing world history, Hegel attempts to explain what, at the present
time, the political structure of an ideal state would be like. The existence or

possible existence, of such a state is a consequence of the transition from pre-modern to modern society. For Hegel this state represents the end of world history (McCarney, 2000). A major issue in the interpretation of Hegel's political thought concerns the question of whether Hegel thought that this end had already been achieved when he published the *Philosophy of Right* in 1821. There are two opposing views on this question. Each plays on the ambiguity of what Hegel says about the *end* of history. Does Hegel mean by this the chronological termination point of world historical development? Or does he mean, rather, the ultimate purpose or goal of that process of development? The traditional interpretation of Hegel asserts that when Hegel talks about the end of history he is using the expression in the first of these two senses. The particular state which he associates with the end of history in this sense, and which he therefore believes is ideally representative of the modern era, is the absolutist Prussian state of 1821. On this reading it is Hegel's view that the historical development of the state, from ancient times to the present day, has now reached its termination in this Prussian state, which is therefore a perfect state. The end of history has arrived and Hegel is basically defending the political *status quo*. His aim in the *Philosophy of Right* is indeed to sanctify the existing social and political order. In the recent literature this interpretation of Hegel is most strongly associated with the work of Karl Popper. Historically, however, it goes back to the nineteenth century. As Engels points out in his essay on Feuerbach, this was the interpretation of Hegel presented by the Old or Right Hegelians in Germany in the 1840s (Engels, 1958, pp. 361–5; McLellan, 1969; McLellan, 1972, pp. 35–6; McLellan, 1973, pp. 30–1).

The Radical Interpretation: The End of History has not Arrived
Employing the terminology of Engels, according to the radical interpretation of Hegel if we wish to understand the political message of Hegel's philosophy we must focus not on Hegel's metaphysical system, as the traditional interpretation does, but on his 'dialectic method'. According to both Marx and Engels, this method sees everything as changing and developing all of the time. It could never permanently sanctify any existing state of affairs. Hence it has radical political implications. As Engels puts it, this dialectic method represents the 'revolutionary character of the Hegelian philosophy', provided it is extracted from the idealist metaphysical system with which it is presently associated (Engels, 1958, p. 362). Considered from this point of view, the end of history had certainly not yet arrived in Prussia in 1821. Marx captures this aspect of Hegel's philosophy very well when he suggests that if we look at the world from an Hegelian point of view the *only*

truly permanent thing is change itself. As Marx puts it, from the standpoint of the Hegelian philosophy properly understood, 'the only immutable thing is the abstraction of movement' itself – '*mors immortalis*' (Marx, 1973, p. 96). Marx claims that Hegel's philosophy only *seems* to 'glorify the existing state of things' in Prussia. For although this philosophy certainly does include within 'its comprehension an affirmative recognition of the existing state of things' nevertheless at the same time, Marx argues, it also includes a 'recognition of the negation of that state' and of 'its inevitable breaking up'. This is so because it regards 'every historically developed social form as in fluid movement' and therefore 'takes into its account its transient nature not less than its momentary existence'. Like Engels, Marx concludes that suitably interpreted Hegel's philosophy is for this reason 'in its essence critical and revolutionary' (Marx, 1974, p. 29).

According to this radical interpretation, then, although it is true that Hegel associates an ideal or perfect state with the state at its highest point of historical development, he did not think that this point of termination had yet been reached (either in Prussia or anywhere else) when he published the *Philosophy of Right*. Nor indeed, paradoxical though it might seem, did Hegel think that the 'end of history' in this particular sense could ever be reached. Hegel, therefore, emphatically does not claim that the absolutist Prussian state of his day is an example of an ideal state. On the contrary, it is his view that the historical accomplishment of such a state continues to lie in the (ever receding) future. It remains the 'end of history' in the second of the two senses referred to above. It continues to be world history's ultimate purpose or goal. On this view, the *Philosophy of Right* contains an account of the best state which has evolved in the process of world history so far. Hence it provides what is inevitably merely a provisional sketch of a truly ideal state – a sketch which will need to be modified in the future as further historical developments take place. Nevertheless, this does not prevent the *Philosophy of Right* from being used now as a yardstick for the critical evaluation of all existing states – by comparison with which the absolutist Prussian state of 1821 is open to certain obvious criticisms (Avineri, 1972, pp. 123–30; Hardimon, 1994, pp. 25–6, pp. 53–4; Hook, 1971, pp. 19–20; Kaufmann, 1970, pp. 151–2; Knox, 1970, p. 18; MacGregor, 1998, pp. 17–18; McCarney, 2000, pp. 96–9; Sayers, 1998, pp. 100–4; Wood, 1990, pp. 8–11; Wood, 1991, pp. 389–90).

Evaluation

In my view the traditional interpretation of Hegel's metaphysics is correct. In his *Shorter Logic* he explicitly embraces the standpoint of philosophical idealism and rejects that of materialism (Hegel, 1975, pp. 33–4, p. 37, p. 52, p. 67, p. 73, p. 140, p. 223). Those who suggest that Hegel is a philosophical materialist have not understood what Hegel means by idealism. These commentators are right to claim that Hegel does not deny the existence of physical objects or material things in time and space. Nor does he maintain that our belief in the existence of such things is based on a deception or an illusion. They also correctly perceive that for Hegel those entities which are truly real (ideas and concepts, or what philosophers refer to as universals) are necessarily associated with such existent, material or physical things. These real entities inhere within individual concrete objects all of which possess a material, physical or corporeal aspect. In short, Hegel subscribes to an immanent rather than a transcendent form of idealist metaphysics (Burns, 1998). However, these commentators are wrong to suggest on these grounds that Hegel is a materialist. Those who claim that Hegel is a materialist make the mistake of identifying the categories of *existence* and *reality* in Hegel's thought. Hegel himself, however, distinguishes between those entities which exist and those which are truly real. The principal aim of Hegel's metaphysics is to present an account of the true nature of reality and not that of existence.

Moreover, a grasp of Hegel's metaphysics is indeed necessary for an adequate understanding of his politics. Perhaps the best illustration of this is provided by the *Doppelsatz*. What does Hegel really *mean* when he claims that 'what is rational is actual and what is actual is rational'? Is he justifying the *status quo* in Prussia in 1821 or condemning it? This question is difficult to answer precisely because of the ambiguity and the obscurity of Hegel's philosophical vocabulary. This difficulty has been well captured by the German poet Heinrich Heine. Heine relates how once, when in conversation with Hegel, he 'expressed disapproval of his assertion "everything which exists is rational".' According to Heine, in response to his objection Hegel 'gave a strange smile and said that one might equally say "everything which is rational, must exist"' (Lukács, 1975, p. 462; also McCarney, 2000, pp. 97–8; Sayers, 1998, p. 103).

The traditional interpretation maintains that what Hegel means by the *Doppelsatz* is that what *exists* is inherently rational. Hence, by implication, the Prussian state of 1821 is a good thing. As Engels puts it in his essay on Feuerbach: 'No philosophical proposition has earned more gratitude from narrow-minded governments and wrath from equally narrow-minded liberals' than this one. Hegel's remark about the rationality of the actual 'was tangibly a sanctification of things that be'. At least, according to Engels, that 'is how Frederick William III and how his subjects understood it' (Engels, 1958, p. 361). Adherents of the radical interpretation, on the other hand, claim that the traditional reading lacks an adequate understanding of Hegel's metaphysics. In particular, they allege that this reading wrongly identifies two things which Hegel keeps separate, namely the categories of *actuality* and *existence* (Hegel, 1975: 201–2). In Hegel's vocabulary the term *actuality* is used only to refer to those existent things which are inherently rational – or to things which are *rationally* existent. From this point of view, although it is true that all of those things which are actual necessarily exist, nevertheless it is not true that all of those things which exist are necessarily actual (and hence also rational). In short, these commentators maintain that for Hegel it is possible for an existing state *not* to be actual precisely because it is irrational and hence an ethically *bad* state (*ibid.*, p. 41, p. 135, p. 191, p. 207, p. 237, pp. 275–6; Hegel, 1979, p. 279, p. 280). As Frederick Copleston has put it, in the *Philosophy of Right*, Hegel 'has no intention of suggesting that historical States are immune from criticism' and this applies just as much to the Prussian state of 1821 as it does to any other existing state (Copleston, 1965, p. 256; see also Avineri, 1972, pp. 123–30; Browning, 1999, p. 4; Fackenheim, 1970; Hardimon, 1994, pp. 25–6, pp. 53–4; Hook, 1971, pp. 19–20; Kaufmann, 1970, pp. 151–2; Knox, 1970, p. 18; Knox, 1979, p. 302; MacGregor, 1998, pp. 17–18; McCarney, 2000a, pp. 96–9; Rose, 1995, pp. 79–81; Sayers, 1998, pp. 100–4; Wood, 1990, pp. 8–11; Wood, 1991, pp. 389–90).

The radical interpretation is right to emphasise that Hegel distinguishes between *actuality* and *existence*. It is also right to argue that the *Doppelsatz* does not imply that whatever exists must be rational simply because it exists. The crucial issue, however, is whether this allows us to interpret Hegel as a radical critic of the *status quo* in Prussia in 1821. In my view (*pace* Michael Hardimon) the answer to this question is 'no' (Hardimon, 1994, p. 79). The reason for this is that when discussing possible criticisms of *bad* states like Prussia, Hegel indicates that although there is indeed 'much that fails to satisfy the general requirements of right' and which is 'far from being as it ought to be' in such states, nevertheless this is true only of 'trivial external and transitory' things (Hegel, 1975, p. 10). For Hegel the possibility of criticising existing *bad* states does not apply to anything which he considers to be essential or of fundamental importance. In his opinion there is never any need for the *radical* transformation of an existing state. Even in a *bad* state what is required is not radical change but reform of those features which have been shown to be out of date by the onward march of world history.

On the issue of the state/individual relation, the interpretation of Hegel as a reactionary defender of monarchical absolutism has both strengths and weaknesses. So far as the strengths are concerned, it recognises that there is a distinctly anti-liberal or authoritarian dimension to Hegel's political thought. For example, Hegel objects strongly to the liberal 'social contract' theory of the state (Hegel, 1979, p. 156). Moreover, Hegel also criticises the liberal or *negative* view that freedom amounts to 'doing what one wants'. He contrasts this with the *positive* conception of freedom, which he defines in such a way that being free does in the end amount to doing one's duty (*ibid.*, p. 22, p. 27). Indeed, Hegel often attaches more importance to the value of order or duty than he does to that of liberty in the sense in which classical liberals understand this term (*ibid.*, p. 29, p. 84, pp. 89–2, pp. 106–10, pp. 161–2, p. 194, pp. 209–11). On the other hand, however, this interpretation also has weaknesses. For example, the 'rational state' which Hegel outlines in the *Philosophy of Right* bears little resemblance to the Prussian state as it existed in 1821 (Copleston, 1963, pp. 257–9; Knox, 1970, p. 18; Plamenatz, 1963, p. 263; Singer, 1983, p. 40; Smith, 1991, p. 135; Wood, 1991, pp. ix–xi). It is clear from this text that Hegel shares with classical liberalism a commitment to the rule of law and to constitutional rather than absolute government. Although Hegel does emphasise the principle of 'my station and its duties', nevertheless the duties in question are primarily the historically inherited duties associated with a particular nation's continually evolving political constitution (Hegel, 1979, p. 139, p. 163. p. 164, pp. 178–9, p. 282).

Hegel makes a distinction between the concept of the state understood in a narrow sense (as a bureaucratic institution whose function is to make and enforce laws), which he refers to as the 'strictly political state', and the concept of the state understood in a broad sense, which in the *Philosophy of Right* he more or less identifies with the sphere of 'ethical life', or the complex, articulated organic community which is society as a whole (Hegel, 1979, p. 163; Brod, 1992, p. 8; Copleston, 1963, p. 263; MacGregor, 1998, pp. 60–1, p. 73; McCarney, 2000, pp. 156–7; Pelczynski, 1971, p. 11; Singer, 1983, p. 42; Westphal, 1993, p. 259). It is Hegel's view that the 'state' to which individuals have an over-riding duty to subordinate their own selfish interests (or their liberty, as liberals understand the term) is not the former but the latter. Hegel is emphatically not suggesting, therefore, that the individual subject has an unconditional duty to obey the arbitrary commands of an absolute monarch. It is for these reasons that Allen Wood has gone so far as to argue that the claim that Hegel is a reactionary defender of Prussian absolutism is 'simply wrong' (Wood, 1991, p. ix). However, this interpretation does capture one aspect of Hegel's political thought, namely Hegel's strong emphasis on the values of order and duty. It is deficient simply because it fails completely to capture the parallel emphasis (which Hegel shares with classical liberalism) on the value of liberty, interpreted as implying a commitment to the rule of law and to constitutional government.

There is evidence which supports Pelczynski's interpretation of Hegel. On the other hand, however, this interpretation is also open to criticism. Pelczynski interprets Hegel not simply as a defender of constitutional government but as being a liberal thinker. There is no objection to associating Hegel with the Whig political thought of eighteenth-century England, as Pelczynski does (Plamenatz, 1976, p. 264). Hegel was familiar with English politics and the English constitution. In the year he died he wrote a (highly critical) essay on the English Reform Bill of 1831 (Pelczynski, 1964). Moreover, as Findlay has pointed out, the views on monarchy which Hegel expresses in the *Philosophy of Right* are not only 'in accord with modern British constitutional practice' but actually appear to have been written specifically in order 'to endorse the traditional arrangements of England' (Findlay, 1958, pp. 329–30). Like Montesquieu and many other intellectuals in both France and Germany in the eighteenth century, Hegel considered England *before* the Great Reform Act of 1832 (when it took its first significant step in the direction of democracy) as being in some ways the archetype of a 'free society', precisely because it was a constitutional monarchy. Rather, the problem with Pelczynski's claim is that he links Hegel with Locke rather than with more historically minded Whigs like Edmund Burke. The difference between these two strands of Whig thought is of decisive importance (Dickinson, 1977, pp. 57–79). For Whigs like Locke defend constitutional government by appealing to ahistorical abstract principles which are assumed to be universally valid, whereas Burke defends it by appealing in the final analysis to history, custom and tradition. In associating Hegel with Locke, Pelczynski ignores completely the importance which Hegel attaches to historical argument. The problem with Pelczynski's interpretation is that Hegel is extremely critical of the 'abstract' reasoning of Locke and classical liberalism because of its radical political implications (Hegel, 1979, pp. 156–7, pp. 286–7). Hegel maintains that, at least in the final analysis, constitutional issues 'must be discussed historically or not at all' (*ibid.*, p. 177, p. 179).

Pelczynski's interpretation of Hegel goes too far. Whereas the interpretation of Hegel as a political reactionary and a defender of absolutism attaches exclusive importance to the value of order in Hegel's political thought and ignores completely that of liberty, Pelczynski does the opposite. He does not appreciate the importance which Hegel attaches to the existing social order and to historical custom and tradition. We may conclude that although Hegel is certainly not a political reactionary, he is not a political radical either. His political thought might be said to represent an attempt to steer a middle way between these two extreme positions. Hegel's aim is to synthesise the principle of order with that of liberty. Hegel *does* subordinate the individual to the state in the broad sense, or to the organic community which is society as a whole. At the same time, however, he recognises that, as members of corporate groups, individuals possess historically inherited constitutional rights which serve to protect them from the intrusions of the 'strictly political state', and which therefore provide a guarantee of their liberties. In my view, there is very little difference between Hegel's position with respect to this issue and that of an historically minded Whig like Edmund Burke.

As for Hegel's attitude towards the French Revolution, it is ambivalent. In so far as the Revolution was associated with democracy and communism Hegel was, as the traditional interpretation maintains, opposed to it. In so far as it was associated with the rule of law and the ideal of constitutional government, he was its most enthusiastic supporter. In Hegel's opinion, the vital historical lesson to be learned from the Revolution is that the most appropriate political constitution for the modern era (and for Prussia in 1821) is one which is based, not on the principle of absolute monarchy, or indeed on the opposing principles of republicanism and democracy, but rather on the intermediate principle of constitutional monarchy (Hegel, 1979, p. 176; also p. 288; Brudner, 1981; Cristi, 1983). This is the historically evolved political ideal which Hegel recommends to his readers in the *Philosophy of Right*. For Prussia in 1821 what this amounted to was a call for cautious political reform from above, away from absolute monarchy in the direction of constitutional monarchy.

In the light of the negative opinions about democracy and communism in the text of the *Philosophy of Right* it is difficult to understand why MacGregor claims that Hegel was in favour of these things. To support this claim MacGregor raises some important methodological issues. In his view the advocates of the traditional interpretation of Hegel have misinterpreted the *Philosophy of Right*. The reason for this is that they have not appreciated the historical context within which it was produced, or Hegel's intentions when writing it. In a manner similar to both Strauss and Skinner (Strauss, 1952; Skinner, 1969), MacGregor maintains that an understanding of Hegel's intentions is 'necessary in any account of Hegel's intellectual growth' and hence for an understanding of his mature political thought (MacGregor, 1998, pp. 33–4). After the Karlsbad Decrees of 1819 Prussia was a 'police state' with very strict censorship laws. Hence, according to MacGregor, Hegel felt it necessary to communicate his real views to his readers in a coded form (MacGregor, 1998, p. 100; see also McCarney, 2000, p. 99). In support of this claim MacGregor appeals again to the authority of Heinrich Heine. According to Heine, Hegel usually spoke 'in very obscure and abstruse signs so that not everyone could decipher them – I sometimes saw him looking anxiously over his shoulder for fear that he had been understood' (MacGregor, 1998, p. 64; also Lukács, 1975, p. 462; McCarney, 2000, p. vi; Sayers, 1998, p. 103). This possibility evidently poses problems for anyone interpreting Hegel's mature political thought. For it implies that there is more than one Hegel and more than one *Philosophy of Right*. There are, MacGregor suggests, two different versions of the text. There is the published version, which is the one which is usually taken at its face value by those who read it and there is the text 'as it was read between the lines' by Hegel's friends and followers and 'interpreted in the context of the events that constrained it'. According to MacGregor, it is the *Philosophy of Right* in the latter sense which truly reflects Hegel's own views. In MacGregor's opinion, this *real* Hegel is a political radical, a democrat and a communist (MacGregor, 1998, p. 100).

MacGregor's thesis should not be dismissed out of hand. But his claim that the mature Hegel was really a democrat and a communist is highly speculative. To be substantiated it would require external historical evidence derived from our knowledge of Hegel's personal life, his correspondence, his journal, or the written testimony of his friends or close acquaintances to corroborate it. Relying heavily on the work of Jacques d'Hondt, MacGregor does present at least some evidence of this sort to back up his claim (MacGregor, 1998, pp. 52–3, p. 64, p. 76, pp. 97–9; see also d'Hondt, 1988, pp. 2–3, p. 68, p. 129, p. 135, p. 172, pp. 191–2, p. 195), although this includes the anecdotal testimony of Heinrich Heine, who is widely considered to be an unreliable source (Lukács, 1975, p. 462; McCarney, 2000, p. 99). In my view, McGregor's assertion that we are justified in ignoring completely what Hegel actually says about democracy and communism in the *Philosophy of Right*, and that we may safely conclude that the mature Hegel was actually in favour of these things, despite the explicit statements to the contrary which are to be found in the text itself, is not sufficiently well supported by this evidence.

Finally, on Hegel's idea of the 'end of history', Engels is right to associate the distinction between Hegel's idealist philosophical system and his dialectic method with the split in the 1830s and 1840s between the Right and the Left Hegelians (Engels, 1958, pp. 361–5; see also Avineri, 1972, p. 126; Berlin, 1965, pp. 63–5; McLellan, 1972, p. 36; McLellan, 1973, pp. 30–1). He is also right to suggest that the Right Hegelians were committed to the traditional reading of Hegel's views on the end of history, whereas the Left Hegelians adopted the radical interpretation of those views. It could, however, be argued that each of these interpretations is one-sided and oversimplified. Each interpretation captures just one aspect of Hegel's thought and ignores the other. The traditional interpretation focuses exclusively on Hegel's system and ignores his method, whereas the radical interpretation does the opposite. It wrongly presents Hegel as committed to an extreme version of the Heraclitean flux doctrine which states that all things are changing in all respects all of the time (Burns, 1997). Against each of these interpretations it might be suggested, as Sidney Hook has argued, that Hegel's system and his method are in fact 'indissoluble' (Hook, 1971, p. 17). Neither the traditional nor the radical interpretation, therefore, succeeds in capturing the complexity of Hegel's thinking as a whole so far as the 'end of history' is concerned.

In the *Philosophy of Right*, Hegel is certainly not a reactionary defender of the *status quo* in Prussia in 1821. He does not wish to freeze the process of historical development of the absolutist Prussian state at that particular moment in time because he thinks the end of history has actually arrived. Nevertheless, however, the mature Hegel emphatically does *not* call for the violent overthrow of the absolutist state in Prussia along the lines indicated by the French Revolution. In Hegel's view, just as in the case of France, any attempted revolutionary political transformation in Prussia would amount to a demand for far too much change far too quickly. If successful it would completely undermine the existing social and political order and thereby disrupt the principle of historical continuity altogether, with dire consequences for almost all of those affected by it, including inparticular the class of educated property owners. In the final analysis, then, Hegel is nothing more than an advocate of cautious political reform from above. His aim is the peaceful transformation of the absolute monarchy in Prussia into a constitutional monarchy – but emphatically not into a democratic republic, let alone a communist society. According to Hegel, for those living in Prussia in 1821 it is a state of this type which, for the time being at least, represents the end of world history. This is why he claims in the *Philosophy of Right*, that 'the development of the state to constitutional monarchy is the achievement of the modern world' (Hegel, 1979, p. 176).

In sum, I have argued that the traditional and the radical interpretations of Hegel's political thought are both incorrect. In a work appropriately entitled *Between Tradition and Revolution*, Manfred Riedel has rightly suggested that Hegel seeks to steer a middle way between the two extremes of a traditionalist approach to politics, on the one hand, and a revolutionary approach on the other (Riedel, 1984). Of the interpretations considered so far the one which comes closest to capturing Hegel's position is that of Pelczynski. Hegel is indeed an advocate of constitutional government, and specifically of constitutional monarchy. In the English context it is correct to describe him as a Whig. In my view, however, Pelczynski is wrong when he claims that Hegel is a liberal thinker. Rather, the most appropriate home for Hegel is the other branch of English Whiggery linked with the name of Edmund Burke, which today is referred to as traditional conservatism. Hegel is a conservative political thinker (Berki, 1977, p. 172; Cassirer, 1967, p. 251; Hook, 1970b, pp. 87–8, p. 92, p. 96; Lindsay, 1932, p. 52, p. 57; Mannheim, 1986, p. 94, p. 144; Mehta, 1968, pp. 126–7, p. 130; Nisbet, 1986, p. 2, pp. 19–20, pp. 35–8, p. 49, p. 79, p. 89, p. 111; Schuettinger, 1970, p. 36, p. 119; Scruton, 1988, pp. 135–6, p. 153). It is important to note, however, that Hegel is not committed to the defence of every aspect of the *status quo* in Prussia in 1821. He does not defend existing historical customs and traditions solely on positive grounds or simply because they are old. Nor is he completely opposed to all political reform. The claim that Hegel is a conservative depends on the view that conservatism itself is a modern political movement which seeks to reconcile the conflicting values of order and liberty, permanence and progression, tradition and revolution (Burns, 1995; Burns, 1996; Burns, 1999). It is for this reason that traditional conservatism might be said to be a Hegelian enterprise. The political thought of Hegel may be seen as a sophisticated philosophical defence of this conservative political ideal.

9

Mill (1806–1873)

Jonathan Seglow

Introduction

Published in 1859, Mill described *On Liberty* as 'a philosophical textbook of a single truth': 'the importance, to man and society ... of giving full freedom to human nature to expand itself in innumerable and conflicting directions' (Mill, 1969, p. 150). It remains the most eloquent and passionate defence of individual liberty in all political thought. Though he is sometimes criticised for vagueness and lack of acuity, no one who reads *On Liberty* can miss this central message. Yet Mill was born and brought up in a different guise; he was the self-conscious heir of the utilitarian radicals, a movement centred on the ideas of Jeremy Bentham. For Bentham the only moral good was pleasure; laws and social arrangements should be designed to maximise it and thus engineer the 'greatest good for the greatest number'. Individual liberty was submerged under this wider movement for social reform. Mill's father expected him to carry forward the movement and famously educated him expressly for that purpose. Following a mental crisis in his early twenties Mill rebelled against the more reductionist and rationalist spirit of Benthamite utilitarianism and embraced the need for spontaneity, diversity and richness of life. His own version of that creed was announced in his *Utilitarianism* (1861). The extent to which individual liberty can be derived from the utilitarian system has become a crucial issue for subsequent Mill scholars.

Mill's other political writings include *Considerations on Representative Government* (1861) which argued for the superiority of democratic government and yet included some explicitly elitist measures and *The Subjection of Women* (1869) which expressed liberal feminist sentiments consonant with *On Liberty*. The latter was much inspired by Harriet Taylor whom Mill married in 1851 and whose influence on his work remains controversial.

Mill also applied himself to a wide range of other topics. In *A System of Logic* (1843) he defended an empiricist view of the origin of mathematical and scientific truths. In *The Principles of Political Economy* (1848), he examined laissez-faire economics, and argued for some radical reforms. (His fragmentary *Chapters on Socialism* was published after his death). These works assured Mill's reputation as a philosopher and social critic even before he came to write *On Liberty*. But they are not widely read today and even *Representative Government* and *Subjection of Women* have been eclipsed by his main work's luminous message. It is, therefore, *On Liberty* on which I shall concentrate here.

Mill's topic in the essay is not despotic governments but the tyranny of popular opinion and governments which legislate in its name. The thrust of the essay is a plea for individual freedom against the potentially coercive power of the 'likings and dislikings of society' (1991, pp. 13–14). His opposition to this is total:

The object of this Essay is to assert one very simple principle, as entitled to govern absolutely the dealings of society with the individual in the way of compulsion and control, whether the means used be physical force in the form of legal penalties, or the moral coercion of public opinion. That principle is, that the sole end for which mankind are warranted, individually or collectively, in interfering with the liberty of action of any of their number is self-protection. That the only purpose for which power can be rightfully exercised over any member of a civilised community, against his will, is to prevent harm to others. His own good, whether physical or moral, is not a sufficient warrant (*ibid.*, p. 17).

In this, the most famous passage in the book, Mill offers unqualified protection for the individual against the intrusion of society or law. It says that each person can do as he wishes up to the point where he harms other people. We can persuade, exhort, entreat a person to do as we want, but we cannot compel or coerce him, even for his own good, unless he himself is being prevented from harming another (or being punished for doing so). Following other commentators, I will call this the Harm Principle (though it is sometimes referred to by others as the Liberty Principle). It divides the 'self-regarding' sphere, where the individual is sovereign from the 'other-regarding' sphere where we are accountable to others. Mill further specifies liberty of conscience, thought and expression; liberty of tastes and pursuits – 'of framing the plan of our life to suit our own character' – and liberty of combination and association between individuals as constituting the self-regarding area (*ibid.*, 17).

Freedom of expression is so important that Mill devotes a whole chapter to defend it. The result is perhaps the finest defence of a right to free speech in the corpus of political philosophy. Though his discussion is a long one, Mill's basic point is simple enough. We cannot tell, when she makes it, whether a person's assertion of some opinion is true or false, right or wrong. To silence someone because you believe her opinion false is to assume what you are not entitled to, that you infallibly know the truth. We can only arrive at the truth through the largest possible circulation of opinions and, Mill says, we should even resurrect known falsehoods to challenge truths which have become stale and dead. (I do not consider Mill's defence of freedom of speech further in this chapter. For useful discussions of it see Riley, 1998, pp. 55–72; Skorupski 1989, pp. 369–88; Ten, 1980, pp. 124–43; Haworth, 1998, Part 1.)

Though vital, free speech is not the main purpose of the Harm Principle, which at its most general is intended to provide a sphere of liberty within which each person can develop her individuality as one of the 'chief ingredients' of well-being. In opposition to Victorian conformity, Mill praises energy, vigour, passion, spontaneity, originality, and 'experiments in living'. He derides conformity, prejudice and the dead weight of custom and tradition. 'Human nature', he writes, 'is not a machine to be built after a model ... but a tree, which requires to grow and develop itself on all sides, according to the tendency of the inward forces which make it a living thing' (1991, p. 66). Developed individuals, moreover, would create a diverse society, one where experiments in living had revealed the manifold ways in which human beings could flourish and develop. Though not a relativist, Mill more than most stressed the fact that the truth is plural and many-sided. The Harm Principle was not intended to regulate a society where each person would, as a matter of free choice, decide to follow her peers. It was designed to protect all those who love liberty, new ideas and experiments in living. Since we cannot know, until we have experienced them, which ways of life will turn out to be worthy and valuable, so men and women should follow whatever direction their own search for truth takes them. That we should have the freedom to do so is the central message of the essay as a whole.

Problems and Issues

The first problem we encounter in reading *On Liberty* is deciding what Mill means by harm. The question is a crucial one since harm to others appears as the sole and apparently simple criterion dividing the self- and other-regarding spheres. Yet nowhere is harm precisely defined and hence elucidating Mill's meaning is a task of reconstruction. On one aspect, however, he is unequivocal: offence or dislike of an action cannot count as harm since otherwise the Harm Principle would provide no protection against society's likings and dislikings. Thus a Muslim's distress at a Christian eating pork (to take his well-known example) could not possibly support a ban on the eating of it (1991, pp. 94–5). This sort of harm just doesn't count. On the other hand (and notwithstanding his defence of freedom of speech), a person may be legitimately prohibited from inciting a turbulent crowd since this could foreseeably cause harm to others such as innocent bystanders nearby (*ibid.*, p. 62). Similarly, Mill also makes it clear that we can harm others by our failure to meet a 'distinct and assignable obligation to any other person' even with acts which apparently affect only ourselves. 'No person ought to be punished simply for being drunk; but a soldier or a policeman should be punished for being drunk on duty' for each of them has placed himself under a certain duty to others (*ibid.*, pp. 90–1). The drunken soldier does not directly harm his garrison but he indirectly does so by putting himself in a state that, off-duty, he would be perfectly entitled to. Harm, therefore, though it excludes mere displeasure or dislike, does include reference to rules and common social duties. Mill does not adopt the extreme position where only attacks on one's physical integrity are instances of harm. Finally, it is important to remember that the mere occurrence of harm is not, for Mill, a sufficient reason for interference, but rather a necessary one. There is the further question of whether it is expedient to do so. Success in business or a competitive exam can both cause harm of the relevant sort to others, yet there is no reason to punish them if the greater good of human liberty is our aim (*ibid.*, p. 105).

The problem of harm is further complicated by the fact that, shortly after announcing the Harm Principle at the beginning of the Essay, Mill goes on to say that utility remains the 'ultimate appeal on all ethical questions; but it must be utility in the largest sense, grounded in the permanent interests of man as a progressive being' (*ibid.*, p. 15). The Harm Principle, then, is not a moral right granted us by God or the first axiom of an ethical system, but presumes instead a prior commitment to the utilitarian doctrine, at least in this largest sense. In *Utilitarianism*, Mill offers us a comprehensive moral system intended to govern all our actions and not just those where a person's freedom is in question. 'Utilitarianism or the Greatest Happiness Principle', he writes, 'holds that actions are right insofar as they tend to promote happiness, wrong as they tend to produce the reverse of happiness' (*ibid.*, p. 137). Happiness is the only thing desirable as an end, so everything we think valuable is so because of the happiness it brings. Utilitarianism thus promotes as the only moral quality an experience with which we could scarcely be more familiar. There need be no appeal to Platonic forms, natural rights or other theological mystifications. Happiness is, furthermore, the only criterion of morality in the sense that it alone should guide us in formulating all laws, rules and principles. Here then we have a wider context in which the Harm Principle must be placed.

This changes the way we understand it. For example, in *Utilitarianism* it seems that Mill is committed to one truth above all: he is committed to the utilitarian view that pleasure and the absence of pain are the only things ultimately valuable as ends; all other ends, however diverse, are only valuable in terms of them. But we also know that Mill is the champion of diversity, pluralism and a variety of human situations. So how does a utilitarian approach the question of pluralism? The answer is far from clear. On other issues the two works seem more consistent. Thus in *Utilitarianism* Mill famously defends the 'higher pleasures' that engage the intellect and imagination over the base pleasures we share with beasts – it is 'better to be Socrates dissatisfied than a fool satisfied' (*ibid.*, p. 140). The fool is a prisoner of his own unthinking prejudices, Socrates an individual true to himself and a critic of the society around him. This sentiment is echoed in *On Liberty* where Mill writes that the person who has developed her individual character and enjoys the higher pleasures is 'a noble and beautiful object of contemplation' (*ibid.*, p. 70). Yet noble objects or tall trees (individualists and freethinkers who are often the vanguards for new ways of life) may look down critically on their lesser neighbours. So that is a further issue: whether Mill intended all to achieve individuality or just a dedicated liberal elite?

Elitism, diversity and – especially – the meaning of harm, we shall all revisit shortly, but first we must address more fully why these differences in interpreting Mill have arisen in the first place.

Why Conflicting Interpretations?

Like all great books, *On Liberty* has become a battleground for its interpreters, although it is not immediately clear why this should be so. Mill writes in English. He addresses the concerns of a society not so far removed from our own. He introduces no esoteric or technical terms and is not a system builder. Rather he combines the empiricist virtues of clear, limpid prose with an earnest desire to be understood. The interpretive disputes which plague *On Liberty* sit rather oddly with Mill's 'one very simple principle'. I have already hinted at one cause of dispute: the meaning of harm and Mill's division between self- and other-regarding acts. The problem is that, given a sufficiently expansive notion of harm, every act can be interpreted as other-regarding. I read a book or practise my religion in the privacy of my own home: the mere thought that I am doing so 'harms' those for whom the book is corrupting, the religion a sin. Though Mill wants to exclude society's likings and dislikings in demarcating a self-regarding sphere he does not seem to do this in a sufficiently robust way. Into this failure of definition flow numerous interpretive positions including a denial that the distinction is possible at all. '[T]he attempt to distinguish between self-regarding acts and acts which regard others', wrote Mill's most famous contemporary critic James Fitzjames Stephen, 'is like an attempt to distinguish between acts which happen in time and acts which happen in space' (Fitzjames Stephen, 1967, p. 28). For conservatives like Stephen, this lack of distinction empowers the enforcement of virtue and prevention of vice as legitimate ends of law and public opinion. Conversely, for liberals sympathetic to Mill, the problem has been to delineate the self-regarding sphere in a way that is philosophically cogent and consonant with his intentions.

In fact the criticism goes further, to the heart of Mill's ultimate commitments. For, having established that the self/other-regarding distinction is undrawable, Mill's critics go on to argue that it is undrawable precisely because of his 'ultimate appeal' to utilitarianism. The problem is that the Harm Principle and utilitarianism have quite different logics. The former provides an absolute constraint on how we treat individuals; the latter is interested in the sum of happiness. A society where one person has a great good and two people have none is better than one where a lesser good is divided equitably amongst the three. In principle there is no limit to how we may treat people in order to maximise the total sum; in particular, there is nothing which says we must not harm them. On utilitarian grounds, then, we can subject the individual to whatever coercion is necessary to promote the general happiness. We can silence the dissenter, lock up the innocent, enforce a religion, all manifestly actions which the Harm Principle is designed to outlaw and yet which, given an unpopular or 'sinful' minority, may produce the most happiness. This cannot be what Mill had in mind. But nor, reversing matters now, is it necessarily true that a principle licensing a wide sphere of personal liberty underwrites a society happier than its alternatives. In societies cemented by strong codes on individual conduct there are good utilitarian grounds for preserving the traditional structure of society and not allowing liberty to challenge the common social norms. There can be strong utilitarian reasons, in fact, for stifling diversity. Few of Mill's contemporary readers, however, have endorsed the latter conclusion; as we shall see they have either dismissed utilitarianism on libertarian grounds (maintaining that there is a contradiction at the heart of Mill's thought) or sought arguments which show that, first appearances notwith-standing, the Harm Principle can be derived from the utilitarian system.

Conflicting Interpretations

Utilitarian Paternalist or Radical Libertarian?

The greatest good as a goal seems hard to square with the value of individ-ual liberty. Conversely, a serious commitment to freedom must mean we allow individuals to do as they want whether or not they promote the gen-eral welfare. While most critics of Mill have seen him caught inexorably between these basic principles, two notorious commentaries have each taken one of these principles – utilitarian paternalism or total liberty – to its extreme.

According to Maurice Cowling 'Mill was attempting in *On Liberty* to protect the elite from domination by the mediocrity' (1963, p. 104). This elite is the 'rational clerisy', a dedicated core of intellectuals whose mission of propagating a secular national culture is first set out by Mill in his essay on Coleridge. Welcoming the decline in Christian beliefs, Mill wished to replace the authority of the Church with a new consensus, furnished by the emergent science of sociology. Thus '*On Liberty*, contrary to common opinion, was not so much a plea for individual freedom, as a means of ensuring that Christianity would be superseded by that form of liberal rationalistic utilitarianism which went by the name of the Religion of Humanity' (*ibid.*, p. xiii). The clerisy's task is to elevate the masses and educate them to accept their own moral and scientific values. *On Liberty*, far from being a plea for diversity, is in fact a manifesto for this new rational consensus. Indeed, in his enthusiasm for it, 'Mill may be accused of more than a touch of something resembling moral totalitarianism' (*ibid.*, p. xii).

Cowling's extreme interpretation has been ably criticised by Rees, Ten and others (Ten, 1980, pp. 144–51; Rees, 1985, pp. 126–36). First, Cowling's Mill who believes in the 'homogeneity of all rational judgment' is strangely related to the Mill who championed all his life the 'freedom of human nature to expand itself in innumerable and conflicting directions' (Cowling, 1963, p. 26; Mill, 1969, p. 150). Cowling can only overlook Mill's plea for diversity by glossing over the difference between advocating a substantive doctrine and compelling others to accept it. But this difference is just what *On Liberty* is about! For Cowling's Mill, freedom is merely instrumentally useful for the clerisy to promote our higher natures. But again, this overlooks close internal relationship between freedom and happiness so that choice and experimentation were part of the happiness of all those who had developed their individuality (a point to which I shall return). Mill is, arguably, an elitist of sorts, but hardly a moral totalitarian.

By contrast, Gertrude Himmelfarb (1974) presents us with a libertarian Mill unconcerned with the general welfare. Yet on Mill's dominant concerns, Himmelfarb is close to Cowling. The difference is that Himmelfarb perceives *On Liberty* as an aberrant text which came towards the end of a writing career revealing a rather different attitude to freedom and the individual. Thus in his early essay, *The Spirit of the Age*, Mill distinguishes between transitional and natural periods of history and looks forward to a time when '[t]he most virtuous and best-instructed of the nation will acquire that ascendancy over the opinions and feelings of the rest, by which alone England can emerge from this crisis of transition and enter once again into a natural state of society' (cited in Himmelfarb, 1974, p. 41). This is Cowling's rational clerisy. For this Mill, freedom of discussion is 'at best a very mixed good, at worst a necessary evil' (*ibid.*, p. 41). But *On Liberty* is a *volte-face*. Under his wife's influence, Mill espoused a philosophy 'which made the individual the repository of wisdom and virtue and which made the freedom of the individual the sole aim of social policy' (*ibid.*, p. 91). Individual desires and inclinations are the source of all good whilst the social virtues are rejected (*ibid.*, p. 91). Elsewhere Mill argues for 'a liberty qualified and supplemented by other principles such as duty, morality, discipline, the public good, tradition, community, nationality, society' (*ibid.*, p. 168). In *On Liberty*, however, these are rejected and in their place is prized solely 'the absolute value of liberty, the absolute sovereignty of the individual' (*ibid.*, p. 272).

Yet Himmelfarb's critics have been more inclined to see the *Spirit of the Age* as the deviant product of a younger Mill (he later excluded it from a collection of his essays) and to search for a more charitable interpretation of his other writings which would make them consistent with *On Liberty*. Himmelfarb is impressed with Mill's uncompromising language at the beginning of the essay where the Harm Principle is revealed as an 'absolute' principle protecting the 'sovereign' individual. Thus she tends to interpret it as the sole principle governing the relations between individuals. But much of what Mill says goes against this libertarian reading. We have already seen that no person may violate a 'distinct and assignable obligation' to another and in general Mill calls for 'a great increase of disinterested exertion to promote the good of others' (1991, p. 84). Indeed, he insists that individuals can rightfully be compelled to do good for other people such as give evidence in court, defend the country or save another's life (*ibid.*, p. 15). The Harm Principle, with its absolute ban on moralistic and paternalistic interference in liberty, is intended to leave individuals discretion about how to live. But other kinds of compulsion may be justified, *pace* Himmelfarb, and Mill clearly thinks more altruistically and socially minded lives are more worthy ones. This seems to take him back towards utilitarianism.

Traditional Views: Mill is Inconsistent

Rather than reading into Mill extreme libertarian or utilitarian views, most scholarship has seen both principles animating his work. Indeed that has been just the problem. For on this traditional account Mill is regarded as an inconsistent, eclectic writer, a great advocate of freedom and utility, but not a true philosopher or systematiser of ideas. For Isaiah Berlin, perhaps the greatest twentieth-century liberal writer, *On Liberty* remains the classic statement of individual liberty despite its lack of rigour and many weak arguments. 'At the centre of Mill's thought and feeling lies, not his utilitarianism ... but his passionate belief that men are made human by their capacity for choice' (Berlin, 1969, p. 192). Why then does utility remain Mill's ultimate principle? Does he not see that utilitarianism has nothing to say about choice? Berlin implies as much. Mill is 'officially committed to the exclusive pursuit of happiness' and yet 'his voice is most his own when he describes the glories of individual freedom or denounces whatever seeks to curtail or extinguish it' (*ibid.*, p. 178). For McCloskey, the dominant message of the essay is clouded by the seemingly arbitrary nature of many of Mill's examples and illustrations (McCloskey, 1971, pp. 104–29). His contention that the state could legitimately forbid marriage, for example, if a couple cannot show they have the means for supporting a family, is illiberal and untenable (Mill, 1991, p. 120; McCloskey, 1971, p. 129). Like Berlin, McCloskey sees a thinker clear in his own mind about the importance of liberty, but confused, unsystematic and inconsistent in its applications.

Other writers have made the further criticism that the Harm Principle must be infused with utilitarian reasons for and against interference, none of them, by that token, absolute. Honderich usefully catalogues the several formulations of the Harm Principle variously distributed in the text. He believes that the essay contains a great many utilitarian reasons for interfering with liberty and, in general concludes that 'the matter of intervention must be settled by the Principle of Utility' for this alone is 'the absolute principle to which Mill is committed' (Honderich, 1974, p. 468, p. 467). And yet 'there is little to be said for it' (*ibid.*, p. 467). The Harm Principle, if derived wholly from the principle of utility, can hardly be said to be an advance on the latter. Once again, Mill's intentions are not what he thought they were.

The lengthiest and most perspicuous example of the traditional view is to be found in C. L. Ten's *Mill on Liberty* (1980). Ten's argument hinges on the notion of 'morality-dependent harm', implicit in Mill, and made explicit by Honderich in a later article (1982). The phrase refers to harm which depends for its existence on a belief, on the part of the person harmed, that the action which caused it is wrong. Offence at a shop's Sunday opening or outrage at the gay commune next door are examples. There is no harm independent of the attitudes someone happens to have, something not true if she is physically assaulted and hardly true if she is insulted. Honderich lays great stress on a paragraph in *On Liberty* where Mill refers somewhat elliptically to acts allowable in private but which, if conducted in public, are 'a violation of good manners' and therefore offences against others liable to prohibition (Mill, 1991, pp. 108–9; see also Wolff, 1998). Public sex or nudity seems to be the sort of thing he has in mind. Honderich argues that this shows Mill was not opposed in principle to intervention in cases of morality-dependent harm. Ten argues, on the contrary, that the Harm Principle is a straightforward dismissal of morality-dependent harm and, indeed, that the point of the essay was just to discount these kinds of moral attitudes from dictating the scope of an individual's personal freedom. Certainly, that seems to be consistent with Mill's many examples in *On Liberty* such as Muslims' antipathy to pork. Indeed, one writer calls the exclusion of morality-dependent distress 'the essential Millian claim' and another claims that he positively welcomed it as the source of moral progress (Riley, 1991, p. 23; Waldron, 1987). Ten maintains that Mill's dismissal of such harm is incompatible with the contingent approach of utilitarianism where all sources of (dis)utility must enter into the calculation. According to Ten, this is because Mill is a champion of liberty alone; his utilitarianism is an unfortunate adjunct of his liberalism and cannot be derived from it. Mill should be praised as a champion of liberty; but that is so much the worse for his (or indeed any) utilitarianism. Ten's argument is subtle and often complex but its central argument is encapsulated by him thus: in deciding whether to intervene in liberty 'the facts to be taken into account by the utilitarian will include precisely what Mill was so eager to exclude, namely, the distress of those who are offended simply by the thought that others are … engaged in acts which they regard as wrong or which they merely dislike' (Ten, 1980, p. 34).

Revisionist Views

Despite their objections, Berlin, McCloskey, Honderich and Ten are, generally speaking, allies of Mill, in contrast to Cowling and Himmelfarb who are critics. Hence the problem for the former – that Mill's self-regarding sphere is, or logically should be, infused with utilitarian considerations for and against intervention – becomes one which requires resolution. That Mill does not resolve it is the orthodox or traditional view of Mill – Berlin is perhaps the best representative of this perspective. That orthodoxy, however, came to be challenged in the 1960s, which inaugurated what John Gray calls the 'revisionary' wave of interpretation of Mill (Gray, 1996, p. 10 and see n. 17 pp. 160–1). The revisionist writers believed that Mill was, after all, a consistent thinker, proclaiming in his two great essays a single, harmonious vision. Further excavation of Mill would reveal this, so the revisionist argument goes, and along the way supply his key terms – liberty, utility, harm and self-regarding action – with clear, technical definitions. I will outline these revisionary views and comment on them further in the conclusion.

Rees on Interests

Mill's primary difficulty, that any act could in principle affect and therefore harm others, was famously addressed by John Rees (1991) who is rightly seen as inaugurating the revisionary school of interpretation. Rees aimed to introduce precision by imputing to Mill a distinction between acts which affect others and acts which affect their interests. Mill does indeed use the notion of interests at several points in the essay. He writes, for example, 'that for such actions as are prejudicial to the interests of others, the individual is accountable' (Rees, 1991, p. 104). The point is that whilst almost all our acts affect other people rather fewer of them impinge upon others' *interests* and it is only in these more serious cases that liberty may be restricted. The great many acts affecting others but not their interests we are fully at liberty to commit. Harming another means harming his or her interests. This shifts the burden to what Mill means by interests. Although he uses the notion, Mill never develops it and never specifies just what our interests are. Rees suggests that interests 'depend for their existence on social recognition and are closely connected with prevailing standards about the sort of behaviour a man can legitimately expect from others' (*ibid.*, p. 175). But whether this is an adequate definition we shall investigate later.

Dworkin on External Preferences

Rees's account is important because he tries to firm up the necessary distinction between self- and other-regarding acts. However, he does not directly address the problem of how utilitarianism infects the scope of liberty identified by Ten, Honderich and others. It is this latter issue which has most exercised Mill's readers and in this and the next two sections I shall present three revisionist attempts to reconcile utility and liberty. The first of these is contained in Ronald Dworkin's book, *Taking Rights Seriously* (1977). Dworkin uses the idea of preference utilitarianism where what is maximised is not happiness but the satisfaction of peoples' preferences: the right thing to do is what most people prefer. However, officials trying to maximise the welfare of their society may hesitate to implement a policy based on a majority's preference that homosexuality should be treated with contempt, for example, or that whites should not mix with blacks. Dworkin calls these latter types of preference *external* preferences since they reflect a person's belief for how other people should be treated and not just oneself. They are not merely *personal* preferences (*ibid.*, p. 234). External preferences offend against the ideal of utilitarianism itself since utilitarianism promises to treat each person with equal concern and respect. A person's desire that blacks should not accompany whites at law school, for example, is an external preference that denies black people an opportunity given to whites. It reflects a moralised belief in the superiority of one race over another. Hence Dworkin commends a utilitarianism cleansed of external preferences and faithful to its own ideal of equal concern and respect. And this is eminently consistent with Mill's Harm Principle, which says that my freedom and opportunity should not be at the mercy of other people's likings and dislikings. This is precisely what a utilitarianism reconstructed to exclude external preferences achieves. Hence for Dworkin, 'the arguments of John Stuart Mill in *On Liberty* are not counter-utilitarian but, on the contrary, arguments in service of the only defensible form of utilitarianism' (*ibid.*, p. 276).

Ryan on the Art of Life
For Dworkin, the problem with external preferences is that they are unjust. This takes us into what Mill says about justice and, more generally, a much closer concern than Dworkin with what Mill actually says. Thus in the neglected final chapter of *Utilitarianism* Mill discusses the relationship between justice and utility. 'Justice', he writes, 'is a name for certain social requirements, which, regarded collectively, stand higher in the scale of social utility, and are therefore of more paramount obligation, than any others' (Mill, 1991, p. 200). Mill goes on to analyse justice in terms of moral rights. Two things are noteworthy about his analysis. The first is the affinity between Mill's discussion here and what he says about harm in *On Liberty*. I mentioned earlier that harm includes reference to rules and

social duties: though Mill does not say so he hints at an identification of harm with injustice, both defined in terms of violating rights. Second, we should note the contrast Mill makes between the 'paramount' utilities of justice and utility in general. The implication is that there are many sources of utility which are not matters of justice or morality. The former covers all appraisals of worth, the latter concern only duties and rights.

Alan Ryan's interpretation of Mill hinges on precisely this distinction between evaluation and what others can demand of us. Ryan looks to Mill's *System of Logic* where in a few brief paragraphs he speculates on creating an Art of Life as 'a body of doctrine' for our conduct (Ryan, 1991; Mill, 1973, p. 949). Such an Art would have three departments: 'Morality, Prudence or Policy, and Aesthetics; the Right, the Expedient, and the Beautiful or Noble, in human conduct and works' (*ibid.*, p. 949). These branches exhaustively define the proper subjects of our approbation: we may praise a person's action because it is right, because it is sensible or because it is noble. Utility remains the ultimate standard for appraisal since moral, prudential and aesthetic conduct all promote, in different ways, human happiness (*ibid.*, p. 951).

While aesthetics evaluates the quality of conduct, morality and prudence are concerned with whether our action affects others or ourselves. The subject of prudence is the agent's own good. Morality is concerned with our relations with others and with rules forbidding our harming them. That these three divisions do represent different ways of assessing conduct seems plain enough. As Ryan shows through the example of a man repaying his debt: we may praise him for doing what is right, for acting sensibly in his own interests, or for doing what is noble or brave (1991, p. 165; cf. Ryan, 1987, p. 118). In addition, the Art of Life can explain Mill's distinction between higher and lower pleasures. Higher pleasures are not more moral or prudential than lower ones, but they are of greater aesthetic value, more noble, admirable and so on (Ryan, 1987, pp. 216–17). From the point of view of liberty, the important division is between morality on the one hand, and prudence and aesthetics on the other. The key point is that Mill's categorisation means that morality is, and can only be, about harm to other persons and the enforcement of rules which prevent and punish them. By contrast, the self-regarding sphere is the province of prudence and aesthetics. The task of the Harm Principle is to clear a space for personal and aesthetic ideals to flourish; morality, by definition, has no place there (Ryan, 1991, p. 165). In fact there can be no such thing as private immorality once the self-regarding sphere is taken out of the province of morality altogether. Immorality must be public for it to be immoral: a person acting within his own self-regarding sphere can be behaving imprudently or basely but not immorally. Within this schema, then, there is no place for morality-dependent harm. Rather, 'Mill's point is that moral judgements must be grounded on the harm the agent knowingly does to others; what lies outside this realm is a fit matter for prudence and aesthetics, fit for entreaty, expostulation, exhortation, but not compulsion, not punishment' (Ryan, 1987, p. 240).

It is, therefore, not what a person does in the self-regarding sphere that makes him liable for punishment, but the way his action impacts upon others. The policeman drunk on duty is behaving basely and foolishly but we only punish him because – other-regardingly – he puts the public at risk and hence his behaviour is wrong. As Mill himself puts it, self-regarding acts 'may be proofs of any amount of folly [not prudent], want of personal dignity and self-respect [not admirable], but they are only a subject of moral reprobation when they involve a breach of duty to others' (Mill, 1991, p. 87). Harm is about violating duties and this is all the Harm Principle forbids. In the self-regarding sphere, we maximise happiness by allowing individuals to pursue their own prudential and aesthetic ideals.

The Berger–Gray Strategy

The final and most complex revisionist view of Mill we shall consider integrates many of the ideas we have encountered so far. It begins, however, by considering what Mill really means by happiness. We already know that Mill (in contrast to Bentham) does not hold that all pleasures are equally valuable: the higher pleasures connected with individuality and the intellectual and imaginative faculties are superior in kind. In his *Happiness, Justice, Freedom*, Berger distinguishes between happiness and pleasure in Mill, arguing that the former is the important notion (Berger, 1984, pp. 37–43). While an indeterminate number of goods may come to be elements of a person's happiness, there are also certain permanent requisites of happiness including 'a sense of one's independence and self-determination, a sense of power, [and] of freedom' (*ibid.*, p. 40). These, furthermore, are necessary ingredients in the higher pleasures. Central here is the link made between happiness and freedom. Identifying these two is the crucial move in ridding utilitarianism of other-regarding pains and pleasures. For the person who values her own autonomy morality-dependent harm can have very little weight. Her happiness comes from determining her own life; she may have altruistic feelings towards others but she respects their right to liberty. Mill's ideal liberal utilitarian society consists, then, of men and women who recognise their essential interest in being free (pp. 230–53). Identifying their freedom with their happiness, utility is maximised by each person living as they wish and this is just what the Harm Principle prescribes.

Gray's argument is similar to Berger's but turns on Mill's optimistic belief that individuals will become progressively more enlightened (Gray, 1996). A problem with Berger's argument that, as a matter of fact, people do experience morality-dependent distress, they do wish to limit other's liberty and they sometimes take pleasure (or are saved from pain) in doing so. Gray seeks to overcome this stumbling block and builds on much of the revisionary scholarship on Mill we have encountered so far. His case for the compatibility of utilitarianism and liberty consists of three separate claims. First, he attributes to Mill a theory of *indirect* utilitarianism which evaluates the maxims and precepts of the Art of Life (including morality) but does not itself provide guidance for action. The direct pursuit of happiness is self-defeating. An indirect strategy where utilitarianism is no longer a principle of action incorporates the wisdom that we make ourselves most happy through attachment to worthy or prudential plans and projects rather than ceaselessly striving for happiness itself. It also saves us from the obligation of paternalistically interfering in others' lives in order to make them happier. Thus Gray believes that Mill intended utilitarianism to be a principle of evaluation, but not itself a practical maxim. And indeed in *Utilitarianism*, Mill does distinguish between utility as the ultimate principle and those subordinate principles we apply by it (Mill, 1991, p. 157).

Second, Mill argues that as individuals develop their potential in increasingly advanced societies they will find happiness more and more in the active and energetic pursuit of projects and activities which exercise their powers of autonomy and choice. Far from being a passive Benthamite sensation, happiness for Mill is found through each individual conducting successive experiments in living as she seeks to discover that form of life that best matches her unique individual endowment. In thus steering their lives each person develops their distinctive excellences of character and finds their authentic sources of happiness. Since our excellences and endowments are different a diverse society will be the result. Moreover, the higher pleasures, on this interpretation, are ones that can only be enjoyed autonomously, as human beings employ their capacities of choice and deliberation in diverse and various activities. Moralistic pleasures and antipathies will gradually wither away. For Gray, like Berger, Mill draws a very tight conceptual connection between individuality and happiness.

Third, Gray makes use of the notion of interests first highlighted by Rees. But unlike Rees, Gray attributes to Mill two invariant vital interests in security and autonomy. Security involves the 'reliability of established expectations', the minimal rules of social life which are protected by the moral rights of the final chapter of *Utilitarianism* (Gray, 1996, p. 54). *On Liberty* defends our vital interest in autonomy. Our security once assured, we require autonomy to frame and implement those successive plans of life which bring happiness and develop our natures (*ibid.*, p. 55). The protection of our interest in autonomy is the task of the Harm Principle. It says that each person should have maximum personal liberty circumscribed only by the vital interests of others where these define the meaning of harm. Morality-dependent harm does not count, on this view, since it is a kind of harm more comprehensive than the need to protect the vital interests alone. Thus 'only harm to vital interests can justify restricting liberty' (*ibid.*, p. 68). The vital interests in autonomy and security belong, in fact, to Mill's utility in the largest sense; they are his 'permanent interests of man as a progressive being' (Mill, 1991, p. 15).

Let us put the pieces together. Indirect utilitarianism releases individuals from the endless obligation to promote each other's happiness and opens up a space for subordinate principles. Happiness as autonomy or individuality explains the significance of the higher pleasures and helps defuse the problem of morality-dependent harm. Finally, the vital interest in autonomy is protected by the Harm Principle, a subordinate principle allowable under indirect utilitarianism which prohibits utilitarian appeals to morality-dependent antipathies. Put simply, Gray's argument amounts to the claim that more utility will be produced with the Harm Principle than without it. Granting individuals the freedom to discover their own autonomous sources of happiness, as the Harm Principle seeks to do, will, in the long run, maximize happiness defined in terms of self-development and individuality. Hence, according to Gray, Mill's argument rests on 'an inductive wager about the future of human nature' (1996, p. 120). Happiness as individuality is achieved in a liberal social order underwritten by the Harm Principle, but not in more conservative or traditional societies populated by less developed human beings.

Evaluation

I suggested earlier that it is wrong to regard Mill as either a utilitarian paternalist (Cowling) or radical libertarian (Himmelfarb) since each of these readings over-emphasises one aspect of his thought – utilitarian or liberal – and neglects the other. An adequate interpretation must do justice to both. In particular, it must address the problem I identified earlier, that Mill's self-regarding sphere is ill-defined and prone to utilitarian incursion in the name of the greatest overall happiness. This is what the interpretive strategies of Rees, Dworkin, Ryan, Gray and Berger all attempt to overcome. Dworkin's preference theory is perhaps the least satisfactory since there is nothing in the internal structure of utilitarianism that tells us to endorse personal preferences which concern only oneself whilst rejecting external preferences which do not. The utilitarian's aim is simply to maximise the overall level of preference satisfaction. Utilitarianism treats people with equal concern and respect only insofar as each person's preferences, whether internal, external or whatever, go into the maximising calculation. But whatever policy produces the greatest total satisfaction, even if that includes unpleasant external preferences, must be the one the utilitarian supports. This may be inconsistent with Mill's (and our) liberalism but it is logical and consistent in itself (Ten, 1991, p. 224; cf. Hart, 1979). Rees's attempt to address directly the apparent vagueness of the self-regarding sphere seems a better approach. Through the notion of interests, Rees makes a strong case for thinking Mill to be a more systematic and less confused thinker than was traditionally thought. However, Rees is less convincing when it comes to delineating precisely what our interests are. On Rees's own account – not one, in fact, he explicitly imputes to Mill – interests are referenced to prevailing social standards. But if prevailing standards are the source of interests it is not clear how they can protect against unwarranted invasions of liberty. Interests based on a popular moral code could, in fact, severely curtail the scope of individual freedom. In a society where marriages were arranged, for example, choosing your own marriage partner would violate others' socially recognised interest in society having a certain character – precisely the kind of other-regarding interest which Mill was so keen to exclude in the name of liberty.

Ryan, Gray and Berger, by contrast, attempt to show that there would not be utilitarian intrusion in liberty once utilitarianism is understood in the right way, in the wider context of Mill's thought. But they too face the problem that utilitarianism remains his self-avowedly 'ultimate principle'. Thus it may indeed be, as Ryan argues, that the self-regarding sphere of liberty, as Mill conceives it, is a realm of prudential and aesthetic ideals outside the moral domain. But it remains true that, if utilitarianism is the ultimate principle, it must take precedence even over morality itself and thus even the moral domain bounded the Harm Principle is not safe from utilitarian incursion (Ten, 1980, pp. 42–51). Put bluntly, if it maximises happiness, then utilitarianism commits us to doing the morally wrong thing – including invading a person's self-regarding sphere in order to prevent her from doing what is (in our eyes) base, foolish or imprudent. Similarly, for Gray and Berger, seeking to argue that the Harm Principle can be adopted from within the utilitarian system conceived in Mill's enlightened terms, the relevant question is whether it will, as a matter of fact, produce most utility. Thus we have no reason to discount those illiberal preferences that currently exist in our own relatively enlightened society (not to mention Mill's more conservative one). As Ten points out in an essay re-asserting the traditional view of Mill, there is much evidence that illiberal feelings and preferences will remain even among those who – such as the moral majority in the United States – enjoy liberal freedoms but are unwilling to extend that liberty to others (Ten, 1991, pp. 218–22). Mill's utilitarian wager, he concludes, is just too speculative in the face of this deep-seated illiberalism. Curtailing the liberties of others is always likely to satisfy too many people.

I have been somewhat critical of Mill's critics. Perhaps you will be convinced by their ingenious, though somewhat technical, manoeuvres and decide that one of them genuinely does succeed in bridging the gap between individual liberty and the general welfare. Or you might take a more optimistic view of Mill's wager: that the tyranny of popular opinion will progressively recede. The sources of many people's well-being do indeed seem more individualistic and liberal than before. But my own view is different. I think we should honestly acknowledge that there simply are two great values at work here, on the one hand liberty, freedom, the right to take one's own path; on the other, happiness, well-being, the welfare of society in the aggregate. It is not Mill's failure to overcome these, and nor, in fact, can he do so – the division is simply a feature of the moral universe we inhabit. Mill was exercised by both sides of this dichotomy even if – and here we return to the traditional interpretation – he did not quite appreciate this himself. I am tempted to agree with Ten and Berlin that utilitarianism is more the product of Mill's intellectual inheritance; interesting in its own right but not the authentic voice of the greatest advocate of individuality and diversity. Mill's voice is most his own when he champions the freedom of the individual, to be the one who is different, foolish perhaps, in the eyes of others, sinful, or just plain wrong. From his criticism of the cramped and stifling atmosphere of Victorian social conformity, to his influence on recent political events, the clarity of Mill's earnest voice for liberty continues to speak through interpretive challenge. Whatever contradictions or tensions, self-created or otherwise, remain within it there is no more stirring plea for individual freedom than in the pages of *On Liberty*.

10

Marx (1818–1883)

JULES TOWNSHEND

Introduction

Marx stands apart from many other thinkers assessed in this volume. He did not consider himself a political philosopher. Philosophers, he famously declaimed, merely interpreted the world; the point was to change it. His theoretical enterprise sought to explain the world *in order to* change it, which involved not merely thought but practical activity. This took him into the realms of political economy, rather than political philosophy. Yet in truth Marx was not implicitly anti-philosophical; he merely attempted to underline its *limitations* as a theoretical instrument in the shaping of the practice of human emancipation. Given this, his patently philosophical roots, and the indelible mark his ideas left on twentieth-century politics, he attracted much philosophical attention, inviting philosophical refutation and defence. Marx is still a 'live' thinker. Often commentators wittingly or unwittingly became engaged in a political activity, of attacking, defending or resuscitating Marx. What often became the centre of interpretive disagreement were Marx's claims to truth, whether methodological or substantive claims about history and contemporary capitalist society. At the same time, less politically engaged lines of questioning were advanced, concerning the meaning of certain texts irrespective of truth claims. What we shall see is an uneasy but creative and complex tension between these two interpretive agendas running *through* and *between* the different commentaries, namely, the truth-about-Marx and Marx-as-truth. Such a distinction contains within it the strong possibility that interpreters establishing the truth-about-Marx also assumed Marx-as-truth.

The object of Marx's intellectual labours consisted of theoretical and empirical investigation into the material and social conditions that would enable – and, he thought, impel – working-class self-emancipation.

Capitalism unintentionally created its own 'grave-diggers' – the working class – which had both the interest and potential to create a classless society. Such a society, built upon highly developed labour productivity, would satisfy the diverse and growing needs of all its members. Revolution would occur when capitalist relations of production could no longer sustain the further development of the productive forces (which for Marx included the working class itself). Thus Marx thought that he could demonstrate that the 'real' and the 'good' were coalescing and that there existed a historical *telos*, the product of a successful proletarian class struggle. The role of radical thinkers such as himself was to help the working class by rendering explicit what was implicit in this historical trajectory, thereby making its political activity more effective. All this meant that Marx saw no need to indulge in philosophical speculation and justification. He devoted his theoretical talents to political economy, to understanding the functioning and limitations of capitalism. Marx held that his project was 'scientific' because it was an investigation into how the human world actually was, stripped of any illusions justifying the capitalist status quo or holding out false promises of working-class emancipation. Thus, he was conducting a two-sided analysis: of the world as it was, and of false conceptions, whether conservative or 'utopian'.

Problems and Issues

The problems and issues which arose for Marx's interpreters stemmed from either his explanatory/factual postulates, or his implicit and explicit value positions, which he thought he had successfully united in his teleological vision of history. Out of these two broad areas Marx scholarship in the postwar period has focused on four connected, yet discrete, problems and issues. The first concerns Marx's claim that his project was 'scientific', that he was offering an objective account of the world, which could be proved or disproved by reason and experience, rather than by appealing to faith or belief in the goodness of humankind. What did Marx mean by 'science', and was his theory of history and capitalism in fact scientific? Within the 'scientific' domain a another interpretive difference arose, about whether Marx's theory of history was excessively technologically deterministic, denying the importance of human agency. The issue was whether this was true textually, and, if so, whether it was defensible. A third area of dispute concerned the relation between his 'scientific' narrative and the normative content of his thought. This focused concretely on Marx's intellectual development, whether he had abandoned the normative beliefs and concepts of his youth, in adopting a 'scientific' standpoint. Did his thinking undergo a fundamental epistemological and ontological shift? The fourth zone of interpretive discord concerned the precise nature of his normative commitments: what exactly were his values, and their role within his overall theoretical structure, especially given his impatience with philosophising and moralising?

Why Conflicting Interpretations?

There are two underlying and connected reasons for interpretive disagreement over Marx's *oeuvre* in the English-speaking world in the post-war period. The first relates to the texts themselves – the tensions or ambiguities within and between them. This problem was exacerbated because, until the 1960s, Marx's early works, especially what became known as the *Economic and Philosophic Manuscripts*, along with his later *Grundrisse* (notebooks for *Capital*) had not been widely available in the Anglophone world. This raised issues about Marx's intellectual development and his normative commitments. Tensions were also visible in his later works as between his schematic 'Preface' to a *Contribution to a Critique of Political Economy* (hereafter 'Preface') and empirically rich *Capital*. Moreover, there are meanings of crucial concepts which are not clear and invite speculation.

Yet these textual issues would not have been as pronounced, had it not been for the changing political and intellectual contexts of the interpreters themselves. From the end of the Second World War until the late 1960s in the Anglophone world the standard view of Marx and Marxism was taken as that promulgated by the Soviet Union, known as 'Marxism – Leninism'. The Continental, 'independent' Marxists – Lukacs, Korsch, Gramsci and the Frankfurt School – forerunners of so-called 'Western Marxism', were relatively unknown. In the Cold War climate the most famous 'refutation' of Marx was by Karl Popper (Popper, 1966), followed by H. B. Acton (Acton, 1955) and John Plamenatz (Plamenatz, 1954, 1963).

Marxist scholarship, however, underwent profound transformation in the 1960s and 1970s. The upsurge in student radicalism led to a great deal of interest in 'independent', that is, non-Soviet, Marxism. English translations of Marx's *Economic and Philosophic Manuscripts* (1959) and *The Grundrisse* (1973), Lukacs' *History and Class Consciousness* (1971) Gramsci's *Prison Notebooks* (1971) became available. All these writings emphasised Marx's humanistic, ethical dimension, his Hegelian affinity (the problem of alienation and use of dialectical analysis), and challenged the dominant Soviet version of Marx as essentially a 'scientific' thinker

(Merquior, 1986). And crucially it meant that radicalised students could claim to be Marxist and anti-capitalist without having to identify themselves with the Soviet Union. In reaction to the rise of humanistic Marxism, the French philosopher Louis Althusser, although not a Stalinist, aimed to reaffirm Marx's scientific credentials by presenting him as a structuralist (Althusser, 1969, 1970). Althusser postulated an 'epistemological break' in his thought, and that the 'real', mature Marx was truly scientific. Marx's scientificity was also later defended by G. A. Cohen, who, reacting to the earlier onslaught by Acton and Plamenatz, gave Marx functionalist gloss (Cohen, 1978). Whilst these philosophers seemed to be concerned about two questions – Marx-as-truth and the truth-about-Marx, ultimately they were more interested in the former. Those who rejected their interpretations were usually more interested in the converse, although there could be a political motive: to distance Marx from the 'scientific' Marxism – with its potential elitism – held responsible for Stalinism. The debate on Marx's ethical thought from the 1970s onwards, inspired by questions posed by Rawlsian liberalism, was perhaps the least politically motivated: scholars were genuinely trying to make sense of his normative utterances, given his seeming inconsistencies.

Conflicting Interpretations

Marx as Scientist

Popper's Critique

Popper saw the scientific pretensions of Marx and Marxism (he often conflated the two) as bogus. Although he held Marx's *intentions* as scientific, Marx was guilty of propounding the false science of 'historicism', which 'aims at predicting the future course of economic and power-political developments, especially revolutions' (Popper, 1966, pp. 82–3). Marx, Popper claimed, wrongly assumed that a 'rigid scientific method' entailed a 'rigid determinism' (*ibid.*, p. 85). Revolutions were supposedly the product of the 'inexorable laws' of history. In his preface to *Capital*, Marx talked about the 'natural laws' of movement and 'natural phases of development' of society, and its 'economic law of motion', and stated that political action could only 'shorten and lessen the birth-pangs' in the creation of a communist society (Marx, 1976, p. 92). Marx's prediction of the transition of capitalism into communism was based upon the 'law of increasing misery' for the working class, upon which the 'whole prophetic argument hinges' (Popper, 1966, p. 169). Marx's and Marxism's failure lay in the inability to distinguish between 'scientific prediction' and 'unconditional historical prophecies' (Popper, 1969, p. 339). So when uncomfortable facts, such as working-class material improvement threatened to refute such predictions, an 'auxiliary hypothesis' explaining this away was introduced, such as the emergence of colonial exploitation (Popper, 1966, p. 187). Marxism was therefore unfalsifiable and could not count as a scientific hypothesis, which for Popper *forbids* things from happening, rather than searches for confirming evidence (Popper, 1969, p. 36). Not only did Marxism as a hypothesis become unfalsifiable, but historical evidence falsified Marx's substantive prediction of conditions that would precipitate proletarian revolution. 'Democratic piecemeal interventionism' restrained capitalist exploitation of the working class, and created full employment (Popper, 1966, pp. 122–9, p. 179, p. 193). Thus Marx could not predict that workers would compromise with capitalism (*ibid.*, p. 155). At the heart of Marx's inability to predict was his economic determinism, which could not fully take into account the way in which ideas, and particularly the political superstructure, can shape economic forces (Popper, 1969, p. 332; Popper, 1966, p. 119). Indeed, Marx's 'economism' was ironically falsified by the Russian revolution itself, which was very much the product of a Marxist idea moulding economic conditions, rather than the converse (Popper, 1966, p. 108).

Cornforth's Defence
Maurice Cornforth (who also used the terms 'Marx' and 'Marxism' interchangeably), an exponent of 'Marxism – Leninism', sought to reaffirm Marx's scientific credentials, in a way that was truer to Marx's intentions – his attempt to unite his theory with (proletarian) political practice. The purpose of theory was to understand the terrain in order to determine the limits and possibilities of political action (Cornforth, 1968, p. 135). Marx was not a 'prophet or a fortune-teller', but spoke as a 'practical organiser' (*ibid.*, p. 153). And such a unity of theory and practice demanded an open-mindedness so that ideas could be tested (*ibid.*, p. 126). Not surprisingly Cornforth rejected the notion that Marx was postulating a thesis of fatalistic, unconditional historical causality, which ignored human agency. Rather, quoting Marx, 'Men make their own history, but ... under circumstances directly encountered, given and transmitted from the past' (*ibid.*, p. 133). Predictions could only be conditional. And the prediction of socialism, premised upon the future fettering of the forces of production by capitalist property relations and developing class struggle, ultimately depended upon the effectiveness of revolutionary political organisation (*ibid.*, pp. 140–9).

Thus, prediction could not be made 'irrespective of human intentions and strivings', as in astronomy (*ibid.*, p. 149), but was conditional, 'based on estimates of probabilities' (*ibid.*, p. 150). Cornforth, however, admitted that making unconditional predictions could make 'very good propaganda' in the struggle for socialism (*ibid.*, p. 149).

Marxism, he argued, was a research hypothesis that sought to understand the social – material problems that people faced. Its guiding idea was the 'adaptation of relations of production to forces of production' (*ibid.*, p. 138). How successful this adaptation was depended upon human intervention (*ibid.*, p. 151). In the light of this, Marxism could offer a falsifiable hypothesis: the full and sustained utilisation of productive forces was 'forbidden' to happen where these forces were privately owned (*ibid.*, pp. 20–1). He admitted that the phenomenon of post-war full employment in Britain had to be explained, but *existing* Marxist theory could explain these temporary 'special conditions'. If, however, a 'supplementary hypotheses' had to be introduced with no evidential basis, then the theory itself would have to be abandoned (*ibid.*, p. 22). As for the Russian Revolution refuting Marxist theory, it 'started where Marxism permitted it to … ' and could be explained in the light of Marxist theory. An examination of material conditions suggested that it was the 'weakest link' within a world capitalist system. Certainly, if a socialist revolution had broken out in Central Africa or the Far East, then Marxism would have been falsified (*ibid.*, p. 22).

Recent Accounts

Recent commentators have argued that Marx's self-understanding clearly departed from the stringent tests for science demanded by Popper. They noted that Marx in using the term 'science' would have employed the German word '*Wissenschaft*' which meant systematically organised knowledge of nature, society, culture and different forms of thought (Ball, 1984, p. 242; Thomas, 1976, p. 7). Perhaps for this reason Marx has been conceived of as a 'methodological pluralist'. He used 'classical and Hegelian logic, and the techniques of mathematical, sociological, economic, historical, and political analysis' (Carver, 1984, p. 276). Moreover, they portrayed him as implicitly or explicitly anti-positivist, especially if positivism is construed as searching for empirically and inductively based universal laws, which could explain both natural and social phenomena. This was apparent in a variety of ways. First, the type of laws he was attempting to formulate were historically specific. Thus, he sharply criticised political economists who wanted to 'naturalise' capitalism, by suggesting that it was an expression of human nature and could be formulated in timeless, abstract conceptual categories. Rather, these categories themselves arose out of specific social relations, which were subject to change (Ball, 1984, p. 246). Moreover, in historical terms Marx opposed explanations derived from any 'general historico-philosophical theory' (Thomas, 1976, p. 11). In terms of Marx's self-understanding, science was needed precisely because causal mechanisms were not readily apparent to the senses: 'All science would be superfluous if the form of appearance of things directly coincided with their essence' (Marx, 1981, p. 956; Little, p. 94; Thomas, p. 12). This was so especially under capitalism, whose workings were concealed by 'commodity fetishism' (Little, 1986, pp. 100–1). This essence/appearance distinction has been taken up by those interpreting Marx's scientific method, resting on dialectics and materialism, as 'realist'. Unlike positivist accounts that prioritise prediction over explanation, inner causal mechanisms are introduced to explain phenomena, for example, profit which arises from the 'hidden structure of exploitation' (Walker, 2000, p. 170).

Nevertheless, other interpreters emphasise the need for the activity of abstraction to be corroborated by empirical observation, as Marx's detailed observations in *Capital* testified (Sayer, 1979, p. 81; Little, 1986, p. 176). This combination of abstraction and empirical analysis has been termed Marx's 'Galilean empiricism' (Little, p. 123, Suchting, 1972, p. 245). Some commentators, following Lakatos, have suggested that Marx's scientific practice was similar to other scientists: he initiated a 'research programme' that consisted of a 'hard core' theory, and a 'protective belt' of auxiliary hypotheses which hopefully produces a further 'positive heuristic' if the research programme is 'progressive', enabling a greater understanding of the phenomenon in question. The 'hard core' of Marx's analysis of capitalism consisted of class, economic structure and crisis. The 'protective belt' consisted of countervailing tendencies to the falling rate of profit (Little, 1986, pp. 184–6; Callinicos, 1985, pp. 124–6).

Marx as Technological Determinist

The Cohen thesis

This interpretive disagreement initiated by Cohen (1978) was over the meaning of pivotal concepts and their interrelation in Marx's 'preface', regarded as the 'classic' exposition of his theory of history. In the 'preface' Marx described the 'guiding thread' of his studies in terms of history conceived as a succession of modes of production which rose and fell according to whether the constitutive production relations facilitated the development of the productive forces. Unfortunately, the brevity of Marx's account left the key concepts undefined, and they had to be decoded from statements he made elsewhere. The problem was compounded because the 'productivist' thrust of the 'preface' also happened to be at odds with what he said elsewhere. The contested terms and their causal relations were 'productive forces', 'production relations' 'economic structure' and 'superstructure'.

Cohen used this passage to establish it as Marx's definitive self-understanding, as well as an intelligible and plausible account of history – the truth-about-Marx and Marx-as-truth. Cohen sought to rebut Acton and Plamenatz, who saw this passage as either incoherent and therefore unverifiable as a theory of history, or, insofar as it was coherent, untrue. Plamenatz held that production relations seemed to mean either work relations or property relations (Plamenatz, 1965, p. 24). Marx also appeared confused about whether property relations were part of the 'base' or 'superstructure' (Plamenatz, 1963, pp. 279–80). This created the 'problem of legality' because the superstructure, which included institutions that regulated and protected property relations, could not be simultaneously the product of an economic structure which included those relations. Acton saw further difficulties with the meaning of production relations. If they meant work relations then the productive force/production relation relationship was tautologous, because envisaged changes in productive forces simultaneously entailed changes in work relations (Acton, 1955, p. 161). And the 'material' productive forces could not be separated from the 'social' production relations in causal terms, since as Marx admitted outside the 'preface' that, 'social' – work-related – co-operation itself could be a (material) productive force (Acton p. 167, Marx, 1965, p. 41). Indeed, productive activity involved law, morals and politics, so these too could be regarded as productive forces. Thus, there existed no clearly identifiable hypothesis that could be empirically corroborated, and because in reality productive forces were not autonomous they could not assume explanatory primacy.

Cohen defended the 'preface' as *the* definitive account of Marx's theory of history, according productive forces explanatory primacy. Cohen also claimed that all the terms in the 'preface' were distinct and potentially unambiguous and the relations between them intelligible in the light of Marx's utterances outside the 'preface'. And Marx's account also happened to be true. Fundamental to working up the meaning of the different terms was a distinction in Marx's work between 'material' and 'social', or 'natural' and 'social'. Productive forces were material, and the property of an object (Cohen, 1978, p. 28), and consisted of the means of production (raw materials, instruments of production, labour power and science) which are used by a producing agent to transform nature (*ibid.*, p. 32). Thus *contra*

Acton, laws, morals and government were not productive forces; they were not directly used in production, merely to motivate workers (*ibid.*, p. 32). Production relations on the other hand were 'social' in giving 'social' form to the material content of productive forces; the 'social' entailed ascribing (non-legal) rights or powers to persons in relation to other persons (*ibid.*, p. 94). For example a working, 'material' individual only becomes a slave in a certain type of society. Similarly, a machine only becomes 'constant' capital, when assuming a particular social form (*ibid.*, p. 89). Work relations are construed as 'material' relations, acts of co-operation, which occur independently of social roles; for instance, as slaves, serfs, proletarians, and so forth (*ibid.*, p. 111). Thus material relations of production had to be distinguished from social relations (*ibid.*, p. 92). Against Acton, the economic structure consists merely of 'social' production relations.

Cohen quoted many passages from Marx both before and after the 'preface' to show that as a definitive account it could be shown that productive forces were primary (*ibid.*, pp. 142–50). Just as significant: when Marx made '*generalisations*' about productive forces/relations, productive forces were always primary, rather than there being a bi-directional relationship (*ibid.*, p. 138, Cohen's emphasis). He admitted that production relations might condition productive forces, but the relationship had to be explained functionally, that is in terms of their beneficial effects on the development of productive forces. Historical change occurred when productive forces could no longer develop, and at some point new production relations would be selected to further their development. Cohen offered historical examples showing how new productive forces (technology) transformed material work relations and then social relations (*ibid.*, pp. 166–7) and, contrary to Acton, the productive force/work relation could be conceived consequentially rather than tautologically (*ibid.*, pp. 168–9). What drove productive force development could be explained in terms of human behaviour: human beings were rationally responding to a historical situation of scarcity, a proposition that was empirically verifiable. Human beings' productive powers had expanded throughout history (*ibid.*, p. 152).

Cohen also answered the 'problem of legality' posed by Acton and Plamenatz, which suggested that if property relations could be part of the economic structure as well as the superstructure, any causal relationship between base and superstructure would be impossible. He distinguished between legal rights as part of superstructure and matching powers as part of the base (*ibid.*, p. 219). Powers and rights do not necessarily entail each other. They only do so in the case of legitimate powers or effective rights. Thus the economic structure could be defined in non-legal terms of power to use the means of production or labour power, or to prevent others using the means of production. Legal relations merely legitimate the economic structure to stabilise it. Thus superstructures are a function of the needs of productive forces.

Cohen's Critics

Only Cohen's unsympathetic critics will be discussed here because they were concerned about his misunderstanding of the truth-about-Marx. His sympathetic critics were more interested in Cohen's *analytical* rescue attempt to demonstrate that Marx made sense, irrespective of Marx's self-understanding (for example, Elster, 1985). One of Cohen's most unsympathetic critics, Sayer (1987), insisted upon the centrality of Marx's dialectical methodology to his self-understanding. Cohen, driven by his analytical method, searched for stable and clear definitions of entities that were 'externally' related. The dialectical account, on the other hand, held that for Marx different phenomena were 'internally' related and that things and their related concepts were subject to change given the fluidity of the historical process. This fluidity arose from human beings' changing nature, the result of their attempt to modify nature in order to meet their material needs. Hence, a generalised, a priori theory of history consisting of stable meanings and causal relationships was implausible. Indeed, philosophy had to yield to the empirical analysis of humans, their productive forces and relations (Sayer, 1987, p. 148). Things could only be understood in their relations and could therefore assume a variety of meanings depending upon what relationship was under consideration. And for Marx ideas themselves could be a 'material force', as could the 'social' division of labour. Thus in reality to distinguish between the material and the social in the productive process was difficult (*ibid.*, p. 25). Marx also saw the superstructure as a production relation (*ibid.*, p. 64; Marx, 1973a, p. 472), and under feudalism the superstructure was seen by Marx as internal to the economic structure (*ibid.*, p. 75). There was the added danger that in emphasising the primacy of the 'material', reification occurred, with productive forces viewed as things rather than as an expression of cooperative human powers. These powers did not necessarily expand as Marx illustrated in his account of 'Asiatic' modes of production (*ibid.*, p. 45). (For example, in ancient China a centralised, despotic state, responsible for the productive infrastructure, especially for irrigation, in tandom with isolated, self-sufficient village communities, laid the basis of economic stagnation.) Hence, Cohen, in endowing the self-expansion of 'material' productive forces with universal historical significance, thereby succumbed to an abstracting process that occurred under specific conditions of capitalist relations of production.

Other critics rejected Cohen's implicit a priorism of productive forces/relations functionalism (Larrain, 1986, p. 15; Miller, 1984, p. 172), and held that methodologically Marx explicitly stated that his account of history in the 'preface' was merely a 'guiding thread' to his studies (Carver, 1982, p. 4; Sayer, 1987, p. 13). Moreover, he explicitly rejected a 'super historical' view of history (Carver, 1982, p. 23). They noted Marx's insistence upon empirical investigation, which could not yield predetermined results (Carver, 1982, p. 22; Rigby, 1987, p. 104). For example, Marx did not see most modes of production in productive force-dynamic terms, especially the Asiatic mode of production (Larrain, p. 83; Miller, 1984, p. 191; Wood, 1995, p. 124). In terms of explaining historical transitions, Cohen's critics indicated that Marx when discussing the collapse of the Roman Empire ascribed it to the economic structure rather than productive forces aspiring to be liberated (McLennan, 1981, p. 56; Miller, p. 214; also, Wood, p. 130). Moreover, Marx in describing the rise of capitalism in Britain, saw production relations, new work relations and superstructural variables as the key rather than technology (Miller, pp. 188–91). Further, Wood argued that Marx saw productive force dynamism as unique to capitalism (Wood, p. 124).

The fact that Marx did not consistently give causal priority to productive forces led many critics to question the weight that Cohen attached to the material, productive force/social, production relation distinction (Carver, 1982, pp. 29–30; Larrain, p. 80; McLennan, 1981, p. 54; Roberts, 1996, p. 65). For example, Marx on numerous occasions saw co-operation itself, especially through the division of labour, as a productive force (Larrain, p. 79, p. 81; McLennan, p. 54; Miller, p. 194; Rigby, 1987, p. 13; A. Wood, 1981, pp. 72–3). In wanting to stipulate work relations as 'material', Cohen had an impoverished definition of the 'social', that went against Marx's own definition, which explicitly included co-operation of individuals (Larrain, p. 80). That Marx could view productive forces as non-material was perhaps not unnatural if the German *Produktivkrafte* was translated less materialistically, not as productive forces, but as productive *powers* expressed in the form of individual or collective ability and capacity for productive activity, thereby inviting a less technological reading of productive forces (A. Wood, 1981, pp. 66–7). And perhaps because he was not prepared to make the material/social as the operative distinction, with the 'social' an epiphenomenon of the 'material', he was quite happy to offer an interactive model of the productive forces/relations relationship (McLennan, p. 57; R. W. Miller, p. 194; Rigby, p. 95; A. Wood, p. 65).

In sum, Cohen's critics, by looking as Marx's theoretical practice as an historian and quotations from his other works, were not therefore prepared to accord the 'preface' its canonical status as *the* account of Marx's theory of history. If, nevertheless, Marx regarded it as such then he was clearly self-contradictory as between the very general claims of the 'preface' and statements made elsewhere (Rigby, p. 52, p. 60; E. Wood, p. 138, p. 160).

Marx's Intellectual Development

Discontinuity: Althusser

Althusser set out his case for discontinuity primarily in *For Marx*. He claimed that an 'epistemological break' occurred in Marx's work around 1845. He aimed to resist the developing 'humanist' tendencies within the international Communist movement after the Soviet Communist Party's denunciation of Stalin's 'cult of personality' in 1956. This 'socialist humanism', which proclaimed the rights of (liberal) 'man' in effect sought accommodation with capitalism, thereby denying the centrality of the class struggle in abolishing exploitation and achieving a 'real' humanism. Advocates of this ethical – humanist turn, Althusser argued, sought legitimation in the works of the young Marx, especially in the *Economic and Philosophic Manuscripts*. Althusser's object was to undermine the 'Marxist' status of such pieces by demonstrating that they were 'ideological' and 'unscientific' in comparison with *Capital*. Thus, there were 'two' Marx's, and only the mature Marx was scientific, in propounding 'historical' and (an undeveloped) 'dialectical' materialism.

Althusser's argument rested upon what he termed a 'symptomatic reading' of Marx, in which the reader was invited to uncover the hidden, or 'silent' 'problematic' of a text, a process akin to a Freudian analyst's examination of a patient's unconscious through interpreting their utterances (Althusser, 1970, p. 316). Hence, not only the explicit, but also the implicit questions in a text had to be identified. Althusser saw in the early Marx a Feuerbachian 'anthropological' and 'historicist' problematic, based upon a concept of human essence or 'species-being', from which people were alienated (Feuerbach's philosophical materialism rejected religion, and the illusion that God made man, rather than the converse. Religion was an expression of human self-alienation, with the love of God preventing the genuine love of humanity). Crucially, Feuerbach and the young Marx had not gone beyond the horizon of the Hegelian problematic, which attempted to reconcile the individual with the modern world through dialectical thinking. They were merely 'inverting' the dialectic. Despite their materialism, they were responding to abstract, philosophical questions, which were 'ideological'. The material conditions and practices that led to the posing and shaping of these questions in the first place went unrecognised. Such a philosophical – idealist problematic did not possess the concepts to yield any genuine knowledge of society. History was seen by the young Marx as unfolding in a teleological form, in terms of the realisation of the human essence.

In the *German Ideology* and *Theses on Feurbach* – the works of the 'break' – Marx reached a new (self)awareness – 'discovery' – that such thoughts were indeed 'ideological'. He no longer viewed human nature as 'anthropological', ahistorical and abstract, but as shaped by society, and a new, scientific problematic emerged, a set of concepts: social formation, mode of production, surplus value, class struggle, and so on, which could used to understand the different kinds of practical activities in which human beings were engaged. Marx established a new *'science'* of the 'history of social formations' (Althusser, 1969, p. 13. Althusser's emphasis). In doing so he was not 'superseding' Hegel. Rather he was turning to 'real history' as expressed in his involvement in the labour movement (*ibid.*, p. 76). Inverting Hegel's dialectic meant a *de facto* rejection of Hegel, because it entailed the development of concepts with which to really grasp reality (*ibid.*, p. 73). Althusser, in *Reading Capital* and elsewhere, sought to show that Marx was in effect a structuralist, with the relations between different economic, political and ideological practices within a given society determined by the overall structure. That a hiatus occurred in Marx's intellectual development was confirmed by Marx himself. As he reported in the 'preface', *The German Ideology* constituted a settling of accounts with his and Engels' 'erstwhile' philosophical consciences in criticising the post-Hegelian radicals (Althusser, 1969, p. 33). Thus, the 'break' was where Marx said it was.

The Unity of Marx's Thought – Althusser's Critics
Although Althusser's account of Marxism angered many Marxists who considered themselves to be humanist Marxists, such as E. P. Thompson, (Thompson, 1978), what will be considered here are those critics that worked at the exegetical level to refute his interpretation of Marx's intellectual development. We should note that two authors who made the strongest case for continuity, Ollman (1971) and Meszaros (1970) would probably have said substantially more than they did about Althusser if their works had not been published so soon after *For Marx* appeared in English. More developed critiques of Althusser were left to others. At the level of textual fidelity critics had a fairly easy job in refuting Althusser's account, because the 'epistemological break' thesis was 'uncorroborated' (Elliot, 1987, p. 138). Thus, Geras could show, whatever the virtues in contrasting the earlier and later Marx, there was little change in Marx's conception of human nature before and after the break. It was both generic and particular,

'historically modified in each epoch', because human beings could only be conceived of in their specific relations (social activities) with others (Geras, 1983, p. 80). Marx opposed 'ideological' conceptions of human nature which were abstracted from their concrete relations (*ibid.*, pp. 78–80).

Secondly, critics demonstrated that alienation was a recurrent theme in Marx's early and later works. For example, John E. Elliott quoted from *Capital*, vol. 1, how the worker becomes 'a fragment of a man … an appendage of a machine'. The capitalists 'estrange from him the intellectual potentialities of the labour-process' (Elliott, 1979, p. 340); in the *Grundrisse*, his conception of exploitation rested on this theory of alienation (*ibid.*, p. 353), and his later works were redolent in calls for the supersession of alienation (*ibid.*, pp. 354–8).

Marx's Normative Thought

Capitalism Not Unjust

On what grounds did Marx condemn capitalism, given his well-known reluctance to engage in ethical discourse in his 'mature' period? Did Marx in particular think capitalism unjust? The debate focused on the particular issue of his view of the wage relation, but broadened into questions of Marx's attitude towards morality in general.

Allen Wood (1980a), who did most to initiate the debate, argued that on whatever grounds Marx condemned capitalism, it was not on account of its injustice. Marx's *explicit* views revealed a narrow, juridical conception of justice, associated with '*Recht*', which was part of the capitalist superstructure and functional to its economic base. As such, justice would be unnecessary in a classless society in which the state was abolished (A. Wood, 1980a, pp. 4–12). Further viewed functionally, each mode of production with its resultant class system, had its own standard of justice. For Wood and other commentators the test case was Marx's view of the wage relation. Marx, in *Capital*, held that the capitalist appropriation of surplus value created by workers was 'good fortune for the buyer [of labour power], but no injustice at all to the seller' (*ibid.*, p. 22). Quoting from the *Critique of the Gotha Programme*, Wood demonstrated that Marx did not think workers as unjustly paid, because wages were a form of distribution based upon the 'juridical relations' of capitalism (*ibid.*, p. 25). Since justice was internal to different modes of production, no external standard could be applied to condemn capitalism. In any case, to make reality conform to such an external ideal was unrealistic, as it was not based upon an analysis of social reality (*ibid.*, p. 29). Marx believed that ultimately in a classless society there would be no need for a juridical system dispensing justice and upholding rights (*ibid.*, p. 30). Not surprisingly, Marx had little interest in justice, and called 'equal right' and 'just distribution' 'outdated verbal trivia' (*ibid.*, p. 31). Later Wood conceded that Marx did condemn capitalism in terms of self-actualisation, community and freedom, which were 'non-moral goods', associated with needs and wants, rather than conscience-derived moral imperatives (A. Wood, 1980b, pp. 121–2).

Capitalism Unjust

Husami admitted that Marx's 'direct and explicit statements' condemning capitalism as unjust were 'few and far between'. Nevertheless, Marx used language 'typically used in philosophical discourse on justice and seems to be condemning capitalism for its injustice' (Husami, 1980, p. 43). Marx described worker exploitation as 'robbery', 'usurpation', 'embezzlement', 'plunder', 'booty', 'theft', 'snatching' and 'swindling' (*ibid.*, p. 45). He agreed with Wood that Marx had a 'sociology of morals', but suggested that he failed to note that for Marx morality, justice and the like were not only part of the capitalist superstructure. Capitalism could be condemned from a critical, 'proletarian standpoint', in terms of 'self-realisation, humanism, community, freedom, equality and justice' refusing to endorse the ruling class's attempt at ideological legitimation (*ibid.*, p. 54). From this standpoint workers were robbed. Marx also invoked an external standard of condemnation based upon a higher form of society (*ibid.*, p. 50). In the *Critique of the Gotha Programme*, Marx's account of the lower and higher stages of communism implicitly saw capitalism as violating two distributive norms, either according to labour contribution or need (*ibid.*, pp. 72–4, p. 77). Husami further argued that Wood had mistakenly confused explanation with evaluation, implying that Marx was merely explaining justice as part of the capitalist superstructure, and avoiding comment. Husami held that Marx not only saw the worker as 'robbed' in the labour process, but took great pains to explain why (*ibid.*, p. 76). On the wage relation, where Marx portrays the capitalist appropriation of the surplus as 'good luck', he was satirizing capitalism. He then says it was 'embezzled, because abstracted without return of an equivalent' (*ibid.*, p. 63). This non-equivalence arises for Marx in the exploitative sphere of production, not in the sphere of circulation, of legal transactions, where equivalents are indeed exchanged. Exploitation is therefore concealed (*ibid.*, pp. 66–8). Marx, then, worked on two levels: at the juridical – explanatory, meaning that capitalism could not be condemned in its own terms, and the proletarian – ethical where it did stand condemned (*ibid.*, p. 77).

Capitalism Just and Unjust

Lukes and Geras held that Marx's general attitude towards morality and his specific view of the wage/capital relation was complex. Lukes, building upon Wood's position, viewed Marx's attitude as 'paradoxical'. This paradox was manifested in, and explained by, Marx's conception of the morality of '*Recht*', associated with rights and justice of the capitalist superstructure, either institutionally or ideologically (Lukes, 1985, p. 24). Such a morality, an expression of a capitalist 'civil society', licensed the individualism of property owners in a situation of relative scarcity. The morality of '*Recht*' would be unnecessary in a classless society of relative abundance. Here Marx's other notion of morality came into play. The morality of 'emancipation' was realised in both individual and communal forms in such a society (*ibid.*, pp. 9–10). As for the wage relation, Lukes argued that Marx's stance was implicitly 'multi-perspectival': capitalism was just within its own terms, whilst 'immanently' unjust because the wage relation also contained an 'exchange' of non-equivalents. From the external perspective of the lower stage of communism, capitalism was unjust because distribution was not according to labour contribution (minus various social deductions). And in the higher phase of communism of relative abundance justice could be dispensed with altogether because distribution would be completely needs-driven (*ibid.*, p. 58).

Geras asserted even more strongly than Lukes that Marx's attitude towards justice and morality was paradoxical: 'Marx did think capitalism unjust, but did not think that he thought so' (Geras, 1985, p. 70). He rejected the 'two moralities' solution of Lukes, because Marx consistently displayed an 'impatience with the language of norms and values' (*ibid.*, p. 85), stating, for example, that workers had 'no ideals to realise' (*ibid.*, p. 84). From the standpoint of the 'immanent movement', even the ideals of freedom, self-realisation and community were rejected (*ibid.*, p. 84). Yet, these 'repressed' ethical commitments, 'denied publicly,' along with justice, kept returning. Marx seemed deeply concerned with distributive issues: the benefits and burdens under capitalism, the distribution of freedom and opportunities for self-development, and of the means of production. Even the needs principle of the higher stage of communism entailed a distributive criterion of equality of need rather than of individual endowment (*ibid.*, pp. 80–1). Geras further maintained that on the justice of the wage relation, Marx was genuinely 'equivocal' in his treatment (*ibid.*, p. 63). For example, in *Capital* (Marx, 1976, p. 729, p. 730). Marx attempted to resolve the question through 'dialectical wizardry' of the 'dialectical inversion' from an exchange of equivalents (justice) to non-reciprocity (injustice) of 'robbery' in the labour process (Geras, 1985, p. 64).

Evaluation

What we have seen is that interpretive difference has revolved around two potentially conflicting research agendas: the truth-about-Marx, and Marx-as-truth. Bearing this in mind, the four main areas of disagreement will be evaluated.

Concerning Marx's scientificity, Popper certainly highlighted the problematic nature of some of Marx's historical projections, and raised the question of the criterion for scientific validity. Against Popper, Cornforth and others argued that using auxiliary hypotheses did not mean that a theory was invalid in the sense of becoming unfalsifiable, because the core theory might be developed to explain the 'anomaly', thereby adding to the explanatory reach of the core theory (Little, 1986, p. 183). Marx's actual scientific practice of a 'research programme' did not significantly differ from other scientists, although this still leaves unanswered the question of how *true* Marx's theory actually is, whether in terms of coherence or empirical veracity. Many economists of varying political persuasions have had difficulty with Marx's theory of value and the falling rate of profit (Howard and King, 1992, chapter 7, 12, 13, and 14). If the question is seen in terms of Marx's self-understanding, Cornforth, in stressing the theory/practice relation and the conditionality of Marx's predictions, all of which makes them provisional, is closer to the mark. Marx was no fatalist standing outside the historical process. His commitment to historical inevitability was, he thought, based upon the revolutionary, communist potential of the working class and the crisis-ridden nature of the capitalist economy, which he held as plausible owing to his empirically derived assumptions. Nevertheless, the rhetorical utterances of unconditional 'inevitability' cannot be ignored. That he was a methodological pluralist is also readily apparent. Marx thought there was more to science than its ability to predict, especially if the 'realist' essence/appearance distinction is fully acknowledged, although his historical teleology, with its predictive implications, should not be underestimated. Yet for him, scientific method of whatever methodological stripe was the key to both understanding political possibility and exposing the shortcomings of 'conservative' and 'progressive' ideological thinking.

On the issue of determinism, what Cohen's critics demonstrated was the difficulty of simultaneously interpreting Marx as a technological determinist and affirming the truth of technological determinism. Too many of Marx's utterances did not match up to the stringent analytic criteria set by Cohen. Some of Marx's self-understanding was sacrificed so that he could be held as making sense in terms of conceptual clarity and logical consistency.

Marx perhaps made himself unwittingly vulnerable as a result of his penchant for generalisation, aphorism and metaphor. The meaning of production relations remained unstable. Yet perhaps an answer to Plamenatz's objection that they could be work *or* property relations is to remind ourselves of the importance of the division of labour for Marx. Although it was the ultimate origin of alienation, it also constituted the basis of human co-operation. Thus the technical and social division of labour could be viewed as two different forms of productive co-operation, with the latter developing out of the former. If relations of production are seen in this evolutionary way, perhaps the 'problem of legality' may not have been a problem for Marx. The property system could be seen as the result of an exchange relations embedded in the social division of labour (itself the outcome of the technical division of labour) pre-dating the institution of the state. This would lend support to Cohen's distinction between *de facto* powers and *de jure* rights legitimated and enforced by the state.

As for the base/superstructure metaphor, this obscured his historical method, rather than illuminated it, and his generalisations in the 'preface' were unhelpful in unravelling his investigative method, which rejected a priori foundations other than those derived from the needs and capacities of human beings. Whilst the 'preface' served as a 'guiding thread' to his studies, his outline involved unequivocal, substantive claims about historical development and implied historical laws of a functional kind as suggested by Cohen. Cohen's critics, even if they were able to demonstrate that the 'preface' was not definitive, could not deny the productive force determinist element in Marx. However, his willingness to be open minded about the causal primacy of productive forces and production relations suggests a far more 'relational' and empirical approach. This raises questions about the causal primacy of productive forces grounded upon the 'material'/'social' distinction necessary for his functional analysis. Even in the 'preface' Marx talks of the 'contradictions of material life' as a 'conflict between the *social* productive forces and the relations of production' (emphasis added). Nevertheless, the tension between his historical teleology and desire for conceptually rigorous and empirically informed analysis remained.

On the question of Marx's intellectual development, Althusser's critics showed that the 'two-Marx' claim could not be substantiated. Marx's theory of human nature and his call for the realising of individual and communal potentials through transcending alienation remained a constant motif in his thought. Moreover, Marx probably used the *Economic and Philosophic Manuscripts* when writing the *Grundrisse* (McLellan, 1980, p. 122). Yet Althusser seemed aware that his developmental narrative might not have been wholly accurate. In the glossary he approved in the English translation of *Reading Capital*, the 'epistemological break' was not 'punctual', but a 'continuous break', and applied 'even to the latest of Marx's works, which "flirt" with Hegelian expressions and contain pre-Marxist "survivals"' (Althusser, 1970, p. 323). Rather than rely on Marx's own understanding of his intellectual development, Althusser effectively introduced an unresolved 'problematic' uncovered by a 'symptomatic' reading. No longer does the 'pre-Marxist' problematic exist temporally; even the 'old' Marx became a pre-Marxist. Nevertheless, as Althusser suggests, something happened around 1845: philosophy could only interpret and justify, but not explain and change the world. Marx's new, practically oriented, materialist theory he put at the service of his new found political ally: the proletariat. Yet the alienation *theme* still resonated, even if expressed in more accessible and concrete language, and in the concept of 'commodity fetishism'. Marx did not bother to establish the concept philosophically; he believed that 'history', that is, proletarian political activity in favourable conditions, would inevitably overcome alienation. His 'mature' concern was with an analysis of the concrete social, economic and political conditions under which disalienation was possible. Yet, although critics indicate that Althusser illicitly separated facts and values in Marx's work (Geras, 1986, p. 130), he does talk about a 'real' humanism subsequent to the prosecution of a successful class struggle (Althusser, 1969, pp. 242–7). Beyond this we encounter a problem already witnessed in Cohen's account, namely, of combining two tasks: a reading of Marx that is true to his self-understanding and that is also authentically 'scientific' (Benton, 1984, p. 31). Althusser's notion of a 'problematic' enabled him to disentangle what he held as the non-scientific from the scientific elements in Marx's thought, but in so doing we lose sight of its unity.

Whilst there were obvious differences between commentators in interpreting what Marx had to say about moral discourse in general and justice in particular, some measure of implicit agreement exists. Although Wood consistently held an 'anti-justice' viewpoint, all commentators agreed that when Marx discussed justice specifically he did so in a narrow juridical sense. They also agreed with him that Marx did condemn capitalism in terms of freedom, self-actualisation and community, although not necessarily as 'non-moral' values. Wood's position then allowed Lukes to describe Marx as 'paradoxical' on the subject. Yet both Husami and Geras, against Wood, were keen to indicate that, at least implicitly, Marx had not lost the distributive justice plot, whether from an external or 'proletarian' standpoint. Also contra Wood, these commentators accepted that Marx held the wage relation as effectively unjust, as 'robbery', although Geras argued that he 'equivocated'. Finally, perhaps the disagreement between Lukes and

Geras over Marx's paradoxical attitude was of degree rather than difference. Lukes was as equally aware of Marx's 'impatience' with moral discourse (Lukes, pp. 5–8).

In assessing respective positions on the justice of the wage relation, although Marx did not use the term, even the so-called 'equivocal' passages suggest an 'injustice' interpretation, and there is nothing obscure about the meaning of 'dialectical inversion'. Marx deploys his labour theory of value to reveal the exploitative essence of the seemingly equitable worker/ capitalist transaction involved in the sale of labour power (for example, Marx, 1976, pp. 729–30). On the wider question of Marx's overall stance towards normative discourse, Wood perhaps too keenly expunged all traces of moralism in Marx's work. Husami fully demonstrated its existence. Lukes and Geras were more alert to the complexity of Marx's position. Yet in terms of Marx's *self-understanding* the question of how contradictory or paradoxical his attitude to, and use of, moral discourse is, is far from settled. Both Lukes and Geras do go some way in *explaining* the tensions in Marx's attitude: his 'moral realism', his scepticism over the efficacy of ideals in promoting human emancipation (Geras, 1985, p. 85) and his teleological view of history, meaning that the 'real' and the 'good' were visibly in the process of objectively coalescing (Lukes, pp. 43–4). If we add to these explanations the centrality of human practice as criterial in determining normative relevance, then Marx was not rejecting ideals *per se*. Rather, he was insisting upon the recognition and examination of the material and practical conditions of moral possibility as broadly construed. Perhaps in terms of Marx's self-understanding his view was less paradoxical, but becomes more so depending on the extent to which we invoke an external criteria of coherence required by philosophical 'practice'. We then ask whether justice can be simultaneously relative and transhistorical. Putting the question in this way helps us understand why one commentator has described him as a 'qualified relativist', as if to underline the paradox (Wilde, 1998).

In sum, Marx's thought has been the site of sharp contestation as a result of the intermingling of two interpretive objectives, either the truth-about-Marx (self-understanding), or Marx-as-truth (external evaluation). These two perspectives have either divided interpreters or have existed within one interpretation, such as Cohen's. Marx's philosophical commentators generally were more interested in Marx-as-truth (or as-falsehood), which often entailed a super-imposition of their own conception of truth or falsity. So Popper imposed his own version of science, of falsifiability, to demonstrate Marx's 'unscientificity'; for Althusser, the later Marx became a structuralist, and for Cohen, Marx was a functionalist. Whatever insights these views revealed, the truth-about-Marx commentators demonstrated that they were often bought at the price of textual infidelity. Yet the more textually oriented often *in effect* exposed deep-seated tensions in Marx's work, between an historical teleology and commitment to the proletarian cause on the one hand and an equally strong commitment to empirical investigation that resisted a priori conceptualisation on the other. Thus, they did not necessarily consider Marx's philosophical or contemporary political and sociological value, or why he is of continuing interest. In interpretive terms this unstable relationship between the truth-about-Marx and Marx-as-truth is likely to remain a frustrating yet fruitful one.

Bibliography

Acton, H. B. (1955), *The Illusion of the Epoch* (London: Routledge and Kegan Paul).

Allen, G. O. (1962), ' "La volonté de tous" and "la volonté générale": a distinction and its significance', *Ethics*, 73: 263–75.

Althusser, L. (trans. Ben Brewster) (1969), *For Marx* (Harmondsworth: Penguin).

Althusser, L. (with E. Balibar) (trans. Ben Brewster) (1970), *Reading Capital* (London: New Left Books).

Anglo, S. (1969), *Machiavelli: A Dissection* (London: Victor Gollancz).

Arendt, H. (1981), *Kant's Political Philosophy* (Chicago: University of Chicago Press).

Ashcraft, R. (1986), *Revolutionary Politics and Locke's Two Treatises of Government* (Princeton, NJ: Princeton University Press).

Ashcraft, R. (1987), *Locke's Two Treatises of Government* (London: Unwin Hyman).

Avineri, S. (1972), *Hegel's Theory of the Modern State* (Cambridge: Cambridge University Press).

Ball, T. and Farr, J. (eds) (1984), *After Marx* (Cambridge: Cambridge University Press).

Ball, T. (1984), 'Marxian Science and Positivist Politics', in Ball and Farr (1984), pp. 235–60.

Baron, H. (1961), 'Machiavelli: The Republican Citizen and the Author of "The Prince" ', *English Historical Review*, 16: 215–53.

Barry, B. (1965), *Political Argument* (London: Routledge and Kegan Paul).

Barry, N. (1995), 'Hume, Smith and Rousseau on Freedom', in R. Wokler (ed.), *Rousseau and Liberty*.

Baumgold, D. (1988), *Hobbes's Political Theory* (Cambridge: Cambridge University Press).

Baynes, K. (1989), 'Kant on Property Rights and the Social Contract', *The Monist*, 72: 433–53.

Beiser, F. (ed.) (1993), *The Cambridge Companion to Hegel* (Cambridge: Cambridge University Press).

Benton, T. (1984), *The Rise and Fall of Structural Marxism* (London: Macmillan).

Berger, F. (1984), *Happiness, Justice, Freedom: The Moral and Political Philosophy of John Stuart Mill* (Berkeley: University of California Press).

Berki, R. N. (1977), *The History of Political Thought: A Short Introduction* (London: Dent).

Berlin, I. (1965[1939]), *Karl Marx* (Oxford: Oxford University Press).

Berlin, I. (1969), *Four Essays on Liberty* (Oxford: Oxford University Press).

Berlin, I. (1972), 'The Originality of Machiavelli', in Myron P. Gilmore (ed.), *Studies on Machiavelli* (Florence: Sansoni).

Blakemore, S. (1988), *Burke and the Fall of Language: The French Revolution as a Linguistic Event* (Hanover, NH: Brown University Press).

Blakemore, S. (ed.) (1992), *Burke and the French Revolution: Bicentennial Essays* (Athens, GA: University of Georgia Press).

Bohman, J. and Lutz-Bachmann M. (eds) (1997), *Perpetual Peace. Essays on Kant's Cosmopolitan Ideal* (Cambridge, MA: MIT Press).

219

Bosanquet, B. (1923, 4th edn), *The Philosophical Theory of the State* (London: Macmillan).
Brod, H. (1992), *Hegel's Philosophy of Politics: Idealism, Identity and Modernity* (Boulder, San Francisco and Oxford: Westview Press).
Browning, G. (1999), *Hegel and the History of Political Philosophy* (London: Macmillan).
Browning, R. (1984), 'The Origin of Burke's Ideas Revisited?', *Eighteenth Century Studies*, 18(1): 57–71.
Brudner, A. (1981), 'Constitutional Monarchy as The Divine Regime: Hegel's Theory of The Just State', *History of Political Thought*, 2/1: 120–40.
Buckle, S. (1991), *Natural Law and the Theory of Property: Grotius to Hume* (Oxford: Clarendon Press).
Burgess, G. (1990), 'Contexts for the Writing and Publication of Hobbes's *Leviathan*', *History of Political Thought*, 11/4: 675–702.
Burke, E. (1906), *The Works of the Right Honourable Edmund Burke* (London: Oxford University Press).
Burke, E. (1958) (ed. J. T. Boulton), *A Philosophical Enquiry into the Origin of our Ideas of the Sublime and Beautiful* (London: Routledge and Kegan Paul).
Burke, E. (1962) (ed. J. M. Robson), *An Appeal from the New to the Old Whigs* (Indianapolis: Bobbs-Merrill).
Burke, E. (1968) (ed. C. C. O'Brien), *Reflections on the Revolution in France* (Harmondsworth: Penguin).
Burke, E. (1987) (ed. J. G. A. Pocock), *Reflections on the Revolution in France* (Indianapolis: Hackett).
Burnham, J. (1943), *The Machiavellians* (New York: The John Day Co).
Burns, T. (1995), 'The Ideological Location of Hegel's Political Thought', in J. Lovenduski and J. Stanyer (eds), *Contemporary Political Studies: 1995* (The Political Studies Association of Great Britain), 3: 1301–08.
Burns, T. (1996), *Natural Law and Political Ideology in the Philosophy of Hegel* (Aldershot: Avebury Press).
Burns, T. (1997), 'Hegel's Interpretation of the Philosophy of Heraclitus: Some Observations', in G. Stoker and J. Stanyer (eds), *Contemporary Political Studies: 1997* (The Political Studies Association of Great Britain), I: 228–39.
Burns, T. (1998), 'Metaphysics and Politics in Aristotle and Hegel', in A. Dobson and G. Stanyer (eds), *Contemporary Political Studies: 1998* (The Political Studies Association of Great Britain), 1: 387–99.
Burns, T. (1999), 'John Gray and the Death of Conservatism', *Contemporary Politics*, 5/1: 7–24.
Burns, T. (2000), 'The Purloined Hegel: Semiology in the Thought of Saussure and Derrida', *History of the Human Sciences*, 13/4: 1–24.
Burns, T. and Fraser, I. (eds) (2000), *The Hegel–Marx Connection* (London: Macmillan).
Burns, T. and Fraser, I. (eds) (2000a), 'Introduction: An Historical Survey of the Hegel–Marx Connection', in *The Hegel–Marx Connection*.
Butterfield, H. (1940), *The Statecraft of Machiavelli* (London: Bell).
Cairns, H. (1949), *Legal Philosophy from Plato to Hegel* (Baltimore: Johns Hopkins University Press).
Callinicos, A. (1985), *Marxism and Philosophy* (Oxford: Oxford University Press).

Cameron, D. (1973), *The Social Thought of Rousseau and Burke: A Comparative Study* (Toronto: University of Toronto Press).

Canavan, F. (1995), *The Political Economy of Edmund Burke: The Role of Property in his Thought* (New York: Fordham University Press).

Carver, T. (1982), *Marx's Social Theory* (Oxford: Oxford University Press).

Carver, T. (1984), 'Marxism as Method', in Ball and Farr (1984).

Cassirer, E. (1946, 1967), *The Myth of the State* (New Haven, Conn.: Yale University Press).

Cassirer, E. (1989, 2nd edn), *The Question of Jean-Jacques Rousseau* (Bloomington: Indiana University Press).

Chabod, F. (1958), *Machiavelli and the Renaissance* (Cambridge, MA: Harvard University Press).

Chapman, J. W. (1956), *Rousseau: Totalitarian or Liberal?* (New York: AMS Press).

Chitty, A. (ed.) (1994), *Has History Ended? Fukuyama, Marx, Modernity* (Aldershot: Avebury Press).

Cobban, A. (1960), *Edmund Burke and the Revolt Against the Eighteenth Century: A Study of the Political and Social Thinking of Burke, Wordsworth, Coleridge and Southey* (London: Allen and Unwin).

Cobban, A. (1964, revised edn), *Rousseau and the Modern State* (London: Allen and Unwin).

Cohen, G. A. (1978), *Karl Marx's Theory of History: A Defence* (Oxford: Oxford University Press).

Cohen, G. A. (1995), 'Marx and Locke on Land and Labour', in *Self-ownership, Freedom and Equality* (Cambridge: Cambridge University Press).

Cohen, J. (1986), 'Reflections on Rousseau: Autonomy and Democracy', *Philosophy and Public Affairs*, 15/1: 275–97.

Cohen, M., Nagel, T. and Scanlon, T. (eds) (1980), *Marx, Justice and History* (Princeton, NJ: Princeton University Press).

Colletti, L. (1972) (trans. J. Merrington and J. White), *From Rousseau to Lenin: Studies in Ideology and Society* (London: New Left Books).

Conniff, J. (1994), *The Useful Cobbler: Edmund Burke and the Politics of Progress* (Albany: State University of New York Press).

Copleston, F. (1963), *A History of Philosophy*, vol. 7, *Modern Philosophy*, Part 1, *Fichte to Hegel* (New York: Doubleday).

Cornforth, M. (1968), *The Open Philosophy and the Open Society* (New York: International Publishers).

Cowling, M. (1963), *Mill and Liberalism* (Cambridge: Cambridge University Press).

Cristi, F. R. (1983), 'The *Hegelische Mitte* and Hegel's Monarch', *Political Theory*, 11/4: 601–22.

Croce, B. (1925), *Elimenti di Politica* (Bari: Laterza).

Croce, B. (1949), 'Una questione che forse non si chiuderà mai: la questione de Machiavelli', *I. Quaderni della 'Critica'*, 19: 1–9.

Crocker, L. G. (1968), *Rousseau's Social Contract: An Interpretive Essay* (Cleveland: Case Western Reserve Press).

Crocker, L. G. (1995), 'Rousseau's soi-disant liberty', in R. Wokler (ed.), *Rousseau and Liberty*, 244–66.

Crowe, I. (ed.) (1997), *Edmund Burke: His Life and Legacy* (Dublin: Four Courts Press).

d'Hondt, J. (1998) (trans. J. Burbidge), *Hegel in His Time* (Peterborough, Ontario: Broadview Press).

Dagger, R. (1981), 'Understanding the General Will', *Western Political Quarterly*, 34: 359–71.

Dagger, R. (1997), *Civic Virtues: Rights, Citizenship, and Republican Virtue* (Oxford: Oxford University Press).

Dallmayr, F. (1993), *G. W. F. Hegel: Modernity and Politics* (London: Sage).

De Bruyn, F. (1996), *The Literary Genres of Edmund Burke: The Political Uses of Literary Form* (Oxford: Clarendon Press).

Della Volpa, G. (1978) (trans. J. Fraser), *Rousseau and Marx* (London: Lawrence & Wishart).

Dent, N. (1988), *Rousseau* (Oxford: Blackwell).

Dent, N. (1992), *A Rousseau Dictionary* (Oxford: Blackwell).

Derathé, R. (1970, 2nd edn), *Rousseau et la science politique de son temps* (Paris: Vrin).

Dickinson, H. T. (1977), *Liberty and Property: Political Ideology in Eighteenth Century England* (London: Methuen).

Dinwiddy, J. R. (1992), *Radicalism and Reform in Britain 1780–1850* (London: The Humbledon Press).

Dinwiddy, J. R. (1974–5), 'Utility and Natural Law in Burke's Thought: A Reconsideration', *Studies in Burke and His Time*, 16/2: 105–28.

Dreyer, F. A. (1979), *Burke's Politics: A Study in Whig Orthodoxy* (Waterloo, Ont.: Wilfrid Laurier University Press).

Dunn, J. (1968), 'Justice and the Interpretation of Locke's Political Theory', *Political Studies*, 16: 68–87.

Dunn, J. (1969), *The Political Thought of John Locke: An Historical Account of the Argument of the 'Two Treatises of Government'* (Cambridge: Cambridge University Press).

Dunn, J. (1984), *Locke* (Oxford: Oxford University Press).

Dworkin, R. (1977), *Taking Rights Seriously* (London: Duckworth).

Eagleton, T. (1997, 4 July), 'Saving Burke From the Tories?', *New Statesman*.

Eagleton, T. (1998), *Crazy John and the Bishop and Other Essays on Irish Culture* (Indiana: University of Notre Dame Press).

Ebbinghaus, J. (1967), 'Interpretation and Misinterpretation of the Categorical Imperative', in R. P. Wolff (ed.), *Kant: A Selection of Critical Essays* (Indiana: University of Notre Dame Press).

Eccleshall, R. (1990), *English Conservatism Since the Restoration: An Introduction and Anthology* (London: Unwin Hyman).

Ellenburg, S. (1976), *Rousseau's Political Philosophy: An Interpretation From Within* (Ithaca: Cornell University Press).

Elliot, G. (1987), *Althusser: A Detour of Theory* (London: Verso).

Elliott, J. E. (1979), 'Continuity and Change in the Evolution of Marx's Theory of Alienation: from the Manuscripts through the *Grundrisse* to *Capital*', *History of Political Economy*, 11/3: 317–62.

Elster, J. (1985), *Making Sense of Marx* (Cambridge: Cambridge University Press).

Engels, F. (1935) (trans. E. Burns), *Anti-Dühring* (London: Martin Lawrence).

Engels, F. (1958), *Ludwig Feuerbach and the End of Classical German Philosophy*, in K. Marx and F. Engels (eds), *Selected Works*, vol. II (Moscow: Foreign Languages Printing House).

Fackenheim, E. (1970), 'On the Actuality of the Rational and the Rationality of the Actual', *Review of Metaphysics*, 13: 690–8.

Fasel, G. W. (1983), *Edmund Burke* (Boston: Twayne's Publishers).

Filmer, R. (1991), *Patriarcha and Other Writings* (Cambridge: Cambridge University Press).

Findlay, J. N. (1958), *Hegel: A Re-Examination* (New York: Collier Books).

Fiore, S. R. (1990), *Niccolò Machiavelli: An Annotated Bibliography of Modern Scholarship and Criticism* (New York: Greenwood).

Fitzjames Stephen, J. (1967[1873]) (ed. R. J. White), *Liberty, Equality and Fraternity* (Cambridge: Cambridge University Press).

Flikschuh, K. (2000), *Kant and Modern Political Philosophy* (Cambridge: Cambridge University Press).

Forbes, D. (1975), *Hume's Philosophical Politics* (Cambridge: Cambridge University Press).

Forbes, D. (1982), 'Natural Law and the Scottish Enlightenment', in R. H. Campbell and A. S. Skinner (eds), *The Origins and Nature of the Scottish Enlightenment* (Edinburgh: Donald).

Fralin, R. (1978), *Rousseau and Representation* (New York: Columbia University Press).

Franklin, J. H. (1978), *John Locke and the Theory of Sovereignty: Mixed Monarchy and the Right of Resistance in the Political Thought of the English Revolution* (Cambridge: Cambridge University Press).

Fraser, I. (1998), *Hegel and Marx: The Concept of Need* (Edinburgh: Edinburgh University Press).

Freeman, M. (1980), *Edmund Burke and the Critique of Political Radicalism.* (Oxford: Blackwell).

Fukuyama, F. (1992), *The End of History and the Last Man* (London: Hamish Hamilton).

Furniss, T. (1993), *Edmund Burke's Aesthetic Ideology: Language, Gender and Political Economy in Revolution* (Cambridge: Cambridge University Press).

Gadamer, H. G. (1975), *Truth and Method* (London: Sheed and Ward).

Gauthier, D. P. (1969), *The Logic of Leviathan: the Moral and Political Theory of Thomas Hobbes* (Oxford: Clarendon Press).

Geras, N. (1983), *Marx and Human Nature: Refutation of a Legend* (London: Verso).

Geras, N. (1985), 'The Controversy about Marx and Justice', *New Left Review*, 150: 47–85.

Geras, N. (1986), *The Literature of Revolution* (London: Verso).

Germino, D. (1966), 'Second Thoughts on Leo Strauss's Machiavelli', *Journal of Politics*, 28: 794–817.

Germino, D. (1969), 'Hegel as a Political Theorist', *Journal of Politics*, 31: 293–313.

Gert, B. (1996), 'Hobbes's Psychology', in Tom Sorell (ed.), *The Cambridge Companion to Hobbes* (Cambridge: Cambridge University Press).

Gilbert, A. H. (1938), *Machiavelli's 'Prince' and its Forerunners: The Prince as a Typical Book de Regime Princepum* (Durham, NC: Duke University Press).

Gilbert, A.H. (1965), *Machiavelli: The Chief Works and Others* (Durham, NC: Duke University Press).

Gilbert, F. (1939), 'The Humanist Concept of The Prince and The Prince of Machiavelli', *Journal of Modern History*, 11: 449–83.

Gilbert, F. (1965), *Machiavelli and Guicciardini* (Princeton, NJ: Princeton University Press).

Goldie, M. (1997), 'Introduction' to *Locke: Political Essays* (Cambridge: Cambridge University Press).

Goldsmith, M. M. (1966), *Hobbes's Science of Politics* (New York: Columbia University Press).

Goldsmith, M. M. (1980), 'Hobbes's "Mortal God": Is there a Fallacy in Hobbes's Theory of Sovereignty?', *History of Political Thought*, 1: 33–50.

Goldsmith, M. M. (1996), 'Hobbes on Law', in T. Sorell (ed.), *The Cambridge Companion to Hobbes* (Cambridge: Cambridge University Press).

Gough, J. W. (1950), *John Locke's Political Philosophy* (Oxford: Clarendon Press).

Gray, J. and Smith, G. W. (eds) (1991), *Mill on Liberty: In Focus* (London: Routledge).

Gray, J. (1996, 2nd edn), *Mill on Liberty: A Defence* (London: Routledge).

Grotius, Hugo (1925) (trans. F. W. Kelsey), *De Jure Belli ac Pacis Libri Tres*, vol. 2 (Oxford: Clarendon).

Guyer, P. (ed.) (1992), *The Cambridge Companion to Kant* (Cambridge: Cambridge University Press).

Guyer, P. (2000), *Kant on Freedom, Law, and Happiness* (Cambridge: Cambridge University Press).

Haakonsen, K. (1993), 'Republicanism', in R. Goodin and P. Pettit (eds), *A Companion to Contemporary Political Philosophy* (Oxford: Blackwell).

Hampsher-Monk, I. (1987), *The Political Philosophy of Edmund Burke* (London: Longman).

Hampsher-Monk, I. (1988), 'Rhetoric and Opinion in the Politics of Edmund Burke', *History of Political Thought*, 9/3: 455–84.

Hampsher-Monk, I. (1992), *A History of Modern Political Thought: Major Political Thinkers from Hobbes to Marx* (Oxford: Blackwell).

Hampsher-Monk, I. (1995), 'Rousseau and Totalitarianism – With Hindsight?', in R. Wokler (ed.), *Rousseau and Liberty*.

Hampton, J. (1986), *Hobbes and the Social Contract Tradition* (Cambridge: Cambridge University Press).

Hancock, K. (1935), 'Machiavelli in Modern Dress', *History*, 20: 197–210.

Hancock, R. N. (1974), *Twentieth Century Ethics* (New York: Columbia University Press).

Hannaford, I. (1972), 'Machiavelli's Concept of Virtù in "The Prince" and "The Discourses" Reconsidered', *Political Studies*, 20: 185–9.

Hardimon, M. O. (1994), *Hegel's Social Philosophy: The Project of Reconciliation* (Cambridge: Cambridge University Press).

Harris, H. S. (1972), *Hegel's Development: Toward the Sunlight* (Oxford: Oxford University Press).

Harris, I. (1994), *The Mind of John Locke: A Study of Political Theory in Its Intellectual Setting* (Cambridge: Cambridge University Press).

Harris, P. and Morrow, J. (eds) (1986), *T. H. Green: Lectures on the Principles of Political Obligation and Other Writings* (Cambridge: Cambridge University Press).

Hart, H. L. A. (1979), 'Between Utility and Rights', in A. Ryan (ed.), *The Idea of Freedom: Essays in Honour of Isaiah Berlin* (Oxford: Oxford University Press).

Haworth, A. (1998), *Free Speech* (London: Routledge).

Hazlitt, W. (1819), *Political Essays* (London: William Hone).

Held, D. (1996, 2nd edn), *Models of Democracy* (Cambridge: Polity Press).

Hegel, G. W. F. (1964) (ed. Z. A. Pelczynski, trans. T. M. Knox), *Hegel's Political Writings* (Oxford: Clarendon Press).

Hegel, G. W. F. (1975) (trans. W. Wallace), *Logic: Being Part One of the Encyclopaedia of the Philosophical Sciences* (Oxford: Oxford University Press).

Hegel, G. W. F. (1979) (trans. T. M. Knox), *Philosophy of Right* (Oxford: Oxford University Press).

Hegel, G. W. F. (1991) (ed. A. Wood), *Elements of the Philosophy of Right* (Cambridge: Cambridge University Press).

Herzog, D. (1998), *Poisoning the Minds of the Lower Orders* (Princeton, NJ: Princeton University Press).

Himmelfarb, G. (1974), *On Liberty and Liberalism: The Case of John Stuart Mill* (New York: Alfred A. Knopf).

Hindson, P. and Gray, T. (1988), *Burke's Dramatic Theory of Politics* (Aldershot, England, Brookfield, VT: Avebury Press).

Hoag, R. W. (1986), 'Happiness and Freedom: Recent Work on John Stuart Mill', *Philosophy and Public Affairs*, 15: 188–99.

Hobbes, T. (1928) (ed. Ferdinand Tönnies), *The Elements of Law* (Cambridge: Cambridge University Press).

Hobbes, T. (1983) (ed. H. Warrender), *De Cive* (Oxford: Clarendon Press).

Hobbes, T. (1996) (ed. Richard Tuck), *Leviathan* (Cambridge: Cambridge University Press).

Höffe, O. (1989), 'Kant's Principle of Justice as Categorical Imperative of Law', in Y. Yovel (ed.), *Kant's Practical Philosophy Reconsidered* (Amsterdam: Kluwer Academic Publishers).

Höffe, O. (1992), 'Even a Nation of Devils Needs a State', in H. Williams (ed.), *Kant's Political Philosophy* (Cardiff: University of Wales Press).

Höffe, O. (1994), *Immanuel Kant* (Albany: State University of New York Press).

Höffe, O. (1995), 'Völkerbund oder Weltrepublik?', in O. Höffe (ed.), *Zum Ewigen Frieden* (Berlin: Akademie Verlag).

Honderich, T. (1974), 'The Worth of J. S. Mill On Liberty', *Political Studies,* 22: 463–70.

Honderich, T. (1982), ' "On Liberty" and Morality-Dependent Harms', *Political Studies*, 30: 504–14.

Hont, I. (1993), 'The Rhapsody of Public Debt: David Hume and Voluntary State Bankruptcy', in Nicholas Phillipson and Quentin Skinner (eds), *Political Discourse in Early Modern Britain* (Cambridge: Cambridge University Press).

Hood, F. C. (1964), *The Divine Politics of Thomas Hobbes* (Oxford: Oxford University Press).

Hook, S. (1970a), 'Hegel Rehabilitated?', in W. Kaufmann (ed.), *Hegel's Political Philosophy*.

Hook, S. (1970b), 'Hegel and his Apologists', in W. Kaufmann (ed.), *Hegel's Political Philosophy*.

Hook, S. (1971, 4th edn), *From Hegel to Marx: Studies in the Intellectual Development of Karl Marx* (Ann Arbor: University of Michigan Press).

Hope Mason, J. (ed.) (1979), *The Indispensable Rousseau* (London: Quartet Books).

Hope Mason, J. (1995), 'Forced to be Free', in R. Wokler (ed.), *Rousseau and Liberty*, 121–38.

Howard, M. C. and King, J. E. (1992), *A History of Marxian Economics*, vol. 11, 1929–1990 (Basingstoke: Macmillan).

Hulliung, M. (1983), *Citizen Machiavelli* (Princeton, NJ: Princeton University Press).

Hume, David (1975, 3rd edn), *Enquiry Concerning the Principles of Morals* (L. A. Selby-Bigge and P. H. Nidditch) (Oxford: Clarendon Press).

Hume, David (1978, 2nd edn), *A Treatise of Human Nature* (eds L. A. Selby-Bigge and P. H. Nidditch) (Oxford: Clarendon Press).

Hume, David (1994) (ed. K. Haakonssen), *Political Essays* (Cambridge: Cambridge University Press).

Husami, Z. I. (1980), 'Marx on Distributive Justice', in M. Cohen *et al.*: 41–79.

Huxley, T. H. (1898), 'Government: Anarchy or Regimentation', in T. H. Huxley, *Collected Essays*, vol. 1 (London: Macmillan).

Hyppolite, J. (1973), *Studies on Marx and Hegel* (New York: Harper Torchbooks).

Jolley, N. (1999), *Locke: His Philosophical Thought* (Oxford: Oxford University Press).

Jones, W. T. (1987), 'Rousseau's General Will and the Problem of Consent', *Journal of the History of Philosophy*, 25: 105–30.

Kant, I. (1964), *Groundwork to the Metaphysics of Morals* (New York: Harper Torchbooks).

Kant, I. (1970) (ed. H. Reiss), *Kant's Political Writings* (Cambridge: Cambridge University Press).

Kant, I. (1991), *The Metaphysics of Morals* (Cambridge: Cambridge University Press).

Kaufmann, W. (ed.) (1970), *Hegel's Political Philosophy* (New York: Atherton Press).

Kaufmann, W. (1970a), 'The Hegel Myth and its Method', in *Hegel's Political Philosophy*.

Kelly, G. A. (1978), *Hegel's Retreat From Eleusis: Studies in Political Thought* (Princeton: Princeton University Press).

Kendall, W. (1941), *John Locke and the Doctrine of Majority Rule* (Urbana Illinois: University of Illinois Press).

Kirk, R. (1960, 3rd edn), *The Conservative Mind* (Chicago: Henry Regnery).

Knox, T. M. (1970), 'Hegel and Prussianism', in W. Kaufmann (ed.), *Hegel's Political Philosophy*.

Knox, T. M. (1979), 'Translator's Foreword and Notes' to Hegel, *Philosophy of Right*.

Kramer, M. H. (1997), *John Locke on the Origins of Private Property: Philosophical Explorations of Individualism, Community and Equality* (Cambridge: Cambridge University Press).

Kramnick, I. (1974), *Edmund Burke* (Englewood Cliffs, NJ: Prentice-Hall).

Kramnick, I. (1977), *The Rage of Edmund Burke: Portrait of an Ambivalent Conservative* (New York: Basic Books).

Kramnick, I. (1990), *Republicanism and Bourgeois Radicalism: Political Ideology in Late Eighteenth-Century England and America* (Ithaca, NY: Cornell University Press).

Kramnick, I. (ed.) (1999), *The Portable Burke* (Harmondsworth: Penguin).

Larrain, J. (1986), *A Reconstruction of Historical Materialism* (London: Allen and Unwin).

Laski, H. (1961[1920]), *Political Thought in England from Locke to Bentham* (London: Williams & Norgate).

Laslett, P. (1998[1960]), 'Introduction' to *John Locke: Two Treatises of Government* (Cambridge: Cambridge University Press).

Lenin, V. I. (1961), *Collected Works*, vol. 38, *Philosophical Notebooks* (Moscow: Foreign Languages Publishing House).

Lenin, V. I. (1961a), 'Conspectus of Hegel's *Science of Logic*', in *Philosophical Notebooks*.

Lenin, V. I. (1961b), 'Conspectus of Hegel's *Lectures on the History of Philosophy*', in *Philosophical Notebooks*.

Levin, M. and Williams, H. (1987), 'Inherited Power and Popular Representation: A Tension in Hegel's Political Theory', *Political Studies*, 35: 105–15.

Levine, A. (1976), *The Politics of Autonomy: A Kantian Reading of Rousseau's Social Contract* (Amherst: University of Massachusetts Press).

Levine, A. (1993), *The General Will: Rousseau, Marx and Communism* (Cambridge: Cambridge University Press).

Lindsay, A. D. (1932), 'Hegel the German Idealist', in F. J. C. Hearnshaw (ed.), *The Social and Political Ideas of Some Representative Thinkers of the Age of Reaction and Reconstruction* (London: Harrap).

Little, D. (1986), *The Scientific Marx* (Minneapolis: University of Minneapolis Press).

Lively, J. and Reeve, A. (eds) (1989), *Modern Political Theory from Hobbes to Marx: Key Debates* (London: Routledge).

Lloyd Thomas, D. (1995), *Locke on Government* (London: Routledge).

Locke, J. (1998[1960]) (ed. P. Laslett), *Two Treatises of Government* (Cambridge: Cambridge University Press).

Lovejoy, A. O. (1956), *The Great Chain of Being: A Study of the History of an Idea* (Cambridge, MA.: Harvard University Press).

Lukács, G. (1975), *The Young Hegel: Studies in the Relations Between Dialectics and Economics* (London: Merlin Books).

Lukes, S. (1985), *Marxism and Morality* (Oxford: Oxford University Press).

Lyotard, J. F. (1984), *The Postmodern Condition: A Report on Knowledge* (Manchester: Manchester University Press).

MacAdam, J. I. (1989), 'The Discourse on Inequality and The Social Contract', in J. Lively and A. Reeve (eds), *Modern Political Theory from Hobbes to Marx: Key Debates*.

Macedo, S. (1990), *Liberal Virtues: Citizenship, Virtue, and Community in Liberal Constitutionalism* (Oxford: Clarendon Press).

McCarney, J. (2000), *Hegel: On History* (London: Routledge).

McCloskey, H. J. (1971), *John Stuart Mill: A Critical Study* (London: Macmillan).

MacGregor, D. (1984), *The Communist Ideal in Hegel and Marx* (Toronto and Buffalo: University of Toronto Press).

MacGregor, D. (1998), *Hegel and Marx After the Fall of Communism* (Cardiff: University of Wales Press).

Mackie, J. L. (1980), *Hume's Moral Theory* (London: Routledge and Kegan Paul).

McLellan, D. (1969), *The Young Hegelians and Karl Marx* (London: Macmillan).

McLellan, D. (1972), *Marx Before Marxism* (Harmondsworth: Penguin).

McLellan, D. (1973), *Karl Marx: His Life and Thought* (London: Macmillan).

McLellan, D. (1980, 2nd edn), *The Thought of Karl Marx* (London: Macmillan).

McLennan, G. (1981), *Marxism and the Methodologies of History* (London: Verso).

McNeilly, F. S. (1968), *The Anatomy of Leviathan* (London: Macmillan).

Macpherson, C. B. (1962), *The Political Theory of Possessive Individualism: Hobbes to Locke* (Oxford: Oxford University Press).

Macpherson, C. B. (1966), *The Real World of Democracy* (Oxford: Clarendon Press).

Macpherson, C. B. (1973), *Democratic Theory: Essays in Retrieval* (Oxford: Clarendon Press).

Macpherson, C. B. (1980), *Burke* (Oxford: Oxford University Press).

Mannheim, K. (1986) (eds D. Kettler, V. Meja and N. Stehr), *Conservatism: A Contribution to the Sociology of Knowledge* (London: Routledge).

Mansfield Jr, H. C. (1984), *Selected Letters of Edmund Burke* (Chicago: University of Chicago Press).

Marcuse, H. (1973), *Reason and Revolution: Hegel and the Rise of Social Theory* (London: Routledge).

Maritain, J. (1942), 'The End of Machiavellianism', *Review of Politics*, 4: 1–33.

Martinich, A. P. (1995), *A Hobbes Dictionary* (Oxford: Oxford University Press).

Marx, K. and Engels, F. (1962), *Selected Works*, (2 vols) (Moscow: Foreign Languages Publishing House).

Marx, K. (1965), *The German Ideology* (London: Lawrence and Wishart).

Marx, K. (1967) (trans. M. Milligan), *Economic and Philosophical Manuscripts of 1844* (Moscow: Progress Publishers).

Marx, K. (1973a) (trans. M. Nicolaus), *Grundrisse* (Harmondsworth: Penguin Books).

Marx, K. (1973b[1846]), *The Poverty of Philosophy: Answer to 'The Philosophy of Poverty' by M. Proudhon* (Moscow: Progress Publishers).

Marx, K. (1974) (ed. F. Engels, trans. S. Moore and E. Aveling), *Capital: A Critical Analysis of Capitalist Production*, vol. 1 (London: Lawrence and Wishart).

Marx, K. (1976), *Capital*, vol. 1 (Harmondsworth: Penguin).

Marx, K. (1981), *Capital* vol. 3 (Harmondsworth: Penguin).

Masters, R. D. (1968), *The Political Philosophy of Rousseau* (Princton, NJ: Princeton University Press).

Mehta, V. R. (1968), *Hegel and the Modern State* (New Delhi: Associated Publishing House).

Meinecke, F. (1957), *Machiavellianism: The Doctrine of Raison d'état and its place in Modern History* (London: Routledge).

Melzer, A. M. (1983), 'Rousseau's Moral Realism: Replacing Natural Law with the General Will', *American Political Science Review*, 77: 633–51.

Merquior, J. G. (1986), *Western Marxism* (London: Paladin Books).

Meszaros, I. (1970), *Marx's Theory of Alienation* (London: Merlin).

Mill, J. S. (1969[1873]) (J. Stillinger, ed.), *Autobiography* (Boston: Houghton Mifflin).

Mill, J. S. (1973) (J. M. Robson, ed.), *A System of Logic* (Books I–III), in *Collected Works*, vol. VII (Toronto: University of Toronto Press).

Mill, J. S. (1991) (J. Gray, ed.), *On Liberty and Other Essays* (Oxford: Oxford University Press).

Miller, D. (1981), *Philosophy and Ideology in Hume's Political Thought* (Oxford: Clarendon Press).

Miller, D. (1982), 'The Macpherson Version', *Political Studies*, 30: 120–7.

Miller, J. (1984), *Rousseau: Dreamer of Democracy* (New Haven: Yale University Press).

Miller, R. W. (1984), *Analyzing Marx* (Princeton, NJ: Princeton University Press).

Moore, James (1976), 'Hume's Theory of Justice and Property', *Political Studies*, 24: 103–19.

Mulholland, L. (1990), *Kant's System of Rights* (New York: Columbia University Press).

Nagel, T. (1959), 'Hobbes's Concept of Obligation', *Philosophical Review*, 68: 68–83.

Nisbet, R. (1986), *Conservatism* (Milton Keynes: Open University Press).

Nozick, R. (1974), *Anarchy, State and Utopia* (Oxford: Blackwell).

Oakeshott, M. (ed.) (1960), *Leviathan* (Oxford: Oxford University Press).

O'Brien, C. C. (1992), *The Great Melody: A Thematic Bibliography and Commented Anthology of Edmund Burke* (Chicago: University of Chicago Press).

O'Gorman, F. (1973), *Edmund Burke: His Political Philosophy* (London: Allen and Unwin).

O'Gorman, F. (1986), *British Conservatism: Conservative Thought From Burke to Thatcher* (London: Longman).

Ollman, B. (1971), *Alienation* (Cambridge: Cambridge University Press).

Olschki, L. (1945), *Machiavelli the Scientist* (Berkeley: University of California Press).

O'Neill, O. (1989), *Constructions of Reason* (Cambridge: Cambridge University Press).

O'Neill, O. (1991), 'Transnational Justice', in D. Held (ed.), *Political Theory Today*, (Oxford: Polity Press).

O'Neill, O. (1996), *Towards Justice and Virtue* (Cambridge: Cambridge Univeristy Press).

Pappin, J. L. (1993), *The Metaphysics of Edmund Burke* (New York: Fordham University Press).

Parkin, C. (1968), *The Moral Basis of Burke's Political Thought, 1500–1800* (New York: Russell and Russell).

Parry, G. (1978), *John Locke* (London: George Allen and Unwin).

Parry, G. (1998), 'The Sovereign as Educator: Thomas Hobbes's National Curriculum', *Paedogogica Historica: International Journal of the History of Education*, 34/3: 711–30.

Pateman, C. (1985), *The Problem of Political Obligation: A Critique of Liberal Theory* (Cambridge: Polity Press).

Pateman, C. (1988), *The Sexual Contract* (Cambridge: Polity Press).

Pelczynski, Z. A. (1964), 'Editor's Introduction' to G. W. F. Hegel, *Hegel's Political Writings*.

Pelczynski, Z. A. (1970), 'Hegel Again', in W. Kaufmann (ed.), *Hegel's Political Philosophy*.

Pelczynski, Z. A. (1971), 'The Hegelian Doctrine of the State', in *Hegel's Political Philosophy: Problems and Perspectives* (Cambridge: Cambridge University Press.

Peters, R. S. (1956), *Hobbes* (London: Penguin).

Phillipson, N. (1993), 'Propriety, Property and Prudence: David Hume and the Defence of the Revolution', in N. Phillipson and Q. Skinner (eds), *Political Discourse in Early Modern Britain* (Cambridge: Cambridge University Press).

Pitkin, H. (1984), *Fortune is a Woman: Gender and Politics in the Thought of Niccolò Machiavelli* (Berkeley: University of California Press).

Plamenatz, J. (1952), *The Revolutionary Movement in France, 1815–71* (London: Longmans).

Plamenatz, J. (1958), *The English Utilitarians* (Oxford: Oxford University Press).

Plamenatz, J. (1963, 1976), *Man and Society*, vol. 2. (London: Longmans).

Plamenatz, J. (1965), *German Marxism and Russian Communism* (New York: Harper and Row).

Plamenatz, J. (1972a), 'In Search of Machiavellian *Virtù*', in A. Parel (ed.), *The Political Calculus* (Toronto: University of Toronto Press).

Plamenatz, J. (1972), 'Ce qui ne signifie autre chose sinon qu'on le forcera d'être libre', in M. Cranston and R. S. Peters (eds), *Hobbes and Rousseau: A Collection of Critical Essays* (New York: Anchor Books).

Plant, R. (1973), *Hegel* (London: Unwin).

Pocock, J. G. A. (1975), *The Machiavellian Moment: Florentine Political Thought and the Atlantic Republican Tradition* (Princeton, NJ: Princeton University Press).

Pocock, J. G. A. (1979), 'Hume and the American Revolution: The Dying Thoughts of a North Briton', in D. F. Norton, N. Capaldi and W. L. Robinson (eds), *McGill Hume Studies* (San Diego: Austin Hills Press).

Pocock, J. G. A. (1983), 'Cambridge paradigms and Scotch philosophers: a study of the relations between the civic humanist and the civil jurisprudential interpretations of eighteenth-century social thought' in I. Hont and M. Ignatieff (eds), *Wealth and Virtue: The Shaping of Political Economy in the Scottish Enlightenment* (Cambridge: Cambridge University Press).

Pocock, J. G. A. (1985), *Virtue, Commerce and History: Essays in Political Thought and History, Chiefly in the Eighteenth Century* (Cambridge, New York: Cambridge University Press).

Pocock, J. G. A. (ed.) (1993), *The Varieties of British Political Thought, 1500–1800* (Cambridge, New York: Cambridge University Press).

Pogson-Smith, W. G. (ed.) (1909), *Leviathan* (Oxford: Clarendon Press).

Polin, R. (1953), *Politique et Philosophie chez Thomas Hobbes* (Paris: Presses Universitaires de France).

Popper, K. (1966, 1969[1945]), *The Open Society and Its Enemies*, vol. 2: Hegel and Marx. (London: Routledge).

Popper, K. (1969[1963]), *Conjectures and Refutations* (London: Routledge and Kegan Paul).

Porter, R. (2000), *Enlightenment: Britain and the Creation of the Modern World* (London: Allen Lane).

Post, G. (1964), 'Ratio publicae utilitatis, ratio status and "reasons of state", 1100–1300', in *Studies in Medieval Legal Thought* (Princeton, NJ: Princeton University Press).

Prezzolini, G. (1967) (trans. G. Savini), *Machiavelli* (London: Robert Hale).

Price, R. (1973), 'The Senses of *Virtù* in Machiavelli', *European Studies Review*, 3: 315–46.

Pufendorf, Samuel (1934) (trans. C. H. Oldfather and W. A. Oldfather), *De Jure Naturae et Gentium libri octo*, vol. 2 (Oxford: Clarendon Press).

Raphael, D. D. (1977), *Hobbes: Morals and Politics* (London: Allen and Unwin).

Rawls, J. (1972), *A Theory of Justice* (Oxford: Oxford University Press).

Rawls, J. (1980), 'Kantian Constructivism in Moral Theory', *Journal of Philosophy*, 77(9): 515–72.

Rawls, J. (1993), *Political Liberalism* (New York: Columbia University Press).

Raz, J. (1986), *The Morality of Freedom* (Oxford: Clarendon Press).

Rees, J. C. (1985), *John Stuart Mill's On Liberty* (Oxford: Clarendon Press).

Rees, J. C. (1991), 'A Re-Reading of Mill on Liberty', in J. Gray and G. W. Smith (eds), *Mill on Liberty: in focus* (London: Routledge).

Reid, C. (1985), *Edmund Burke and the Practice of Political Writing* (New York: St. Martin's Press).

Reiss, H. (ed.) (1991, 2nd edn), *Kant: Political Writings* (Cambridge: Cambridge University Press).

Renaudet, A. (1942), *Machiavel: Etude d'histoire des Doctrines Politiques* (Paris: Gallimard).

Ridolfi, R. (1963) (trans. C. Grayson), *The Life of Niccolò Machiavelli* (Chicago: University of Chicago Press).

Riedel, M. (1984), *Between Tradition and Revolution: The Hegelian Transformation of Political Philosophy* (Cambridge: Cambridge University Press).

Rigby, S. (1987), *Marxism and History* (Manchester: Manchester University Press).

Riley, J. (1991), 'One Very Simple Principle', *Utilitas*, 3: 1–35.

Riley, J. (1998), *Mill on Liberty* (London: Routledge).

Riley, P. (1973), 'On Kant as the Most Adequate of the Social Contract Theorists', *Political Theory*, 1: 450–71.

Riley, P. (1982), *Will and Political Legitimacy: A Critical Exposition of Social Contract Theory in Hobbes, Locke, Rousseau, Kant and Hegel* (Cambridge, MA: Harvard University Press).

Riley, P. (1983), *Kant's Political Philosophy* (Totowa: Rowman and Littlefield).

Ritter, J. (1982), *Hegel and the French Revolution: Essays on the Philosophy of Right* (Cambridge, MA: MIT Press).

Roberts, M. (1996), *Analytical Marxism: A Critique* (London: Verso).

Robertson, John (1983), 'The Scottish Enlightenment at the limits of the civic tradition', in I. Hont and M. Ignatieff (eds), *Wealth and Virtue: The Shaping of Political Economy in the Scottish Enlightenment* (Cambridge: Cambridge University Press).

Rose, G. (1995), *Hegel Contra Sociology* (London: Athlone Press).

Rousseau, J.-J. (1974) (trans. by B. Foxley), *Émile* (London: Dent).

Rousseau, J.-J. (1979), 'Letter to Christophe de Beaumont', in J. Hope Mason (ed.), *The Indispensable Rousseau*.

Rousseau, J.-J. (1997a) (ed. and trans. Victor Gourevitch), *The Social Contract and Other Later Political Writings* (Cambridge: Cambridge University Press).

Rousseau, J.-J. (1997b) (ed. and trans. Victor Gourevitch), *The Discourses and Other Early Political Writings* (Cambridge: Cambridge University Press).

Russell, B. (1946), *A History of Western Philosophy* (London: Unwin).

Ryan, A. (1965), 'Locke and the Dictatorship of the Bourgeoisie', *Political Studies*, 13: 219–30.

Ryan, A. (1987, 2nd edn), *John Stuart Mill* (London: Routledge).

Ryan, A. (1988a), 'Hobbes and Individualism', in G. A. J. Rogers and A. Ryan (eds), *Perspectives on Thomas Hobbes* (Oxford: Clarendon Press).

Ryan, A. (1988b), 'A More Tolerant Hobbes?', in Susan Mendus (ed.), *Justifying Toleration: Conceptual and Historical Perspectives* (Cambridge: Cambridge University Press).

Ryan, A. (1991), 'John Stuart Mill's Art of Living', in Gray and Smith (eds).

Sasso, G. (1952), 'Sul setimo capitolo del Principe', *Revista storica italiana*, 64: 177–207.

Sasso, G. (1958), *Niccolò Machiavelli* (Naples: Instituto italiano per gli studi storici), 10.

Sayer, D. (1979), *Marx's Method* (Brighton: Harvester).

Sayer, D. (1987), *The Violence of Abstraction, The Analytical Foundations of Historical Materialism* (Oxford: Blackwell).

Sayers, S. (1998), *Marxism and Human Nature* (London: Routledge).

Sayers, S. (1990), 'Marxism and the Dialectical Method: A Critique of G. A. Cohen', in S. Sayers and P. Osborne (eds).

Sayers, S. and Osborne, P. (eds) (1990), *Socialism, Feminism and Philosophy* (London: Routledge).

Scaglione, A. (1956), 'Machiavelli the Scientist', *Symposium*, 10: 43–4.

Schuettinger, R. L. (1970), *The Conservative Tradition in European Thought* (New York: Putnam).

Scruton, R. (1988), 'G. W. F. Hegel', in R. Scruton (ed.), *Conservative Thinkers: Essays From the Salisbury Review* (London: Claridge).

Seliger, M. (1968), *The Liberal Politics of John Locke* (London: Allen and Unwin).

Shklar, J. N. (1957), *After Utopia: The Decline of Political Faith* (Princeton, NJ: Princeton University Press).

Shklar, J. N. (1985, 2nd edn), *Men and Citizens: A Study of Rousseau's Social Theory* (Cambridge: Cambridge University Press).

Simmons, A. J. (1992), *The Lockean Theory of Rights* (Princeton, NJ: Princeton University Press).

Simmons, A. J. (1993), *On the Edge of Anarchy: Locke, Consent, and the Limits of Society* (Princeton, NJ: Princeton University Press).

Singer, P. (1983), *Hegel* (Oxford: Oxford University Press).

Skinner, Q. (1965), 'The Ideological Context of Hobbes's Political Thought', *Historical Journal*, 9: 286–317.

Skinner, Q. (1969), 'Meaning and Understanding in the History of Ideas', *History and Theory*, 8: 3–53.

Skinner, Q. (1974), 'Some Problems in the Analysis of Political Thought and Action', *Political Theory*, 2: 227–303.

Skinner, Q. (1981), *Machiavelli* (Oxford: Oxford University Press).

Skinner, Q. (1996), *Reason and Rhetoric in the Philosophy of Hobbes* (Cambridge: Cambridge University Press).

Skinner, Q. (1999), 'Hobbes and the Purely Artificial Person of the State', *The Journal of Political Philosophy*, 7/1: 1–29.

Skorupski, S. (1989), *John Stuart Mill* (London: Routledge).

Smith, S. B. (1991), *Hegel's Critique of Liberalism: Rights in Context* (Chicago: University of Chicago Press).

Sorell, T. (1986), *Hobbes* (London: Routledge and Kegan Paul).

Spellman, W. M. (1997), *John Locke* (London: Macmillan).

Spragens, T. A. (1973), *The Politics of Motion: the World of Thomas Hobbes* (London: Croom Helm).

Sreenivasan, G. (1995), *The Limits of Lockean Rights in Property* (Oxford: Oxford University Press).

Stanlis, P. J. (1991), *Edmund Burke: The Enlightenment and Revolution* (New Brunswick, NJ: Transaction Publishers).

Strauss, L. (1952), *Persecution and the Art of Writing* (Glencoe, Ill.: Free Press).

Strauss, L. (1953), *Natural Right and History* (Chicago: University of Chicago Press).

Strauss, L. (1958), *Thoughts on Machiavelli* (Glencoe, Ill.: The Free Press).

Strauss, L. (1963), *The Political Philosophy of Hobbes: its Basis and its Genesis* (Chicago: University of Chicago Press).

Suchting, W. (1972), 'Marx, Popper and "Historicism"', *Inquiry*, 15: 235–66.

Sullivan, R. (1994), *An Introduction to Kant's Ethics* (Cambridge: Cambridge University Press).

Suter, J. F. (1971), 'Burke, Hegel and the French Revolution', in Z. A. Pelczynski, (ed.), *Hegel's Political Philosophy*.

Talmon, J. L. (1952), *The Origins of Totalitarian Democracy* (London: Secker and Warburg).

Taylor, A. E. (1938), 'The Ethical Doctrine of Hobbes', *Philosophy*, 13: 406–24.

Taylor, C. (1989), *Sources of the Self* (Cambridge: Cambridge University Press).

Taylor, C. (1989a), *Hegel* (Cambridge: Cambridge University Press).

Taylor, C. (1991), *The Ethics of Authenticity* (Cambridge, MA: Harvard University Press).

Ten, C. L. (1980), *Mill on Liberty* (Oxford: Clarendon Press).

Ten, C. L. (1991), 'Mill's Defence of Liberty', in Gray and Smith (eds).

Thomas, K. (1965), 'The Social Origins of Hobbes' Political Thought', in K. C. Brown (ed.), *Hobbes Studies* (Oxford: Blackwell).

Thomas, P. (1976), 'Marx and Science', *Political Studies*, 24/1: 1–24.

Thompson, E. P. (1978), *The Poverty of Theory* (London: Merlin Press).

Townshend, J. (2000), *C.B. Macpherson and the Problem of Liberal Democracy* (Edinburgh: Edinburgh University Press).

Tuck, R. (1979), *Natural Rights Theories: their Origin and Development* (Cambridge: Cambridge University Press).

Tuck, R. (1990), 'Hobbes and Locke on Toleration', in Mary G. Dietz (ed.), *Thomas Hobbes and Political Theory* (Lawrence, Kansas: University Press of Kansas).

Tully, J. (1980), *A Discourse on Property: John Locke and His Adversaries*, (Cambridge: Cambridge University Press).

Tully, J. (ed.) (1988), *Meaning and Context: Quentin Skinner and His Critics* (Cambridge: Polity Press).

Tully, J. (1993), *An Approach to Political Philosophy: Locke in Contexts* (Cambridge: Cambridge University Press).

Vaughan, C. E. (1915), *The Political Writings of Jean-Jacques Rousseau*: vol. I. (Cambridge: Cambridge University Press).

Villari, P. (trans. L. Villari), *The Life and Times of Niccolò Machiavelli* (London: Fisher Unwin, n.d).

Viroli, M. (1988), *Jean-Jacques Rousseau and the 'Well-ordered' Society* (Cambridge: Cambridge University Press).

Viroli, M. (1990), 'Machiavelli and the Republican Idea of Politics', in G. Block, Q. Skinner and M. Viroli (eds), *Machiavelli and Republicanism* (Cambridge: Cambridge University Press): 143–71.

Waldron, J. (1979), 'Enough and as Good Left for Others', *Philosophical Quarterly*, 29: 319–28.

Waldron, J. (1982), 'The Turfs My Servant Has Cut', *Locke Newsletter*, 13: 9–20.

Waldron, J. (1983), 'Two Worries About Mixing One's Labour', *Philosophical Quarterly*, 33: 37–44.

Waldron, J. (1987), 'Mill and the Value of Moral Distress', *Political Studies*, 35: 410–23.

Waldron, J. (1988), 'Locke's Discussion of Property', in *The Right to Private Property* (Oxford: Clarendon Press).

Walker, D. M. (2000), *Marx, Methodology and Science* (Aldershot: Ashgate).

Warrender, H. (1957), *The Political Philosophy of Hobbes: His Theory of Obligation*, (Oxford: Clarendon Press).

Watkins, J. W. N. (1965), *Hobbes's System of Ideas* (London: Hutchinson).

Weale, A. (1999), *Democracy* (London: Macmillan).

Weinstock, D. (1996), 'Natural Law and Public Reason in Kant's Political Philosophy', *Canadian Journal of Philosophy*, 26: 389–411.

Westphal, K. (1993), 'The Basic Context and Structure of Hegel's *Philosophy of Right*', in Beiser (ed.), *The Cambridge Companion to Hegel*.

Whale, J. (ed.) (2000), *Edmund Burke's Reflections on the Revolution in France: New Interdisciplinary Essays* (Manchester: Manchester University Press).

Whelan, F. G. (1985), *Order and Artifice in Hume's Political Philosophy* (Princeton: Princeton University Press).

White, S. (1993), 'Burke on Politics, Aesthetics and the Dangers of Modernity', *Political Theory*, 21: 507–27.

White, S. (1994), *Edmund Burke: Modernity, Politics, and Aesthetics* (California: Sage Publications).

Whitfield, J. H. (1947), *Machiavelli* (Oxford: Oxford University Press).

Wilde, L. (1998), 'Marx and Justice Revisited: The Greek Dimension', *Studies in Marxism*, 5: 93–113.

Wilkins, B. T. (1967), *The Problem of Burke's Political Philosophy* (Oxford: Clarendon Press).

Williams, H., Sullivan, D. and Matthews, G. (1997), *Francis Fukuyama and the End of History* (Cardiff: University of Wales Press).

Williams, M. (1996), 'Burkean "Description" and Political Representation: A Reappraisal', *Canadian Journal of Political Science*, 29/1: 23–45.

Winch, D. (1983), 'Adam Smith's, "enduring particular result": A political cosmo-politan perspective' in Istvan Hont and Michael Ignatieff (eds), *Wealth and Virtue: The Shaping of Political Economy in the Scottish Enlightenment* (Cambridge: Cambridge University Press).

Winch, D. (1985), 'The Burke–Smith Problem and Late Eighteenth-Century Political and Economic Thought', *The Historical Journal*, 28/1: 231–47.

Wokler, R. (ed.) (1995), *Rousseau and Liberty* (Manchester: Manchester University Press).

Wolff, J. (1998), 'Mill, Indecency and the Harm Principle', *Utilitas*, 10: 1–16.

Wood, A. (1980a), 'The Marxian Critique of Justice' reprinted in M. Cohen, *et al.*: 3–41.

Wood, A. (1980b) , 'Marx on Right and Justice: A Reply to Husami', in Cohen, *et al.*: 106–34.

Wood, A. (1981), *Karl Marx* (London: Routledge and Kegan Paul).

Wood, A. (1990), *Hegel's Ethical Thought* (Cambridge: Cambridge University Press).

Wood, A. (1991), 'Editor's Introduction' to Hegel, *Elements of the Philosophy of Right*.

Wood, E. (1995), *Democracy against Capitalism* (Cambridge: Cambridge University Press).

Wood, N. (1967), 'Machiavelli's Concept of Virtù Reconsidered', *Political Studies*, 15: 159–72.

Wood, N. (1984), *John Locke and Agrarian Capitalism* (Berkeley, California: University of California Press).

Zerilli, L. (1994), *Signifying Woman: Culture and Chaos in Rousseau, Burke and Mill* (Ithaca, NY: Cornell University Press).

Index

Acton, H. B., 200, 201, 205, 206
Agathocles, 36
Allen, G. O., 111
Althusser, L., 201, 209–10, 215–16, 217
Anglo, S., 26, 28, 37
Aquinas, T., 15, 129, 131
Arendt, H., 153
Aristotle, 15, 28, 129, 130, 164, 167
Ashcraft, R., 65–7, 70–2, 79–80
Avineri, S., 166, 168, 169, 171, 173

Ball, T., 203, 204
Baron, H., 31, 32, 38
Barry, B., 112
Barry, N., 111
Baumgold, D., 46, 56, 57
Bentham, J., 111, 180, 193, 194
Berger, 193–6
Berki, R. N., 179
Berlin, I., 14, 28, 35, 105–6, 188,
    189–90, 197
Blakemore, S., 126, 137, 139
Bodin, J., 27
Bolingbroke, 82, 93
Borgia, C., 36
Bosanquet, B., 105, 111
Brod, H., 168, 174
Browning, G., 163, 173
Browning, R., 137
Brudner, A., 168, 176
Buckle, S., 89–90
Burd, L. A., 28
Burgess, G., 59
Burke, E., 6, 7, 8, 14–15, 105, 107,
    114, **121–42**, 175, 176, 179
  as conservative and liberal, 127–8
  as natural law conservative, 129–30,
    142
  as no liberal, 136–7
  as 'Old Whig', 142

as opponent of tyranny, 135–6
as political economist, 133–6
as rhetorician and dramatist, 137–9,
    141
as sceptic, 128–9, 140
not a natural law theorist, 130–33
Burnham, J., 25
Burns, A., 162, 164, 178, 179

Cairns, H., 166
Callinicos, A., 204
Cambridge School, 2–5
Cameron, D., 124
Canavan, F., 124, 134
Carver, T., 203, 208
Cassirer, E., 26, 28, 29, 30, 103, 113,
    114, 166, 179
Castro, F., 115
Chabod, F., 25, 27, 31
Chapman, J. W., 108, 110, 111, 112
Chitty, A., 163
Civil War, 41, 46, 71
Clarke, Samuel, 87
Cobban, A., 108, 128
Cohen, G. A., 67, 70, 210, 204–9, 215,
    217
Cohen, J., 109, 117
Coleridge, 186
Colletti, L., 116, 117, 120
Conniff, J., 131
Copleston, F., 173, 174
Cornforth, M., 202–3, 214
Cowling, M., 186–8, 189, 195
Cristi, F. R., 168, 176
Croce, B., 25, 27, 40
Crocker, L. G., 104, 105, 106, 107, 115
Crowe, I., 122

Dagger, R., 111, 113
Dallmayr, F., 165